1914

1914
The Early Campaigns of the Great War by the British Commander

Sir John French

1914: the Early Campaigns of the Great War by the British Commander
by Sir John French

Leonaur is an imprint of Oakpast Ltd

Text in this form and material original to this edition
copyright © 2009 Oakpast Ltd

ISBN: 978-1-84677-652-6 (hardcover)
ISBN: 978-1-84677-651-9 (softcover)

http://www.leonaur.com

Publisher's Notes

The opinions expressed in this book are those of the author and are not necessarily those of the publisher.

Contents

Preface	9
Preliminary	11
The British Expeditionary Force	23
The Sailing of the Expeditionary Force	38
The Retreat from Mons	58
Further Course of the Retreat	78
The Battle of the Marne	103
The Battle of the Aisne	126
The Siege and Fall of Antwerp	152
The Aisne and Northwards	167
The Battle of Ypres	183
The Battle of Ypres	201
The Battle of Ypres	217
The Battle of Ypres	233
Entry of the Territorial Army	241
After the First Battle of Ypres	252
The Operations of December 14th-19th, 1914	267
The Close of the Year 1914	277
Ammunition	289
Maps	301

This book is dedicated to
The Rt. Hon. David Lloyd George, M.P.
to whose prevision, energy and tenacity
the army and the empire owe so much.

Preface

Le Maréchal French commandait en Chef l'Armée Britannique au début de la Guerre.

Comme on le sait, les allemands ont cherché en 1914 à profiter de leur supériorité numérique et de l'écrasante puissance de leur armement, pour mettre hors de cause les Armées Alliées d'Occident, par une manoeuvre enveloppante, aussi rapide que possible.

Après avoir cherché en vain la décision à la Marne, puis à l'Aisne et à la Somme, ils la poursuivent successivement à Arras, sur l'Yser et à Ypres.

À mesure que dans cette course à la mer, le terrain disponible se restreint devant eux, les coups se précipitent et se répètent plus violents, les réserves s'engagent, de nouveaux Corps d'Armée entrent en ligne nombreux et intacts. La reddition d'Anvers assure d'ailleurs à l'ennemi d'importantes disponibilités.

Mais déjà l'Armée Belge, appuyée de troupes françaises, arrête les allemands sur l'Yser, de Nieuport à Dixmude. Après avoir pris part aux actions de l'Aisne, l'Armée Britannique a été transportée dans le Nord. C'est ainsi qu'elle s'engage progressivement de la Bassée à Ypres, s'opposant partout à l'invasion.

Bref, les allemands, après avoir vainement développé leurs efforts de la Mer à la Lys, dès le 15 octobre, sont dans l'obligation, à la fin du mois, de vaincre à Ypres, ou bien leur manoeuvre échoue définitivement, leur offensive expire en Occident et la Coalition reste debout.

Ainsi sont-ils amenés, sur ce point d'Ypres, dans une lutte

acharnée, à concentrer leurs moyens, une forte artillerie lourde largement approvisionée, renforcée de minenwerfers, de corps d'armée nombreux et renouvelés.

Quant aux Alliés, ils sont réduits à recevoir le choc avec des effectifs restreints, des munitions comptées et rares, une faible artillerie lourde. Toute relève leur est interdite par la pénurie de troupes, quelle que soit la durée de la bataille. Pour ne citer qu'un exemple, le premier corps britannique reste engagé du 20 octobre au 15 novembre—au milieu des plus violentes attaques et malgré de formidables pertes.

Mais à cette dernière date la bataille était gagnée. Les Alliés avaient infligé un retentissant échec à l'ennemi: ils avaient sauvé les communications de la Manche et par là fixé le sort et l'avenir de la Coalition.

Si l'union étroite du Commandement Allié et la valeur des troupes ont permis ces glorieux résultats, c'est que le Maréchal French a déployé la plus entière droiture, la plus complète confiance, la plus grande énergie: résolu à se faire passer sur le corps plutôt qu'à reculer.

La Grande-Bretagne avait trouvé en lui un grand soldat. Il avait maintenu ses troupes à la hauteur de celles de Wellington.

Avec l'émotion d'un souvenir profond et toujours vivant, je salue le vaillant compagnon d'armes des rudes journées et les glorieux drapeaux Britanniques de la Bataille d'Ypres.

F. Foch

Maréchal de France

CHAPTER 1

Preliminary

For years past I had regarded a general war in Europe as an eventual certainty. The experience which I gained during the seven or eight years spent as a member of the Committee of Imperial Defence, and my three years tenure of the Office of Chief of the General Staff, greatly strengthened this conviction.

For reasons which it is unnecessary to enter upon, I resigned my position as Chief of the Staff in April, 1914, and from that time I temporarily lost touch with the European situation as it was officially represented and appreciated.

I remember spending a week in June of that year in Paris, and when passing through Dover on my return, my old friend, Jimmie Watson (Colonel Watson, late of the 60th Rifles, A.D.C. to the Khedive of Egypt), looked into my carriage window and told me of the murder of the Archduke Francis Ferdinand and his Consort. I cannot say that I actually regarded this tragedy as being the prelude which should lead ultimately to a great European convulsion, but in my own mind, and in view of my past experience, it created a feeling of unrest within me and an instinctive foreboding of evil. Then came a few weeks of the calm which heralded the storm—a calm under cover of which Germany was vigorously preparing for "the day."

One afternoon, late in July, I was the guest at lunch of the German Ambassador, Prince Lichnowski. It was a small party, comprising, to the best of my recollection, only Princess Henry of Pless, Lady Cunard, Lord Kitchener, His Excellency and myself. The first idea I got of the storm which was brewing came from a short conversation which I had with the Ambassador in a corner of the room after lunch. He was very unhappy and perturbed, and he plainly told me that he feared all Europe would be in a blaze before we were a fortnight older. His feeling was prophetic. His surprising candour foreshadowed the moral courage with which Prince Lichnowski subsequently issued his famous apologia.

On July 28th Austria-Hungary declared war on Serbia. The military preparations of the Dual Monarchy inevitably led to a partial mobilisation by Russia against Austria, whereupon the German Emperor proclaimed the *Kriegsgefahrszustand* on July 31st, following this up by declaring war against Russia on August 1st. On August 2nd German troops entered Luxemburg and, without declaration of war, violated French territory. Great Britain declared war against Germany on August 4th and against Austria on August 12th, France having broken off relations with Austria two days earlier.

On Thursday, July 30th, I was sent for by the Chief of the Imperial General Staff, and was given private intimation that, if an expeditionary force were sent to France, I was to command it. On leaving the room I found some well-known newspaper correspondents in the passage. I talked a little with them and found that great doubt existed in their minds as to whether this country would support France by force of arms. This doubt was certainly shared by many.

I remember well that on the morning of Saturday, August 1st, the day upon which Germany declared war on Russia, and it was known that the breaking out of hostilities between Germany and France was only a question of hours, I received a visit from the Vicomte de la Panouse, the French Military Attaché in London. He told me that the Ambassador was much disheartened in mind by these doubts and fears. We talked matters over, and he came to dinner with me that night. Personally, I felt perfectly sure that so long as Mr. Asquith remained Prime Minister, and Lord Haldane, Sir Edward Grey and Mr. Winston Churchill continued to be members of the Cabinet, their voices would guide the destinies of the British Empire, and that we should remain true to our friendly understanding with the *Entente* Powers. As the result of the long conversation I had with the Vicomte de la Panouse, I think I was successful in causing this conviction to prevail at the French Embassy.

England declared war on Germany on Tuesday, August 4th, and on the 5th the mobilisation of Regulars, Special Reserve and Territorials was ordered. On Wednesday, August 5th, a Council of War was held at 10, Downing Street, under the Presidency of the Prime Minister. Nearly all the members of the Cabinet were present, whilst Lord Roberts, Lord Kitchener, Sir Charles Douglas, Sir Douglas Haig, the late Sir James Grierson, General (now Sir Henry) Wilson and myself were directed to attend. To the best of my recollection the two main subjects discussed were:

1. The composition of the Expeditionary Force.
2. The point of concentration for the British Forces on their arrival in France.

As regards 1

It was generally felt that we were under some obligation to France to send as strong an army as we could, and there was an idea that one Cavalry Division and six Divisions of all arms had been promised. As to the exact number, it did not appear that we were under any definite obligation, but it was unanimously agreed that we should do all we could. The question to be decided was how many troops it was necessary to keep in this country adequately to guard our shores against attempted invasion and, if need be, to maintain internal order.

Mr. Churchill briefly described the actual situation of the Navy. He pointed out that the threat of war had come upon us at a most opportune moment as regards his own Department, because, only two or three weeks before, the Fleet had been partially mobilised, and large reserves called up for the great Naval Review by His Majesty at Spithead and the extensive naval manoeuvres which followed it. So far as the Navy was concerned, he considered Home Defence reasonably secure; but this consideration did not suffice to absolve us from the necessity of keeping a certain number of troops at home. After this discussion it was decided that two Divisions must for the moment remain behind, and that one Cavalry Division and four Divisions of all arms should be sent out as speedily as possible. This meant a force of approximately 100,000 men.

As regards 2

The British and French General Staffs had for some years been in close secret consultation with one another on this subject. The German menace necessitated some preliminary understanding in the event of a sudden attack. The area of concentration for the British Forces had been fixed on the left flank of the French, and the actual detraining stations of the various units were all laid down in terrain lying between Maubeuge and Le Cateau. The Headquarters of the Army were fixed at the latter place.

This understanding being purely provisional and conditional upon an unprovoked attack by Germany, the discussion then took the turn of overhauling and reviewing these decisions, and of making arrangements in view of the actual conditions under which war had broken out. Many and various opinions were expressed; but on this day no final decisions were arrived at. It was thought absolutely necessary to ask the French authorities to send over a superior officer who should be in full possession of the views and intentions of the French General Staff. It was agreed that no satisfactory decision could be arrived at until after full discussion with a duly accredited French Officer. I think this is the gist of the really important points dealt with at the Council.

During the week the Headquarters of the Expeditionary Force were established in London at the Hotel Metropole, and the Staff was constituted as follows:

Chief of Staff	Gen. Sir Archibald Murray
Sub-Chief	Brig.-Gen. H. H. Wilson
Adjutant-General	Maj-Gen. Neville Macready
Quartermaster-General	Maj-Gen. Sir William Robertson
Director of Intelligence	Brig.-Gen. Macdonogh
C.R.A.	Major-Gen. Lindsay

C.R.E.	Brig.-Gen. Fowke
Military Secretary	Col. the Hon. W. Lambton
Principal Medical Officer	Surg.-Gen. T. P. Woodhouse
Principal Veterinary Officer	Brig.-Gen. J. Moore

It was about Thursday the 7th, or Friday the 8th, August, that Lord Kitchener was appointed Secretary of State for War, and on Monday, the 10th, the Mission sent by the French Government arrived. It was headed by Colonel Huguet, a well-known French Artillery Officer who had recently been for several years French Military Attaché in London.

As before mentioned, one of the most important matters remaining for discussion and decision was finally to determine whether the original plan as regards the area of concentration for the British Forces in France was to be adhered to, or whether the actual situation demanded some change or modification. There was an exhaustive exchange of views between soldiers and Ministers, and many conflicting opinions were expressed. The soldiers themselves were not agreed. Lord Kitchener thought that our position on the left of the French line at Maubeuge would be too exposed, and rather favoured a concentration farther back in the neighbourhood of Amiens. Sir Douglas Haig suggested postponing any landing till the campaign had actively opened and we should be able to judge in which direction our co-operation would be most effective.

Personally, I was opposed to these ideas, and most anxious to adhere to our original plans. Any alteration in carrying out our concentration, particularly if this meant delay, would have upset the French plan of campaign and created much distrust in the minds of our Allies. Delay or hanging back would not only have looked like hesitation, but might easily have entailed disastrous consequences by permanently separating our already inferior forces. Having regard to what we subsequently knew of the German plans and preparations, there can be no doubt that any such delayed landing might well have been actively opposed. As will be seen hereafter, we were at first hopeful of carrying out a successful offensive, and, had those hopes been justified, any change or delay in our original plans would have either prevented or entirely paralysed it. The vital element of the problem was speed in mobilisation and concentration, change of plans meant inevitable and possibly fatal delay.

Murray, Wilson, Grierson and Huguet concurred in my views, and it was so settled.

The date of the embarkment of the Headquarters Staff was fixed for Friday, August 14th.

During the fateful days which intervened, daily and almost hourly reports reached us as to the progress of mobilisation both of our Allies and our Enemies. From the first it became quite evident that the German system of mobilisation was quicker than the French. There was reason to believe that Germany had partly mobilised some classes of her reserves before formal mobilisation. The splendid stand made by the Belgians in defence of their frontier fortresses is well known, and the course of the preliminary operations on the Belgian and Luxemburg frontiers, as well as those in the neighbourhood of Nancy, gave us hope that the wonderful army of which we had heard so much, was not altogether the absolutely invincible war machine we had been led to expect and believe. During this most critical time, my mind was occupied day and night with anxious thought. I will try to recall those days of the first half of August, 1914, and crystallise the result of my meditations. This will serve to show the doubts, fears, hopes and aspirations, in short the mental atmosphere in which I awaited the opening of the campaign.

In the ten years previous to the War, I had constantly envisaged the probable course of events leading up to the outbreak of this world-war, as well as the manner of the outbreak itself. In imagination I had seen the spark suddenly emitted in some obscure corner of Europe, followed by the blowing-up of one huge magazine, such as the declaration of war between Russia and Austria would prove to be, then the conflagration spreading with lightning speed, and I had seemed to have a foretaste amid it all of the anxious hesitation which would precede our entry into the war.

I have been a member of the Committee of Imperial Defence since 1906, and have assisted at the innumerable deliberations of that Aulic Council. It was somewhere about 1908 that the certainty of a war was forced upon my mind. Lord Haldane was then Secretary of State for War and I was Inspector-General of the Forces. Lord Haldane was himself alive to the possibility of war; but, while he hoped to ward it off by diplomacy and negotiation, he fully acquiesced in the desirability of making every preparation which could be carried out in complete secrecy. He told me that were he in power, if and when the event occurred, he would designate me to command the Expeditionary Force, and requested me to study the problem carefully and do all I could to be ready. It thus fell out that in August, 1914, the many possibilities and alternatives of action were quite familiar to my mind.

It is now within the knowledge of all that the General Staffs of Great Britain and France had, for a long time, held conferences, and that a complete mutual understanding as to combined action in certain eventualities existed.

Belgium, however, remained a "dark horse" up to the last, and it is most unfortunate that she could never be persuaded to decide upon her attitude in the event of a general war. All we ever had in our mind was *defence* against attack by Germany. We had guaranteed the neutrality of Belgium, and all reports pointed to an intention by Germany to violate that neutrality. What we desired above all things was that Belgium should realise the danger which subsequently laid her waste. We were anxious that she should assist and co-operate in her own defence. The idea of *attacking* Germany through Belgium or in any other direction never entered our heads.

Pre-war arrangements like these were bound in such circumstances to be very imperfect, though infinitely better than none at all.

It will be of interest at this point to narrate a conversation I had with the Emperor William in August, 1911. When His Majesty visited this country in the spring of that year to unveil the statue of Queen Victoria, he invited me to be his guest at the grand cavalry manoeuvres to be held that summer in the neighbourhood of Berlin.

It was an experience I shall never forget, and it impressed

me enormously with the efficiency and power of the German cavalry. It was on about the third day of the manoeuvres that the Emperor arrived by train at five in the morning to find the troops drawn up on the plain close by to receive him. I have never seen a more magnificent military spectacle than they presented on that brilliant August morning, numbering some 15,000 horsemen with a large force of horse artillery, *jäger* and machine guns.

When His Majesty had finished the inspection of the line, and the troops had moved to take up their points for manoeuvre, the Emperor sent for me. He was very pleasant and courteous, asked me if I was made comfortable, and if I had got a good horse. He then went on to say that he knew all our sympathies in Great Britain were with France and against Germany. He said he wished me to see everything that could be seen, but told me he trusted to my honour to reveal nothing if I visited France.

After the manoeuvres of the day were completed, at about 11 or 12 o'clock, I was placed next to His Majesty at luncheon and we had another conversation. He asked me what I thought of what I had seen in the morning and told me that the German cavalry was the most perfect in the world; but he added: "It is not only the Cavalry; the Artillery, the Infantry, all the arms of the Service are equally efficient. The sword of Germany is sharp; and if you oppose Germany you will find how sharp it is."

Before I left, His Majesty was kind enough to present me with his photograph beautifully framed. Pointing to it, he remarked, semi-jocularly: "There is your arch-enemy! There is your disturber of the peace of Europe!"

Reverting to my story. Personally, I had always thought that Germany would violate Belgian neutrality, and in no such half measure as by a march through the Ardennes, which was what our joint plans mainly contemplated. I felt convinced that if ever she took this drastic step, she would make the utmost use of it to pour over the whole country and outflank the Allies.

The principal source of the terrible anxiety I felt took its root in the thought that we were too much mentally committed to meet an attack from the east, instead of one which was to come as it actually did. It reassured me, however, to know that our actual dispositions did not preclude the possibility of stemming the first outburst of the storm so effectively as to ward off any imminent danger which might threaten Northern France and the Channel Ports.

To turn from the province of strategy to the sphere of tactics, a life-long experience of military study and thought had taught me that the principle of the tactical employment of troops must be instinctive. I knew that in putting the science of war into practice, it was necessary that its main tenets should form, so to speak, part of one's flesh and blood. In war there is little time to think, and the right thing to do must come like a flash—it must present itself to the mind as perfectly *obvious*.

No previous experience, no conclusion I had been able to draw from campaigns in which I had taken part, or from a close study of the new conditions in which the war of today is waged, had led me to anticipate a war of positions. All my thoughts, all my prospective plans, all my possible alternatives of action, were concentrated upon a war of movement and manoeuvre. I knew perfectly well that modern up-to-date inventions would materially influence and modify our previous conceptions as to the employment of the three arms respectively; but I had not realised that this process would work in so drastic a manner as to render all our preconceived ideas of the method of tactical field operations comparatively ineffective and useless. Judged by the course of events in the first three weeks of the War, neither French nor German generals were prepared for the complete transformation of all military ideas which the development of the operations inevitably demonstrated to be imperative for waging war in present conditions.

It is easy to be "wise after the event"; but I cannot help wondering why none of us realised what the most modern rifle, the machine gun, motor traction, the aeroplane and wireless telegraphy would bring about. It seems so simple when judged by actual results. The modern rifle and machine gun add tenfold to the relative power of the defence as against the attack. This precludes the use of the old methods of attack, and has driven the attack to seek covered entrenchments after every forward rush of at most a few hundred yards.

It has thus become a practical operation to place the heaviest artillery in position close behind the infantry fighting line, not only owing to the mobility afforded by motor traction but also because the old dread of losing the guns before they could be got away no longer exists. The crucial necessity for the effective employment of heavy artillery is observation, and this is provided by the balloon and the aeroplane, which, by means of wireless telegraphy, can keep the batteries instantly informed of the accuracy of their fire.

I feel sure in my own mind that had we realised the true effect of modern appliances of war in August, 1914, there would have been no retreat from Mons, and that if, in September, the Germans had learnt their lesson, the Allies would never have driven them back to the Aisne. It was in the fighting on that river that the eyes of all of us began to be opened.

New characteristics of offensive and defensive war began vaguely to be appreciated; but it required the successive attempts of Maunoury, de Castelnau, Foch and myself to turn the German flanks in the north in the old approved style, and the practical failure of these attempts, to bring home to our minds the true nature of war as it is today.

About the middle of November, 1914—after three and a half months of war—we were fairly settled down to the war of positions. It was, therefore, in a somewhat troubled frame of mind that I began to play my humble part in this tremendous episode in the history of the world. The new lessons had to be learned in a hard school and through a bitter experience. However, for good or for evil, I have always been possessed of a sanguine temperament. No one, I felt, had really been able to gauge the respective fighting values of the French and German Armies. I hoped for the best and rather believed in it; and in this confident spirit, although anxious and watchful, I landed at Boulogne at 5 p.m. on August 14th, 1914.

It will be a fitting close to this chapter if I add the instructions which I received from His Majesty's Government before leaving.

Owing to the infringement of the neutrality of Belgium by Germany, and in furtherance of the Entente which exists between this country and France, His Majesty's Government has decided, at the request of the French Government, to send an Expeditionary Force to France and to entrust the command of the troops to yourself.

The special motive of the Force under your control is to support and co-operate with the French Army against our common enemies. The peculiar task laid upon you is to assist the French Government in preventing or repelling the invasion by Germany of French and Belgian territory and eventually to restore the neutrality of Belgium, on behalf of which, as guaranteed by treaty, Belgium has appealed to the French and to ourselves.

These are the reasons which have induced His Majesty's Government to declare war, and these reasons constitute the primary objective you have before you.

The place of your assembly, according to present arrangements, is Amiens, and during the assembly of your troops you will have every opportunity for discussing with the Commander-in-Chief of the French Army, the military position in general and the special part which your Force is able and adapted to play. It must be recognised from the outset that the numerical strength of the British Force and its contingent reinforcement is strictly limited, and with this consideration kept steadily in view it will be obvious that the greatest care must be exercised towards a minimum of losses and wastage.

Therefore, while every effort must be made to coincide most sympathetically with the plans and wishes of our Ally, the gravest consideration will devolve upon you as to participation in forward movements where large bodies of French troops are not engaged and where your Force may be unduly exposed to attack. Should a contingency of this sort be contemplated, I look to you to inform me fully and give me time to communicate to you any decision to which His Majesty's Government may come in the matter. In this connection I wish you distinctly to understand that your command is an entirely independent one, and that you will in no case come in any sense under the orders of any Allied General.

In minor operations you should be careful that your subordinates understand that risk of serious losses should only be taken where such risk is authoritatively considered to be commensurate with the object in view.

The high courage and discipline of your troops should, and certainly will, have fair and full opportunity of display during the campaign, but officers may well be reminded that in this, their first experience of European warfare, a greater measure of caution must be employed than under former conditions of hostilities against an untrained adversary.

You will kindly keep up constant communication with the War Office, and you will be good enough to inform me as to all movements of the enemy reported to you as well as to those of the French Army.

I am sure you fully realise that you can rely with the utmost confidence on the wholehearted and unswerving support of the Government, of myself, and of your compatriots, in carrying out the high duty which the King has entrusted to you and in maintaining the great tradition of His Majesty's Army.

Kitchener
Secretary of State

CHAPTER 2

The British Expeditionary Force

I have thought fit to interrupt my narrative here to devote some pages to the composition of the original Expeditionary Force.

The First Expeditionary Force consisted of the First Army Corps (1st and 2nd Divisions) under Lieut.-Gen. Sir Douglas Haig; the Second Army Corps (3rd and 5th Divisions) under Lieut.-Gen. Sir James Grierson (who died shortly after landing in France and was succeeded by Gen. Sir Horace Smith-Dorrien), and the Cavalry Division under Major-Gen. E. H. H. Allenby.

To these must be added the 19th Infantry Brigade, which, at the opening of our operations in France, was employed on our Lines of Communication. The original Expeditionary Force was subsequently augmented by the 4th Division, which detrained at Le Cateau on August 25th. The 4th Division and the 19th Infantry Brigade were, on the arrival of Gen. Pulteney in France, on August 30th, formed into the Third Army Corps, to which the 6th Division was subsequently added.

For the purpose of convenient reference, I have included in this chapter the composition of the 6th Division, which joined us on the Aisne, and of the 7th Division and the 3rd Cavalry Division, which came into line with the original Expeditionary Force in Belgium in the opening stages of the First Battle of Ypres; as also of the Lahore Division of the Indian Corps, which likewise took part in the Battle of Ypres.

THE FIRST EXPEDITIONARY FORCE.

General Officer Commanding-in-Chief:
Field-Marshal Sir J. D. P. FRENCH.

Chief of the General Staff:
Lieut.-Gen. Sir A. J. MURRAY.

Adjutant-General:
Major-Gen Sir C. F N MACREADY.

Quartermaster-General:
Major-Gen. Sir W. R ROBERTSON

First Army Corps:
Lieut.-Gen Sir DOUGLAS HAIG.

1st Division:
Major-Gen. S H. LOMAX,
wounded October 31st, replaced by Brig.-Gen LANDON *(temp)*,
then by Brig.-Gen. Sir D HENDERSON.

1st Infantry Brigade:
Brig.-Gen. F I. MAXSE,
succeeded by Brig.-Gen. FITZCLARENCE, V C. (killed, November 11th). Col. McEwen then took command. Later on, Col Lowther was appointed to command the Brigade.
1st Batt. Coldstream Guards.
1st Batt. Scots Guards.
London Scottish (joined Brigade in November)
1st Batt. Royal Highlanders (the Black Watch).
2nd Batt. Royal Munster Fusiliers (cut to pieces at Etreux, August 29th, replaced by 1st Batt. Cameron Highlanders.

2nd Infantry Brigade :
Brig.-Gen. E. S. BULFIN,
wounded November 1st, succeeded by Col. Cunliffe-Owen (temp.).
Brig.-Gen. WESTMACOTT took command November 23rd.
2nd Batt. Royal Sussex Regt.   1st Batt. Northampton Regt.
1st Batt. N. Lancs Regt.   2nd Batt. K.R.R.

3rd Infantry Brigade :
Brig.-Gen. H. J. S. LANDON,
appointed to command the Division after October 31st, Col. Lovett taking command of Brigade. Brig.-Gen. R. H. K. BUTLER was appointed to command the Brigade November 13th.
1st Batt. The Queen's Royal West Surrey Regt. (cut up October 31st, replaced by 2nd Royal Munster Fusiliers).
1st Batt. S. Wales Borderers.
1st Batt. Gloucester Regt.
2nd Batt. Welsh Regt.

Divisional Cavalry :
" C " Squadron 15th Hussars.   1st Cyclist Co.

Royal Engineers :
23rd & 26th Field Cos.   1st Signal Co.

Royal Artillery :
R.F.A. Batteries—
  XXV. Brigade—113, 114, 115.
  XXVI. Brigade—116, 117, 118.
  XXIX. Brigade—46, 51, 54.
  XLIII. Brigade (Howitzer)—30, 40, 57.

Heavy Battery R.G.A.—26.   1st Divisional Train.

R.A.M.C. : 1st, 2nd, & 3rd Field Ambulances.

2nd Division:

Major-Gen. C. C. MONRO.

4th (Guards) Brigade:

Brig.-Gen. R. SCOTT-KERR,
wounded September 1st and succeeded by Brig.-Gen. the EARL OF CAVAN (arrived September 18th).

2nd Batt. Grenadier Guards.   3rd Batt. Coldstream Guards.
2nd Batt. Coldstream Guards. 1st Batt. Irish Guards.
1st Herts (T.F.) (joined Brigade about November 10th).

5th Infantry Brigade:

Brig.-Gen. R. C. B. HAKING,
wounded on September 16th; succeeded by Lieut.-Col. Westmacott until Haking returned on November 20th.

2nd Batt. Worcester Regt.   2nd Batt. Highland L.I.
2nd Batt. Oxf. & Bucks L.I. 2nd Batt. Connaught Rangers.
                            (2nd Connaughts were amalgamated with their 1st Batt. at the end of November and replaced in the Brigade by 9th H.L.I. (Glasgow Highlanders).)

6th Infantry Brigade:

Brig.-Gen. R. H. DAVIES,
invalided in September; succeeded by Brig.-Gen. FANSHAWE, September 13th.

1st Batt. The King's (Liverpool) Regt.   1st Batt. Royal Berks Regt.
2nd Batt. S. Staffs Regt.   1st Batt. K.R.R.

Divisional Cavalry:

"B" Squadron 15th Hussars.   2nd Cyclist Co.

Royal Engineers:

5th & 11th Field Cos.   2nd Signal Co.

Royal Artillery:

R.F.A. Batteries—
  XXXIV. Brigade—25, 50, 70.
  XXXVI. Brigade—15, 48, 71.
  XLI. Brigade—9, 16, 17.
  XLIV. Brigade (Howitzer)—47, 56, 60.

Heavy Battery R.G.A.—35.   2nd Divisional Train.

R.A.M.C.: 4th, 5th & 6th Field Ambulances.

Second Army Corps:

Lieut.-Gen. Sir JAMES GRIERSON,
died August 17th; succeeded by Gen. Sir HORACE SMITH-DORRIEN.

3rd Division:

Major-Gen. HUBERT I. W. HAMILTON,
killed October 14th; Major-Gen. MACKENZIE in command till end of October; then Major-Gen. WING till November 6th; then Major-Gen. HALDANE.

7th Infantry Brigade:

Brig.-Gen. F. W. N. McCracken.

3rd Batt. Worcester Regt.   1st Batt. Wilts Regt.
2nd Batt. S. Lancs Regt.   2nd Batt. Royal Irish Rifles.

8th Infantry Brigade:

Brig.-Gen. B. J. C. Doran,
invalided October 23rd; Brig.-Gen. Bowes took over command.

2nd Batt. Royal Scots.
2nd Batt. Royal Irish Regt. (Battalion cut up at Le Pilly, October 20th; became G.H.Q. troops, replaced by 2nd Suffolks.)
4th Batt. Middlesex Regt.
1st Batt. Gordon Highlanders. (Employed as G.H.Q. troops during September, being replaced by 1st Devons, but rejoined Brigade at beginning of October.)

9th Infantry Brigade:

Brig.-Gen. F. C. Shaw,
wounded November 12th; succeeded by Lieut.-Col. Douglas Smith, Royal Scots Fusiliers.

1st Batt. Northumberland Fusiliers.
4th Batt. Royal Fusiliers.
1st Batt. Lincolnshire Regt.
1st Batt. Royal Scots Fusiliers.

Divisional Cavalry:

"A" Squadron 15th Hussars.   3rd Cyclist Co.

Royal Engineers:

56th & 57th Field Cos.   3rd Signal Co.

Royal Artillery:

R.F.A. Batteries—
    XXIII. Brigade—107, 108, 109.
    XL. Brigade—6, 23, 49.
    XLII. Brigade—29, 41, 45.
    XXX. Brigade (Howitzer)—128, 129, 130.
Heavy Battery R.G.A.—48.   3rd Divisional Train.

R.A.M.C.: 7th, 8th, & 9th Field Ambulances.

5th Division:

Major-Gen. Sir CHARLES FERGUSSON,
invalided October 22nd; succeeded by Major-Gen. MORLAND.

13th Infantry Brigade:

Brig.-Gen. G. J. CUTHBERT,
invalided about the end of September; succeeded by Brig.-Gen. HICKIE, who went sick October 13th, Col. Martyn getting command (*temp.*).

2nd Batt. K.O. Scottish Borderers.
2nd Batt. (Duke of Wellington's) West Riding Regt.
1st Batt. Royal West Kent Regt.
2nd Batt. K.O. Yorkshire L.I.

14th Infantry Brigade:

Brig.-Gen. S. P. ROLT,
invalided October 29th; succeeded by Brig.-Gen. F. S. MAUDE.
2nd Batt. Suffolk Regt. (replaced by 1st Devons at the beginning of October, and became G.H.Q. troops).
1st Batt. East Surrey Regt.
1st Batt. Duke of Cornwall's L.I.
2nd Batt. Manchester Regt.

15th Infantry Brigade:
Brig.-Gen. Count A. E. W. GLEICHEN.

1st Batt. Norfolk Regt. 1st Batt. Cheshire Regt.
1st Batt. Bedford Regt. 1st Batt. Dorset Regt.

Divisional Cavalry:
" A " Squadron 19th Hussars.

Royal Engineers:
17th & 59th Field Cos. 5th Cyclist Co.

Royal Artillery:
R.F.A. Batteries—
XV. Brigade—11, 52, 80.
XXVII. Brigade—119, 120, 121.
XXVIII. Brigade—122, 123, 124.
VIII. Brigade (Howitzer)—37, 61, 65.

Heavy Battery R.G.A.—108. 5th Divisional Train.

R.A.M.C.: 13th, 14th, & 15th Field Ambulances.

19th Infantry Brigade:
Brig.-Gen. L. G. DRUMMOND,
succeeded early in September by Brig.-Gen. F. GORDON.

[NOTE.—This Brigade was formed from units on Lines of Communication, and was attached successively to the Cavalry Division, Second Corps and Fourth Division during the retreat from Mons and advance to the Aisne. In the Flanders fighting of October–November, 1914, it worked with the Sixth Division.]

2nd Batt. Royal Welsh Fusiliers.
1st Batt. Scottish Rifles.
1st Batt. Middlesex Regt.
2nd Batt. Argyll and Sutherland Highlanders.
19th Field Ambulance.

Cavalry Division:

Major-Gen. E. H. H. ALLENBY, took command of the Cavalry Corps on its formation in October, Brig.-Gen. DE LISLE taking command of the 1st Cavalry Division.

1st Cavalry Brigade:

Brig.-Gen. C. J. BRIGGS.

2nd Dragoon Guards.   5th Dragoon Guards.
11th Hussars.

2nd Cavalry Brigade:

Brig.-Gen. H. DE B. DE LISLE, transferred to command 1st Cavalry Division in October and succeeded by Brig.-Gen. MULLINS.

4th Dragoon Guards.   9th Lancers.
18th Hussars (Queen Mary's Own).

3rd Cavalry Brigade:

Brig.-Gen. HUBERT DE LA POER GOUGH.

4th Hussars.   5th Lancers.   16th Lancers.

4th Cavalry Brigade:

Brig.-Gen. Hon. C. E. BINGHAM.

Household Cavalry (Composite Regt.).
6th Dragoon Guards.   3rd Hussars.

5th Cavalry Brigade:
Brig.-Gen. Sir PHILIP P. W. CHETWODE.
12th Lancers.   20th Hussars.
2nd Dragoons (Scots Greys).

Royal Horse Artillery:
Batteries—" D," " E," " I," " J," " L " (" L " Battery went home to refit after Néry (September 1st), and was replaced by " H," R.H.A., which arrived about the middle of September).

Royal Engineers:
1st Field Squadron.   1st Signal Squadron.

[NOTE.—In September the 2nd Cavalry Division was formed, consisting at first of the 3rd and 5th Cavalry Brigades under Major-Gen. Gough, Brig.-Gen. Vaughan taking command of the 3rd Cavalry Brigade. With these brigades were " D " and " E " Batteries, R.H.A. In October the 4th Cavalry Brigade was transferred to the 2nd Cavalry Division, as was also " J " Battery, R.H.A. The 2nd Cavalry Division had the 2nd Field Squadron R.E. and 2nd Signal Squadron.]

R.A.M.C.: corresponding Cavalry Field Ambulances.

Royal Flying Corps:
Brig.-Gen. Sir DAVID HENDERSON.
Aeroplane Squadrons Nos. 2, 3, 4, and 5.

4th Division:
Major-Gen. T. D. O. SNOW, invalided September; succeeded by Major-Gen. Sir H. RAWLINSON, who was transferred to 4th Army Corps early in October and replaced by Major-Gen. H. F. M. WILSON.

10th Infantry Brigade:

Brig.-Gen. J. A. L. HALDANE,
appointed to command 3rd Division, November 6th; succeeded by Brig.-Gen. HULL.

1st Batt. Royal Warwickshire Regt.
2nd Batt. Seaforth Highlanders.
1st Batt. Royal Irish Fusiliers.
2nd Batt. Royal Dublin Fusiliers.

11th Infantry Brigade:

Brig.-Gen. A. G. HUNTER-WESTON.

1st Batt. Somersetshire L.I.   1st Batt. Hampshire Regt.
1st Batt. E. Lancs Regt.   1st Batt. Rifle Brigade.

12th Infantry Brigade:

Brig.-Gen. H. F. M. WILSON,
in command of the 4th Division in October, and on promotion succeeded by Col. F. G. Anley.

1st Batt. K.O. (R. Lancaster) Regt.
2nd Batt. Lancashire Fusiliers.
2nd Batt. Royal Inniskilling Fusiliers.
2nd Batt. Essex Regt.

Divisional Cavalry:

" B " Squadron 19th Hussars.   4th Cyclist Co.

Royal Engineers:

7th & 9th Field Cos.   4th Signal Co.

Royal Artillery:

R.F.A. Batteries—
    XIV. Brigade—39, 68, 88.
    XXIX. Brigade—125, 126, 127.
    XXXII. Brigade—27, 134, 135.
    XXXVII. Brigade—31, 35, 55.
Heavy Battery, R.G.A.—31.

R.A.M.C.: 10th, 11th, & 12th Field Ambulances.

Lines of Communication and Army Troops:

1st Batt. Devonshire Regt. (transferred to 8th Brigade about middle of September, later to 14th Brigade).
1st Batt. Cameron Highlanders (replaced 2nd Munsters in 1st Brigade about September 6th).

    [NOTE.—The 28th London (Artists' Rifles), 14th London (London Scottish), 6th Welsh and 5th Border Regt. were all in France before the end of the First Battle of Ypres, as was also the Honourable Artillery Company. These battalions were all at first on Lines of Communication.]

6th Division:

Major-Gen. J. L. KEIR.

16th Infantry Brigade:

Brig.-Gen. C. INGOUVILLE-WILLIAMS.

1st Batt. East Kent Regt. (The Buffs).
1st Batt. Leicestershire Regt.
1st Batt. Shropshire L.I.
2nd Batt. York and Lancaster Regt.

17th Infantry Brigade:
Brig.-Gen. W. R. B. DORAN.

1st Batt. Royal Fusiliers.   2nd Batt. Leinster Regt.
1st Batt. N. Staffs Regt.   3rd Batt. Rifle Brigade.

18th Infantry Brigade:
Brig.-Gen. W. N. CONGREVE, V.C.

1st Batt. West Yorks Regt.   2nd Batt. Notts and Derby Regt.
1st Batt. East Yorks Regt.   (the Sherwood Foresters).
2nd Batt. Durham L.I.

Divisional Cavalry:
" C " Squadron 19th Hussars.   6th Cyclist Co.

Royal Engineers:
12th & 38th Field Cos.   6th Signal Co.

Royal Artillery:
R.F.A. Batteries—
  II. Brigade—21, 42, 53.
  XXIV. Brigade—110, 111, 112.
  XXXVIII. Brigade—24, 34, 72.
  XII. Brigade (Howitzer)—43, 86, 87.

Heavy Battery R.G.A.—24.   6th Divisional Train.

R.A.M.C.: 16th, 17th & 18th Field Ambulances.

7th Infantry Division:
Major-Gen. T. CAPPER.

20th Infantry Brigade:
Brig.-Gen. H. G. RUGGLES-BRISE.

1st Batt. Grenadier Guards.   2nd Batt. Border Regt.
2nd Batt. Scots Guards.   2nd Batt. Gordon Highlanders.

21st Infantry Brigade:
Brig.-Gen. H. E. WATTS.

2nd Batt. Bedfordshire Regt.   2nd Batt. Royal Scots Fusiliers.
2nd Batt. Yorkshire Regt.   2nd Batt. Wiltshire Regt.

22nd Infantry Brigade:
Brig.-Gen. S. T. B. LAWFORD.

2nd Batt. The Queen's Royal West Surrey Regt.
2nd Batt. Royal Warwickshire Regt.
1st Batt. Royal Welsh Fusiliers.
1st Batt. S. Staffs Regt.

Divisional Cavalry:

Northumberland Yeomanry (Hussars).   7th Cyclist Co.

Royal Engineers:

54th & 55th Field Cos.   7th Signal Co.

Royal Artillery:
R.H.A. Batteries—" F " and " T."
R.F.A. Batteries—
    XXII. Brigade—104, 105, 106.
    XXV. Brigade—12, 35, 58.
Heavy Batteries R.G.A.—111, 112.

R.A.M.C.: 21st, 22nd and 23rd Field Ambulances.

3rd Cavalry Division:
Major-Gen. The Hon. JULIAN BYNG.

6th Cavalry Brigade:
Brig.-Gen. E. MAKINS.

3rd Dragoon Guards (joined the Division early in November).
North Somerset Yeomanry (attached to the Brigade before the end of First Battle of Ypres).
1st Dragoons (The Royals).
10th Hussars.

7th Cavalry Brigade:
Brig.-Gen. C. T. McM. KAVANAGH.
1st Life Guards.　　　　2nd Life Guards.
Royal Horse Guards (the Blues).

Royal Horse Artillery:
Batteries " C " and " K."

Royal Engineers:
3rd Field Squadron.

R.A.M.C. : 6th, 7th and 8th Cavalry Field Ambulances.

Chapter 3

The Sailing of the Expeditionary Force

I left Charing Cross by special train at 2 p.m. on Friday, August 14th, and embarked at Dover in His Majesty's cruiser *Sentinel*. Sir Maurice FitzGerald and a few other friends were at the station to see me off, and I was accompanied by Murray, Wilson, Robertson, Lambton, Wake, Huguet and Brinsley FitzGerald (my private secretary). The day was dark, dull and gloomy, and rather chilly for August. Dover had ceased to be the cheery seaside resort of peace days, and had assumed the appearance of a fortress expecting momentary attack. Very few people were about, and the place was prepared for immediate action. The fine harbour was crowded with destroyers, submarines, and a few cruisers; booms barred all the entrances and mines were laid down.

It was the first time since war had been declared that I witnessed the outward and visible signs of the great struggle for which we were girding our loins. Not the least evidence of this was the appearance of the officers and men of the *Sentinel*. All showed in their faces that strained, eager, watchful look which told of the severe and continual daily and nightly vigil. This was very marked, and much impressed me.

We sailed a little before 4 and landed at Boulogne about 5.30 in the evening. I was met by the Governor, the Commandant, and the port officials, and we had a very hearty reception. There were several rest camps at Boulogne, and I was able to visit them. Officers and men looked fit and well, and were full of enthusiasm and cheer.

Boulogne was only a secondary port of embarkation, but I can vividly recall the scene. Everyone knows the curious and interesting old town, with its picturesque citadel, situated on a lofty hill. On all sides were evidences of great activity and excitement. Soldiers and sailors, both British and French, were everywhere. All were being warmly welcomed and cheered by the townspeople.

The declining August sun lit up sinuous columns of infantry ascending the high ground to their rest camps on the plateau to the sound of military bands. From the heights above the town, the quays and wharves, where the landing of troops and stores was unceasingly going forward, looked like human beehives. Looking out to sea, one could distinguish approaching transports here and there between the ever wary and watchful scout, destroyer and submarine, which were jealously guarding the route.

Over all towered the monument to the greatest world-soldier—the warrior Emperor who, more than a hundred years before, had from that spot contemplated the invasion of England. Could he have now revisited "the glimpses of the moon," would he not have rejoiced at this friendly invasion of France by England's "good yeomen," who were now offering their lives to save France from possible destruction as a Power of the first class? It was a wonderful and never to be forgotten scene in the setting sun; and, as I walked round camps and bivouacs, I could not but think of the many fine fellows around me who had said good-bye to Old England for ever.

We left Boulogne at 7.20 the same evening, and reached Amiens at 9. There I was met by General Robert (Military Governor) and his staff, the Prefect and officials. Amiens was the Headquarters of General Robb, the Commander of our Line of Communications, and it was also the first point of concentration for our aircraft, which David Henderson commanded, with Sykes as his chief assistant. Whilst at Amiens I was able to hold important discussions with Robb and Henderson as to their respective commands.

I left Amiens for Paris on the morning of the 15th and we reached the Nord Terminus at 12.45 p.m., where I was met by the

British Ambassador (now Lord Bertie) and the Military Governor of Paris. Large crowds had assembled in the streets on the way to the Embassy, and we were received with tremendous greetings by the people. Their welcome was cordial in the extreme. The day is particularly memorable to me, because my previous acquaintance with Lord Bertie ripened from that time into an intimate friendship to which I attach the greatest value. I trust that, when the real history of this war is written, the splendid part played by this great Ambassador may be thoroughly understood and appreciated by his countrymen. Throughout the year and a half that I commanded in France, his help and counsel were invaluable to me.

We drove to the Embassy and lunched there. In the afternoon, accompanied by the Ambassador, I visited M. Poincaré. The President was attended by M. Viviani, Prime Minister, and M. Messimy, Minister for War. The situation was fully discussed, and I was much impressed by the optimistic spirit of the President. I am sure he had formed great hopes of a victorious advance by the Allies from the line they had taken up, and he discoursed playfully with me on the possibility of another battle being fought by the British on the old field of Waterloo. He said the attitude of the French nation was admirable, that they were very calm and determined.

After leaving the President I went to the War Office. Maps were produced; the whole situation was again discussed, and arrangements were made for me to meet General Joffre at his Headquarters the next day.

In the evening I dined quietly with Brinsley FitzGerald at the Ritz, and here it was curious to observe how Paris, like Dover, had put on a sombre garb of war. The buoyant, optimistic nature of the French people was apparent in the few we met; but there was no bombastic, over-confident tone in the conversation around us; only a quiet, but grim, determination which fully appreciated the tremendous difficulties and gigantic issues at stake. The false optimism of *à Berlin* associated with 1870 was conspicuously absent. In its place, a silent determination to fight to the last franc and to the last man.

We left Paris by motor early on the 16th, and arrived at Joffre's Headquarters at Vitry-le-François at noon. A few minutes before our arrival a captured German flag (the first visible trophy of war I had seen) had been brought in, and the impression of General Joffre which was left on my mind was that he possessed a fund of human understanding and sympathy.

I had heard of the French Commander-in-Chief for years, but had never before seen him. He struck me at once as a man of strong will and determination, very courteous and considerate, but firm and steadfast of mind and purpose, and not easily turned or persuaded. He appeared to me to be capable of exercising a powerful influence over the troops he commanded and as likely to enjoy their confidence.

These were all "first impressions"; but I may say here that everything I then thought of General Joffre was far more than confirmed throughout the year and a half of fierce struggle during which I was associated with him. His steadfastness and determination, his courage and patience, were tried to the utmost and never found wanting. History will rank him as one of the supremely great leaders. The immediate task before him was stupendous, and nobly did he arise to it.

I was quite favourably impressed by General Berthelot (Joffre's Chief of Staff) and all the Staff Officers I met, and was much struck by their attitude and bearing. There was a complete absence of fuss, and a calm, deliberate confidence was manifest everywhere. I had a long conversation with the Commander-in-Chief, at which General Berthelot was present. He certainly never gave me the slightest reason to suppose that any idea of "retirement" was in his mind. He discussed possible alternatives of action depending upon the information received of the enemy's plans and dispositions; but his main intention was always to attack.

There were two special points in this conversation which recur to my mind.

As the British Army was posted on the left, or exposed flank, I asked Joffre to place the French Cavalry Division, and two Reserve Divisions which were echeloned in reserve behind, directly under my orders. This the Commander-in-Chief found himself unable to concede.

The second point I recall is the high esteem in which the General Commanding the 5th French Army, General Lanrezac, which was posted on my immediate right, was held by Joffre and his Staff. He was represented to me as the best Commander in the French Army, on whose complete support and skilful co-operation I could thoroughly rely.

Before leaving, the Commander-in-Chief handed me a written memorandum setting forth his views as he had stated them to me, accompanied by a short appreciation of the situation made by the Chief of the General Staff.

We motored to Rheims, where we slept that night. Throughout this long motor journey we passed through great areas of cultivated country. All work, it seemed, had ceased; the crops were half cut, and stooks of corn were lying about everywhere. It was difficult to imagine how the harvest would be saved; but one of my most extraordinary experiences in France was to watch the farming and agriculture going on as if by magic. When, how, or by whom it was done, has always been an enigma to me. There can be no doubt that the women and children proved an enormous help to their country in these directions. Their share of the victory should never be forgotten. It has been distilled from their sweat and tears.

On the morning of the 17th I went to Rethel, which was the Headquarters of the General Commanding the 5th French Army. Having heard such eulogies of him at French G.H.Q., my first impressions of General Lanrezac were probably coloured and modified in his favour; but, looking back, I remember that his personality did not convey to me the idea of a great leader. He was a big man with a loud voice, and his manner did not strike me as being very courteous.

When he was discussing the situation, his attitude might have made a casual observer credit him with practical powers of command and determination of character; but, for my own part, I seemed to detect, from the first time my eyes fell upon him, a certain over-confidence which appeared to ignore the necessity for any consideration of alternatives. Although we arrived at a mutual understanding which included no idea or thought of "retreat," I left General Lanrezac's Headquarters believing that the Commander-in-Chief had over-rated his ability; and I was therefore not surprised when he afterwards turned out to be the most complete example, amongst the many this War has afforded, of the Staff College "pedant," whose "superior education" had given him little idea of how to conduct war.

On leaving Rethel, I motored to Vervins, where I interviewed the Commanders of the French Reserve Divisions in my immediate neighbourhood, and reached my Headquarters at Le Cateau late in the afternoon.

The first news I got was of the sudden death of my dear old friend and comrade, Jimmie Grierson (General Sir James Grierson, Commanding the 2nd Army Corps). He was taken ill quite suddenly in the train on his way to his own Corps Headquarters, and died in a few minutes. I had known him for many years, but since 1906 had been quite closely associated with him; for he had taken a leading part in the preparation of the Army for war throughout that time. He possessed a wonderful personality, and was justly beloved by officers and men alike. He was able to get the best work out of them, and they would follow him anywhere. He had been British Military Attaché in Berlin for some years, and had thus acquired an intimate knowledge of the German Army. An excellent linguist, he spoke French with ease and fluency, and he used to astonish French soldiers by his intimate knowledge of the history of their regiments, which was often far in excess of what they knew themselves. His military acquirements were brilliant, and in every respect thoroughly up-to-date. Apart from the real affection I always felt for him, I regarded his loss as a great calamity in the conduct of the campaign.

His place was taken by Sir Horace Smith-Dorrien, although I asked that Sir Herbert Plumer might be sent out to me to succeed Grierson in command of the 2nd Corps. As a matter of fact, the question of Sir James Grierson's successor was not referred to me at all. The appointment was made at home. Although I knew Sir Horace to be a soldier who had done good service and possessed a fine record, I had asked for Sir Herbert Plumer because I felt he was the right man for this command.

Lord Kitchener had asked me to send him a statement of the French dispositions west of the Meuse. I sent him this in the following letter:

Headquarters
Le Cateau
August 17th, 1914
My Dear Lord K.

With reference to your wire asking for information as to the position of French troops west of the line Givet—Dinant—Namur—Brussels, I have already replied by wire in general terms. I now send full details.

A Corps of Cavalry (three divisions less one brigade), supported by some Infantry, is north of the River Sambre between Charleroi and Namur. This is the nearest French force to the Belgian Army, and I do not know if and where they have established communication with them, nor do the French.

One French Corps, with an added Infantry Brigade and a Cavalry Brigade, is guarding the River Meuse from Givet to Namur. The bridges are mined and ready to be blown up.

In rear of this corps, two more corps are moving—one on Philippeville, the other on Beaumont. Each of these two corps is composed of three divisions. In rear of them a fourth corps assembles tomorrow west of Beaumont. Three Reserve divisions are already in waiting between Vervins and Hirson. Another Reserve division is guarding the almost impassable country between Givet and Mézières.

Finally, other Reserve formations are guarding the frontier between Maubeuge and Lille.

I left Paris on Sunday morning (16th) by motor, and reached the Headquarters of General Joffre (French Commander-in-Chief) at 12. They are at Vitry-le-François. He quite realises the importance and value of adopting a waiting attitude. In the event of a forward movement by the German Corps in the Ardennes and Luxemburg, he is anxious that I should act in echelon on the left of the 5th French Army, whose present disposition I have stated above. The French

Cavalry Corps now north of the Sambre will operate on my left front and keep touch with the Belgians.

I spent the night at Rheims and motored this morning to Rethel, the Headquarters of General Lanrezac, Commander 5th French Army. I had a long talk with him and arranged for co-operation in all alternative circumstances.

I then came on to my Headquarters at this place where I found everything proceeding satisfactorily and up to time. I was much shocked to hear of Grierson's sudden death near Amiens when I arrived here. I had already wired asking you to appoint Plumer in his place, when your wire reached me and also that of Ian Hamilton, forwarded—as I understand—by you. I very much hope you will send me Plumer; Hamilton is too senior to command an Army Corps and is already engaged in an important command at home.

Please do as I ask you in this matter? I needn't assure you there was no 'promise' of any kind.

Yours sincerely

J. D. P. French

P.S.—I am much impressed by all I have seen of the French General Staff. They are very deliberate, calm, and confident. There was a total absence of fuss and confusion, and a determination to give only a just and proper value to any reported successes. So far there has been no conflict of first-rate importance, but there has been enough fighting to justify a hope that the French artillery is superior to the German.

It was on Tuesday, August 18th, that I was first able to assemble the Corps Commanders and their Staffs. Their reports as to the transport of their troops from their mobilising stations to France were highly satisfactory.

The nation owes a deep debt of gratitude to the Naval Transport Service and to all concerned in the embarking and disembarking of the Expeditionary Force. Every move was carried out exactly to time, and the concentration of the British Army on the left of the French was effected in such a manner as to enable every unit to obtain the requisite time to familiarise troops with active service conditions, before it became necessary to make severe demands upon their strength and endurance.

My discussion with the Corps Commanders was based upon the following brief appreciation of the situation on that day. This was as follows:

Between Tirlemont (to the east of Louvain) and Metz, the enemy has some 13 to 15 Army Corps and seven Cavalry Divisions. A certain number of reserve troops are said to be engaged in the offensive of Liége, the forts of which place are believed to be still intact, although some of the enemy's troops hold the town.

These German Corps are in two main groups, seven to eight Corps and four Cavalry Divisions being between Tirlemont and Givet. Six to seven Corps and three Cavalry Divisions are in Belgian Luxemburg.

Of the northern group, it is believed that the greater part—perhaps five Corps—are either north and west of the Meuse, or being pushed across by bridges at Huy and elsewhere.

The general direction of the German advance is by Waremme on Tirlemont. Two German Cavalry Divisions which crossed the Meuse some days ago have reached Gembloux, but have been driven back to Mont Arden by French cavalry supported by a mixed Belgian brigade.

The German plans are still rather uncertain, but it is confidently believed that at least five Army Corps and two or three Cavalry Divisions will move against the French frontiers southwest, on a great line between Brussels and Givet.

The 1st French Corps is now at Dinant, one Infantry and one Cavalry Brigade opposing the group of German Corps south of the Meuse.

The 10th and 3rd Corps are on the line Rethel—Thuin, south of the Sambre. The 18th Corps are moving up on the left of the 10th and 3rd.

Six or seven Reserve French Divisions are entrenched on a line reaching from Dunkirk, on the coast, through Cambrai and La Capelle, to Hirson.

The Belgian Army is entrenched on a line running north-east and south-west through Louvain.

My general instructions were then communicated to Corps Commanders as follows:

> When our concentration is complete, it is intended that we should operate on the left of the French 5th Army, the 18th Corps being on our right. The French Cavalry Corps of three divisions will be on our left and in touch with the Belgians.
>
> As a preliminary to this, we shall take up an area north of the Sambre, and on Monday the heads of the Allied columns should be on the line Mons—Givet, with the cavalry on the outer flank. Should the German attack develop in the manner expected, we shall advance on the general line Mons—Dinant to meet it.

During these first days, whilst our concentration was in course of completion, I rode about a great deal amongst the troops, which were generally on the move to take up their billets or doing practice route marches. I had an excellent opportunity of observing the physique and general appearance of the men. Many of the reservists at first bore traces of the civilian life which they had just left, and presented an anxious, tired appearance; but it was wonderful to observe the almost hourly improvement which took place amongst them. I knew that, under the supervision and influence of the magnificent body of officers and non-commissioned officers which belonged to the 1st Expeditionary Force, all the reservists, even those who had been for years away from the colours, would, before going under fire, regain to the full the splendid military vigour, determination, and spirit which has at all times been so marked a characteristic of British soldiers in the field.

I received a pressing request from the King of the Belgians to visit His Majesty at his Headquarters at Louvain; but the immediate course of the operations prevented me from doing so.

The opening phases of the Battle of Mons did not commence until the morning of Saturday, August 22nd. Up to that time, so far as the British forces were concerned, the forwarding of offensive operations had complete possession of our minds.

During the days which intervened, I had frequent meetings and discussions with the Corps and Cavalry Commanders. The Intelligence Reports which constantly arrived, and the results of cavalry and aircraft reconnaissances, only confirmed the previous appreciation of the situation, and left no doubt as to the direction of the German advance; but nothing came to hand which led us to foresee the crushing superiority of strength which actually confronted us on Sunday, August 23rd.

This was our first practical experience in the use of aircraft for reconnaissance purposes. It cannot be said that in these early days of the fighting the cavalry entirely abandoned that role. On the contrary, they furnished me with much useful information.

The number of our aeroplanes was then limited, and their powers of observation were not so developed or so accurate as they afterwards became. Nevertheless, they kept close touch with the enemy, and their reports proved of the greatest value.

Whilst at this time, as I have said, aircraft did not altogether replace cavalry as regards the gaining and collection of information, yet, by working together as they did, the two arms gained much more accurate and voluminous knowledge of the situation. It was, indeed, the timely warning they gave which chiefly enabled me to make speedy dispositions to avert danger and disaster.

There can be no doubt indeed that, even then, the presence and co-operation of aircraft saved the very frequent use of small cavalry patrols and detached supports. This enabled the latter arm to save horseflesh and concentrate their power more on actual combat and fighting, and to this is greatly due the marked success which attended the operations of the cavalry during the Battle of Mons and the subsequent retreat.

At the time I am writing, however, it would appear that the duty of collecting information and maintaining touch with an enemy in the field will in future fall entirely upon the air service, which will set the cavalry free for different but equally important work.

I had daily consultations with Sir William Robertson, the Quartermaster-General. He expressed himself as well satisfied with the condition of the transport, both horse and mechanical, although he said the civilian drivers were giving a little trouble at first. Munitions and supplies were well provided for, and there were at least 1,000 rounds per gun and 800 rounds per rifle. We also discussed the arrangements for the evacuation of wounded.

The immediate despatch from home of the 4th Division was now decided upon and had commenced, and I received sanction to form a 19th Brigade of Infantry from the Line of Communication battalions.

At this time I received some interesting reports as to the work of the French cavalry in Belgium. Their morale was high and they were very efficient. They were opposed by two divisions of German cavalry whose patrols, they said, showed great want of dash and initiative, and were not well supported. They formed the opinion that the German horse did not care about trying conclusions mounted, but endeavoured to draw the French under the fire of artillery and *jäger* battalions, the last-named always accompanying a German Cavalry Division.

At 5.30 a.m. on the 21st I received a visit from General de Morionville, Chief of the Staff to His Majesty the King of the Belgians, who, with a small staff, was proceeding to Joffre's Headquarters. The General showed signs of the terrible ordeal through which he and his gallant army had passed since the enemy had so grossly violated Belgian territory. He confirmed all the reports we had received concerning the situation generally, and added that the unsupported condition of the Belgian Army rendered their position very precarious, and that the King had, therefore, determined to effect a retirement on Antwerp, where they would be prepared to attack the flank of the enemy's columns as they advanced. He told me he hoped to arrive at a complete understanding with the French Commander-in-Chief.

On this day, August 21st, the Belgians evacuated Brussels and were retiring on Antwerp, and I received the following message from the Government:

> The Belgian Government desire to assure the British and French Governments of the unreserved support of the Belgian Army on the left flank of the Allied Armies with the whole of its troops and all available resources, wherever their line of communications with the base at

Antwerp, where all their ammunition and food supplies are kept, is not in danger of being severed by large hostile forces. Within the above-mentioned limits the Allied Armies may continue to rely on the co-operation of the Belgian troops.

Since the commencement of hostilities the Field Army has been holding the line Tirlemont—Jodoigne—Hammemille—Louvain, where, up to the 18th August, it has been standing by, hoping for the active co-operation of the Allied Army.

On August 18th it was decided that the Belgian Army, consisting of 50,000 Infantry rifles, 276 guns, and 4,100 Cavalry should retreat on the Dyle. This step was taken owing to the fact that the support of the Allies had not yet been effective, and, moreover, that the Belgian forces were menaced by three Army Corps and three Cavalry Divisions (the greater part of the First Army of the Meuse), who threatened to cut their communications with their base.

The rearguard of the 1st Division of the Army having been forced to retire after a fierce engagement lasting five or six hours on August 18th, and the Commander of the Division having stated that his troops were not in a fit state to withstand a long engagement owing to the loss of officers and the weariness of the men; and, moreover, as the Commander of the 3rd Division of the Army, which was so sorely tried at Liége, had similarly come to the conclusion, on August 19th, that the defence of the Dyle was becoming very dangerous, more especially in view of the turning movement of the 2nd Army Corps and 2nd Cavalry Division, it was definitely decided to retreat under the protection of the forts at Antwerp.

The general idea is now that the Field Army, in part or as a whole, should issue from Antwerp as soon as circumstances seem to favour such a movement.

In this event, the Army will try to co-operate in its movements with the Allies as circumstances may dictate.

Exhaustive reconnaissances and intelligence reports admitted of no doubt that the enemy was taking the fullest advantage of his violation of Belgian territory, and that he was protected to the right of his advance, at least as far west as Soignies and Nivelles, whence he was moving direct upon the British and 5th French Armies.

In further proof that, at this time, no idea of retreat was in the minds of the leaders of the Allied Armies, I received late on Friday, the 21st, General Lanrezac's orders to his troops. All his corps were in position south of the Sambre, and he was only waiting the development of a move by the 3rd and 4th French Armies from the line Mézières—Longwy to begin his own advance.

As regards our own troops, on the evening of the 21st, the cavalry, under Allenby, were holding the line of the Condé Canal with four brigades. Two brigades of horse artillery were in reserve at Harmignies. The 5th Cavalry Brigade, under Chetwode, composed of the Scots Greys, 12th Lancers, and 20th Hussars, were at Binche, in touch with the French.

Reconnoitring squadrons and patrols were pushed out towards Soignies and Nivelles.

I visited Allenby's Headquarters in the afternoon of the 21st, and discussed the situation with him. I told him on no account to commit the cavalry to any engagement of importance, but to draw off towards our left flank when pressed by the enemy's columns, and there remain in readiness for action and reconnoitring well to the left.

The 1st Army Corps, under Sir Douglas Haig, was in cantonments to the north of Maubeuge, between that place and Givry. The 2nd Corps, under Sir Horace Smith-Dorrien, was to the north-west of Maubeuge, between that place and Sars-la-Bruyère. The 19th Infantry Brigade was concentrating at Valenciennes.

Turning to our Ally, the 6th and 7th French Reserve Divisions were entrenching themselves on a line running from Dunkirk, through Cambrai and La Capelle, to Hirson. The 5th French Army was on our right, the 18th French Corps being in immediate touch with the British Army. Three Divisions of French cavalry under General Sordet, which had been operating in support of the Belgians, were falling back behind the 18th Corps for rest and refit. The 3rd and 4th French Armies, comprising 8-1/2 Corps, three Cavalry Divisions and some reserve Divisions, were between Mézières and Longwy. The French troops further south had taken the offensive and marched into Alsace. Liége still held out. Namur was intact. The Belgians seemed secure behind the fortifications of Antwerp.

Before going further it would be as well to give some account of the country in which the two opposing forces faced one another on the night of Friday, August 21st, the area Condé—Cambrai—Le Nouvion—Binche:

Distances	
Cambrai to Condé	24 miles
Condé to Binche	26 miles
Cambrai to Le Nouvion	26 miles
Le Nouvion to Binche	31 miles

This region forms part of the Belgian province of Hainault and the French Departments of the Nord and the Aisne, lying approximately between the upper valleys of the Rivers Scheldt and Sambre. Its northern boundary is formed by the basin of the River Haine. This river, formed from three streams which rise in the neighbourhood of Binche, passes Mons and flows into the Scheldt at Condé after a course of 30 miles. Close to its left bank, from Mons to Condé, a canal connects the former place with the Scheldt. Prior to the construction of this canal, the Haine was navigable by means of locks. Several small parallel streams run into it from the south, along sunken valleys in an undulating plateau, over which lie scattered the various mines of the Bérinage coalfield.

West of Mons the valley of the Haine forms a long, low plain, covered with meadows, through which the river meanders in broad bends as far as the Scheldt. Numerous water ditches, cut in the peaty soil and marked out by poplars and willows, drain the land and render the movement off the roads of any troops but infantry quite impracticable.

On the northern boundary of the valley of the Haine, a belt of sand gives rise to a tract of rough uncultivated land which is in many places covered with woods. On its southern boundary the ground rises steeply on the east, and more gently on the west, to the Franco-Belgian frontier, over a rocky subsoil in which the affluents of the river have cut deep valleys.

The Mons-Condé Canal has a length of 16¼ miles, 12¼ of which are in Belgian territory. It has a surface width of 64 feet and its maximum depth is 7 feet. The canal is crossed by 18 bridges, all of which, with the exception of the railway bridge east of St. Ghislain and the railway bridge at Les Herbières, are swing bridges. A metalled towing-path runs along each bank.

The principal passages across the valley of the Haine are at Mons from Brussels, at St. Ghislain from Ath, and near Pommeroeul from Tournai.

The Scheldt, rising near Le Catelet at an altitude of 360 feet above the sea, soon approaches the St. Quentin Canal and runs alongside it as far as Cambrai, where the river and canal flow in one channel and form a navigable connection between the Scheldt and the Somme. Below Cambrai, the now canalised river flows on to Valenciennes, receiving on the way on its left bank the Sensée river and canal, and on its right bank the Ereclin, Selle, Ecaillon, and Rhonelle streams, which flow down in parallel courses from the watershed close to the left bank of the Sambre. From Valenciennes the Scheldt runs to Condé, where, as stated above, it is joined by the Mons-Condé Canal and the River Haine. Immediately afterwards it enters Belgian territory, where it becomes the great river of the Flemish part of the country, just as the Meuse may be said to be the great river of the Walloon portion.

There are 14 locks between Cambrai and Condé, each providing a means of passage over the river. The general breadth of the canalised river is 55 feet and its maximum depth 7 feet. The towing-path follows sometimes one bank and sometimes another. The principal points of crossing of the Scheldt between Cambrai and Condé are at Cambrai, Bouchain, Lourches, Denain, Bouvignies, Thiant, Trith, St. Légers, Valenciennes, and Condé.

While the Scheldt as it grows older flows through country which is for the most part little above sea level, in its upper reaches it cuts through an upland plateau on its way to join the Belgian central plains.

Rising near Fontenelle, 9 miles south-west of Avesnes, the Sambre flows through Landrecies, where it becomes navigable, and where it is connected with the Oise by the Sambre Canal. Flowing past Maubeuge it enters Belgium below Jeumont and traverses thence, in a north-easterly direction, one of the most important industrial districts of Belgium. The country through which the river flows from its source to Charleroi forms a plateau cut up by numerous dales and deep valleys.

Below Landrecies the depth of the river is from 6 to 7 feet, while its breadth is 50 feet; it is nowhere fordable. A towing-path runs in places on the left bank, in places on the right bank. Nine locks regulate the depth of the canal between Landrecies and Jeumont, and afford a means of passage for pedestrians. Communication is amply supplied for wheeled traffic by 22 road and railway bridges, of which the most important are those at Landrecies, Berlaimont, Hautmont, Louvroil, Maubeuge, Jeumont, Erquelinnes, Merbes-le-Château and Lobbes.

South of Landrecies important road bridges cross the Sambre Canal at Catillon and near Oisy.

The principal tributaries of the Sambre, in the area under view, flow into the river from the eastern foothills of the Ardennes; the streams which join it on its left bank are few and insignificant. On the right bank the Rivièrette, the Helpe Mineure, the Helpe Majeure, the Tarsy and the Solre, flowing in parallel courses in a north-westerly direction, lie in deeply cut valleys which broaden out as they reach the main stream. The high ground between these streams offers a succession of defensive positions against an enemy advancing from the north in a south-westerly direction.

The area under review may be divided into two portions. A northern or industrial, with all the inconvenience to military operations characteristic of such a district, and a southern or agricultural with unlimited freedom of movement and view, resembling in many respects the features of Salisbury Plain. The dividing line of these two portions may be taken as a line running through Valenciennes and Maubeuge.

With the exception of the thickly populated Bérinage coalfield, west and south of Mons, the country is open, arable, and undulating. Extensive views are obtainable, the villages, though numerous, are compact, and movement across country is easy.

A notable feature in the southern portions of the area is the Forêt de Mormal and in its neighbourhood the Bois l'Évêque.

The Forêt de Mormal, which is 22,460 acres in extent, is situated on the summit and slopes of the high ground bordering the left bank of the Sambre between Landrecies and Boussières. It is crossed by one first-class road from Le Quesnoy to Avesnes, and several second-class roads.

The forest is also traversed by two railways; that from Paris to Maubeuge, which follows its southern boundary from Landrecies to Sassegnies, and that from Valenciennes to Hirson, which runs from north-west to south-east and joins the former line at Aulnoye. On account of its thick undergrowth, its streams and marshy bottoms, the forest is not passable for troops except by the above-mentioned roads.

Le Bois Levesque (1,805 acres), situated between Landrecies and Le Cateau, may be considered as an extension of the Forêt de Mormal, from which it is only about 2-1/2 miles distant. It is traversed by the railway line from Paris to Maubeuge, by the road from Landrecies to Le Cateau, and the country road from Fontaine to Ors.

In conclusion, let us glance at the principal places of strategic importance in this region which witnessed the opening stages of the retreat from Mons.

In the beginning of the war, Maubeuge, with 20,000 inhabitants, belonged to the second class of French fortresses, which possessed a limited armament and which were destined to act as *points d'appui* for mobile forces acting in their vicinity. The strategic value of Maubeuge is due to the fact that the main lines from Paris to Brussels *via* Mons, and to northern Germany *via* Charleroi and Liége, pass through the town, while from it runs a line towards the eastern frontier *via* Hirson and Mézières, with branch lines leading to Laon and Châlons. It is also a junction of main roads from Valenciennes, Mons, Charleroi, and Laon.

The fortress has a circumference of about 20 miles. The forts, which lie in open country, are mostly small. Shortly before the outbreak of the War the defences of Maubeuge had been strengthened to meet the increased effect of high explosives, and various redoubts and batteries had been constructed in addition to the above-mentioned works.

Mons, the capital of Hainault, had a pre-war population of 28,000 inhabitants, and is situated on a sandhill overlooking the Trovillon. It is the centre of the Bérinage, the chief coal-mining district of Belgium. Main roads from Brussels, Binche, Charleroi, Valenciennes and Maubeuge have their meeting place here, while the railway from Paris to Brussels passes through it. It is also the junction point of the canal from Condé and the Canal Du Centre, which connects the former with the Charleroi Canal and the Sambre.

The town of Binche (12,000 inhabitants), lying 15 miles east-south-east of Mons, is a centre of roads from Charleroi, Brussels, Mons, Bavai, and Beaumont. Through it passes a double line of railway coming from Maubeuge on its way to Brussels.

Condé, a small and old fortified town, owes its military value to its position at the confluence of the Scheldt and the Haine, and to its canal communications with Mons. A single railway line connects it on the north with Tournai and on the south with Valenciennes. The main road from Audenarde to Valenciennes and Cambrai passes here.

The strategetical importance of Valenciennes, a town of 32,000 inhabitants, is due to its being the meeting places of main roads from Cambrai, Lille, Tournai, Condé and Mons. It is also the junction point of the main lines from Paris *via* Cambrai, Hirson, and the north. Its position on the canalised Scheldt has been already referred to.

Cambrai (28,000 inhabitants), lying on the right bank of the Scheldt, which first becomes navigable here, is the centre of main roads from Péronne, Bapaume, Arras, Douai, Valenciennes, Bavai and Le Cateau. It is also important as being the junction point of railways from Paris to Valenciennes and from Douai to St. Quentin.

Le Cateau, where, as I have already said, I established my

first General Headquarters in France, is situated on the Selle. Before the War its population numbered 10,700 and it possessed important woollen mills. It is the junction point of main roads connecting Valenciennes with St. Quentin and Cambrai with Le Nouvion. It also stands on the main line from Paris to Maubeuge, while single-line railways connect it with Cambrai, Valenciennes, and Le Quesnoy.

Lastly, with regard to communications throughout the area, they were good and ample. The principal roads from north to south are those from Condé, through Valenciennes, to Cambrai, Le Cateau, and Landrecies, and from Mons to Binche, to Le Cateau *via* Bavai and to Landrecies through Maubeuge. Numerous second-class roads afford good lateral communications between the above-mentioned roads.

Such, then, was the region in which, on the night of Friday, August 21st, the British Expeditionary Force found itself awaiting its first great trial of strength with the enemy. That night we went to sleep in high hopes. The mobilisation, transport, and concentration of the British Army had been effected without a hitch. The troops had not only been able to rest after their journey, but a few days had been available for practice marches and for overhauling equipment. The condition of the reservists, even those who had been longest away from the colours, was excellent and constantly improving.

The highest spirit pervaded all ranks, and the army with one accord longed to be at grips with the enemy. The cavalry had been pushed well to the front, and such engagements as had taken place between detachments of larger or smaller patrols had foreshadowed that moral superiority of British over German which was afterwards so completely established, and proved of such enormous value in the retreat, the Battles of the Marne and the Aisne, and in the opening phases of the first Battle of Ypres. The French troops had already secured minor successes, and had penetrated into the enemy's territory. The Allied Commanders were full of hope and confidence.

CHAPTER 4

The Retreat from Mons

At 5 a.m. on the 22nd I awoke, as I had lain down to sleep, in high hopes. No evil foreboding of coming events had visited me in dreams; but it was not many hours later that the disillusionment began. I started by motor in the very early hours of a beautiful August morning to visit General Lanrezac at his Headquarters in the neighbourhood of Philippeville.

Soon after entering the area of the 5th French Army, I found my motor stopped at successive cross roads by columns of infantry and artillery moving *south*. After several such delays on my journey, and before I had gone half the distance, I suddenly came up with Captain Spiers of the 11th Hussars, who was the liaison officer at General Lanrezac's Headquarters.

There is an atmosphere engendered by troops retiring, when they expect to be advancing, which is unmistakable to anyone who has had much experience of war. It matters not whether such a movement is the result of a lost battle, an unsuccessful engagement, or is in the nature of a "strategic manoeuvre to the rear." The fact that, whatever the reason may be, it means giving up ground to the enemy, affects the spirits of the troops and manifests itself in the discontented, apprehensive expression which is seen on the faces of the men, and the tired, slovenly, unwilling gait which invariably characterises troops subjected to this ordeal.

This atmosphere surrounded me for some time before I met Spiers and before he had spoken a word. My optimistic visions of the night before had vanished, and what he told me did not tend to bring them back. He reported that the Guard and 7th German Corps had since daybreak advanced on the Sambre in the neighbourhood of Franière, and had attacked the 10th French Corps which was holding the river. The advanced troops had driven the Germans back; but he added that "offensive action was contrary to General Lanrezac's plans," and that this had "annoyed him."

The 10th Corps had had to fall back with some loss, and were taking up ground known as the "Fosse Position," on the south side of the Sambre. Spiers thought that the 10th Corps had been knocked about a good deal. He gave me various items of information gleaned from the Chief of Intelligence of the French 5th Army. These reports went to show that the German turning movement in Belgium was extending far towards the west, the right being kept well forward as though a powerful envelopment was designed. It was evident that the enemy was making some progress in his attempts to bridge and cross the Sambre all along the front of the 5th Army. There appeared to be some difficulty in finding General Lanrezac, and therefore I decided to return at once to my Headquarters at Le Cateau.

I found there that our own Intelligence had received information which confirmed a good deal of what I had heard in the morning. They thought that at least three German Corps were advancing upon us, the most westerly having reached as far as Ath.

The hopes and anticipations with which I concluded the last chapter underwent considerable modification from these experiences and events; but the climax of the day's disappointment and disillusionment was not reached till 11 p.m., when the Head of the French Military Mission at my Headquarters, Colonel Huguet, brought a French Staff Officer to me who had come direct from General Lanrezac. This officer reported the fighting of which Spiers had already informed me, and said that the French 10th Corps had suffered very heavily. When thinking of our estimates of losses in those days, it must be remembered that a dearly bought experience had not yet opened our minds to the terrible toll which modern war exacts.

The position of the 5th French Army extended from Dinant on

the Meuse (just north of Fosse—Charleroi—Thuin back to Trélon) about five Corps in all. Sordet's Cavalry Corps had reported that probably three German Corps were advancing on Brussels.

The German line facing the Anglo-French Army was thought to be *roughly* Soignies—Nivelles—Gembloux, and thence circling to the north of the Sambre, round Namur. A strong column of German infantry was advancing on Charleroi from Fleurus about 3 p.m. on the 21st. There had been heavy fighting at Tamines, on the Sambre, in which French troops had been worsted. General Lanrezac was anxious to know if I would attack the flank of the German columns which were pressing him back from the river.

In view of the most probable situation of the German Army, as it was known to both of us, and the palpable intention of its Commander to effect a great turning movement round my left flank, and having regard to the actual numbers of which I was able to dispose, it is very difficult to realise what was in Lanrezac's mind when he made such a request to me.

As the left of the French 5th Army (Reserve Division of 18th Corps) was drawn back as far as Trélon, and the centre and right of that Army were in process of retiring, the forward position I now held on the Condé Canal might quickly become very precarious.

I, therefore, informed Lanrezac in reply that such an operation as he suggested was quite impracticable for me. I agreed to retain my present position for 24 hours; but after that time I told him it would be necessary for me to consider whether the weight against my front and outer flank, combined with the retreat of the French 5th Army, would not compel me to go back to the Maubeuge position.

I should mention that earlier in the day, on my return to Headquarters after my talk with Spiers, I had despatched the following message to General Lanrezac:

> I am waiting for the dispositions arranged for to be carried out, especially the posting of French Cavalry Corps on my left. I am prepared to fulfil the role allotted to me when the 5th Army advances to the attack.

In the meantime, I hold an advanced defensive position extending from Condé on the left, through Mons to Erquelinnes, where I connect with two Reserve Divisions south of the Sambre. I am now much in advance of the line held by the 5th Army and feel my position to be as forward as circumstances will allow, particularly in view of the fact that I am not properly prepared for offensive action till tomorrow morning, as I have previously informed you.

I do not understand from your wire that the 18th Corps has yet been engaged, and they stand on my inner flank.

I left my Headquarters at 5 a.m. on Sunday the 23rd and went to Sars-la-Bruyère (Headquarters of the 2nd Corps), and there I met Haig, Smith-Dorrien, and Allenby.

The cavalry had, during the 22nd, drawn off towards my left flank after heavy pressure by the enemy's advancing columns, leaving detachments in front of my right to the east of Mons, which was not so severely threatened. These detachments extended in a south-easterly direction south of Bray and Binche, the latter place having been occupied by the enemy. They were in touch with the 5th French Army. Patrols and advanced squadrons had engaged similar bodies of the enemy and had held their own well.

The 2nd Corps occupied the line of the Condé Canal, from that place round the salient which the canal makes to the north of Mons, and extended thence to the east of Obourg, whence that part of the line was drawn back towards Villers-St. Ghislain. The 5th Division was holding the line from Condé to Mariette, whilst the 3rd Division continued the line thence round the salient to the right of the line occupied by the 2nd Corps. The 1st Corps was echeloned on the right and in rear of the 2nd.

I told the commanders of the doubts which had arisen in my mind during the previous 24 hours, and impressed on them the necessity of being prepared for any kind of move, either in advance or in retreat. I discussed exhaustively the situation on our front.

Allenby's bold and searching reconnaissance had not led me to believe that we were threatened by forces against which we could not make an effective stand. The 2nd Corps had not yet been seriously engaged, while the 1st was practically still in reserve.

Allenby's orders to concentrate towards the left flank when pressed by the advance of the enemy's main columns had been practically carried into effect. I entertained some anxiety as to the salient which the canal makes north of Mons, and enjoined on Smith-Dorrien particular watchfulness and care with regard to it.

They all assured me that a quiet night had been passed and that their line was firmly taken up and held.

The air reconnaissance had started at daybreak, and I decided to await aircraft reports from Henderson before making any decided plan.

I instructed Sir Archibald Murray, my Chief of Staff, to remain for the present at General Smith-Dorrien's Headquarters at Sars-la-Bruyère, and gave him full instructions as to arrangements which must be made if a retreat became necessary. I then went on to Valenciennes. General Drummond (Commanding the 19th Infantry Brigade) and the French Commandant at Valenciennes met me at the station.

I inspected a part of the entrenchments which were under construction, and the disposition of the Territorial troops (two divisions under General d'Amade) which were detailed to hold them and to guard our left flank. The 19th Brigade (2nd Batt. R. Welsh Fusiliers, 1st Batt. Scottish Rifles, 1st Batt. Middlesex Regt., and 2nd Batt. Argyle and Sutherland Highlanders) was just completing its detrainment, and I placed Drummond under the orders of General Allenby commanding the Cavalry Division.

During this day (August 23rd) reports continued to reach me of heavy pressure on our outposts all along the line, but chiefly between Condé and Mons.

Sir Horace Smith-Dorrien, it will be remembered, was now in command of the 2nd Corps, having been sent out from England in succession to Sir James Grierson on the latter's untimely death.

After my conference with the Corps Commanders on the morning of the 23rd, I left General Smith-Dorrien full of confidence in regard to his position, but when I returned to my Headquarters in the afternoon, reports came to hand that he was giving up the salient at Mons because the outpost line at Obourg had been penetrated by the enemy, and that he was also preparing to give up the whole of the line of the canal before nightfall. He said that he anticipated a gap occurring in his line between the 3rd and 5th Divisions in the neighbourhood of Mariette, and he went so far as to make a request for help to the 1st Corps.

Up to this time there was no decided threat in any strength on Condé, Sir Horace, therefore, need not have feared an imminent turning movement, and, as regards his front, he was nowhere threatened by anything more than cavalry supported by small bodies of infantry.

At that time no directions for retreat had been issued from Headquarters, although the Chief of the General Staff had been left at Sars-la-Bruyère on purpose to give orders for such a movement if it should become necessary.

The General's anxiety seems to have lessened later in the afternoon, for at 5 p.m. a message from the 2nd Corps said that the commander was "well satisfied with the situation."

The 3rd Division was now effecting a retirement south of the canal to a line running west through Nouvelles, and this movement had the inevitable result of bringing back the 5th Division and handing over the bridges of the canal to the German cavalry.

Every report I was now receiving at Headquarters pointed to the early necessity of a retirement of the British Forces in view of the general strategic situation, and I did not, therefore, deem it desirable to interfere with the 2nd Corps commander.

Reports of German activity on his front continued to be received from the G.O.C. 2nd Corps. At 7.15 p.m. he asked for permission to retire on Bavai; at 9.45 he was again reassured—a Divisional Headquarters which had retired was now "moving forward again"; and at 10.20 p.m. he reported, "casualties in no way excessive; all quiet now."

The line which the 2nd Corps had taken up for the night showed an average retirement of three miles south of the canal. During the late afternoon the advanced troops of the 1st Corps were engaged, but not seriously threatened; they held their ground.

During the late afternoon and evening very disquieting reports had arrived as to the situation on my right. These were confirmed later in a telegram from French Headquarters, which arrived at half-past eleven at night. It clearly showed that our present position was strategically untenable; but this conclusion had been forced upon me much earlier in the evening when I received a full appreciation of the situation as it then appeared at French General Headquarters. General Joffre also told me that his information led him to expect that I might be attacked the next day by at least three German Corps and two Cavalry Divisions.

Appreciating the situation from the point of view which all reports now clearly established, my last hope of an offensive had to be abandoned, and it became necessary to consider an immediate retreat from our present forward position.

I selected the new line from Jerlain (south-east of Valenciennes) eastwards to Maubeuge. This line had already been reconnoitred. The Corps and Divisional Staff Officers who were called into Headquarters to receive orders, especially those of the 2nd Corps, thought our position was much more seriously threatened than it really was and, in fact, one or two expressed doubts as to the possibility of effecting a retirement in the presence of the enemy in our immediate front. I did not share these views, and Colonel Vaughan (Chief of the Staff of the Cavalry Division) was more inclined to accept my estimate of the enemy's forces on or near the canal than the others were. His opportunities of gauging the enemy's strength and dispositions had been greatly enhanced by the fine reconnoitring work done on the previous two or three days by the Cavalry Division. However, I determined to effect the retreat, and orders were issued accordingly.

The 1st Army Corps was to move up towards Givry and to take up a good line to cover the retreat of the 2nd Corps towards Bavai, which was to commence at daybreak. Our front and left flank was to be screened and covered by the cavalry and the 19th Infantry Brigade.

At about 1 a.m. on the 24th, Spiers came in from the Headquarters of the 5th French Army and told me that they were seriously checked all along the line. The 3rd and 4th French Armies were retiring, and the 5th French Army, after its check on Saturday, was conforming to the general movement.

The information previously referred to as arriving from French Headquarters at 11.30 p.m. on the 23rd was as follows:

1. Namur fell this day.

2. The 5th French Army had been attacked all along their front by the 3rd German Corps, the Guard, the 10th and 7th Corps, and was falling back on the line Givet—Philippeville—Maubeuge.

3. Hastière had been captured by the Germans on the 23rd.

4. The Meuse was falling rapidly and becoming fordable in many places, hence the difficulty of defence.

At 5.30 a.m. on the 24th I went out to my advanced Headquarters, which had been established at Bavai, a small village which is strategically important from the circumstance that it is the meeting place of roads from every point of the compass. The orders issued through the night had been carried out. The 1st Corps was on the line Nouvelles—Harmignies—Givry, with Corps Headquarters at Bonnet. They were making an excellent stand to cover the retirement of the 2nd Corps, which was being hard pressed, particularly the 5th Division to the south-east of Condé. In fact, at 10 a.m. General Fergusson, Commanding the Division, found it necessary to call very urgently upon General Allenby for help and support. The 19th Infantry Brigade under Drummond had, it will be remembered, been placed at the disposal of the commander of the Cavalry Division, who, calling this Brigade up in immediate support of the 5th Division, directed Gough's 3rd and De Lisle's 2nd Cavalry Brigades (3rd Cavalry Brigade: 4th Hussars, 5th Lancers, and 16th Lancers; 2nd Cavalry Brigade: 4th Dragoon Guards, 9th Lancers, and 18th Hussars) to threaten and harass the flanks of the advancing German troops, whilst Bingham's 4th Cavalry Brigade remained in observation towards the west.

The intervention of Allenby and Drummond, and the support they rendered, was most effective in taking the severe pressure of the enemy off the 5th Division and enabling it to continue its retreat. About 11.30 a.m. the 2nd Corps Headquarters were retired from Sars-la-Bruyère to Hon.

Soon after arriving at Bavai I visited the Headquarters of the 1st Corps at Bonnet and observed the fighting above mentioned. Our troops in this part of the line were very active and pushing. The 8th Brigade under Davies (2nd Batt. Royal Scots, 2nd Batt. Royal Irish Regt., 4th Batt. Middlesex Regt. and 1st Batt. Gordon Highlanders) was now at Nouvelles, on the left; then came the rest of the 2nd Division, and then the 1st Division under Lomax, on the right.

I went out from Haig's Headquarters to a high ridge, whence the ground slopes down towards the north and north-east, along a gentle declivity stretching almost to the canal which was some distance away. The situation of the 1st Corps was excellent, and the artillery positions were well chosen. From where we stood we could observe the effect of our fire. It was very accurate, and shrapnel could be seen bursting well over the enemy lines and holding his advance in complete check, whilst the German fire was by no means so effective. The infantry were defending their position a long way down the slope with great determination and tenacity. The steadfast attitude and skilful retreat of our right wing at Mons had much to do with the success of our withdrawal, and the short time I spent with the 1st Corps that morning inspired me with great confidence.

The subsequent retirement of the 1st Corps was carried out successfully and with little loss, Haig's Headquarters being established at Riez de l'Erelle at about 1 p.m.

After visiting some important points in the field over which the 2nd Corps was fighting, I determined to seek out General Sordet, Commanding the French Cavalry Corps, which was in cantonments somewhere to the east of Maubeuge. I found Sordet's Headquarters at Avesnes. The scene in the village was very typical of continental war as it has been so often presented to us in pictures of the war of 1870.

The Commander of the French Cavalry Corps and his Staff, whom I met in the central square, formed a striking group against a very suitable background of gun parks and ammunition wagons. One looked in vain for the fire-eating *beau sabreur* of a Murat.

The man who had come back from that first desperate onslaught in Belgium, and had so grandly supported and succoured our hard-pressed Allies in their splendid defence, was a very quiet, undemonstrative, spare little figure of at least 60 years of age. He appeared hard and fit, and showed no sign of the tremendous strain he had already undergone. On the contrary, he was smart and dapper, and looked like the light-weight horseman he is. His clear-cut face and small, regular features, denoted descent from the old *noblesse*, and he struck me in his bright tunic as one who might be most fittingly imaged in a piece of old Dresden china; but added to all this was the bearing of a Cavalry Commander.

His manner was courteous in the extreme; but he showed inflexible firmness and determination.

His Staff were of the pattern of French cavalry officers. I have seen much of them for years past at manoeuvres, etc., and they combine the best qualities of cavalry leaders with the utmost *camaraderie* and good fellowship.

I interviewed the General at some length, pointing out what I had been told by General Joffre and his Chief of Staff, namely, that the Cavalry Corps had been directed to operate on my left or outer flank. I informed him that in my opinion this was the point where his presence was chiefly required, and where his action would be most effective in checking the advance of the enemy. I told the General that I should be very glad of his help in that locality as soon as possible, because in my present forward position, and having regard to the continued retirement of the 5th French Army, I should sorely need all the assistance I could get to establish the Army under my command in their new position.

General Sordet was very courteous and sympathetic. He expressed the utmost desire to help me in every possible way. He added that he had received no orders to move to the left flank and must, therefore, await these instructions before he could march. He further told me that after the arduous time he had experienced when supporting the Belgian Army, his horses stood in the most urgent need of rest, and that, in any case, it would be impossible for him to leave his present position for at least 24 hours. He promised, however, to do all in his power to help me, and, as my story will presently show, he kept his word splendidly.

I then went back to Le Cateau to pick up any messages or news from Joffre or Lanrezac. Here I was gladdened by the sight of the detrainment of the advanced troops of the 4th Division (General Snow).

After a brief halt at Le Cateau, I started again for my advanced Headquarters at Bavai. The experiences of that afternoon remain indelibly impressed on my memory. Very shortly after leaving Le Cateau I was met by streams of Belgian refugees, flying from Mons and its neighbourhood. They were lying about the fields in all directions, and blocking the roads with carts and vans in which they were trying to carry off as much of their worldly goods as possible. The whole country-side showed those concrete evidences of disturbance and alarm which brought home to all our minds what this retreat meant and all that it might come to mean.

After much delay from these causes I reached Bavai about 2.30 p.m., and it was with great difficulty that my motor could wind its way through the mass of carts, horses, fugitives and military baggage trains which literally covered almost every yard of space in the small town. The temporary advanced Headquarters were established in the market place, the appearance of which defies description. The Babel of voices, the crying of women and children, mingled with the roar of the guns and the not far distant crack of rifles and machine guns, made a deafening noise, amidst which it was most difficult to keep a clear eye and tight grip on the rapidly changing course of events.

In a close room on the upper floor of the *Mairie* I found Murray, my Chief of Staff, working hard, minus belt, coat and collar. The heat was intense. The room was filled with Staff Officers bringing reports or awaiting instructions. Some of the Headquarters Staff had not closed their eyes for 48 hours, and were stretched out on forms or huddled up in corners, wrapped in that deep slumber which only comes to brains which, for the time being, are completely worn out.

If some of the armchair critics who so glibly talk of the easy time which Staff Officers, compared with their regimental comrades, have in war—if some of them could have watched that scene, they would be more chary of forming such opinions and spreading such wrong ideas.

Personally, I have always been far more a regimental than a Staff Officer, and I have every reason to sympathise with the former, but when I have witnessed scenes and gone through days such as I am now very imperfectly describing, and when I know such days to be frequent and long drawn out occurrences in war, it makes my blood boil to hear and to read of the calumnies which are often heaped upon the head of the unfortunate Staff.

Murray did splendid work that day and set the best of examples. On my arrival at Bavai he reported the situation fully and clearly to me. The action of the cavalry and the 19th Brigade on the left had greatly relieved the heavy pressure on the 5th Division, and the retirement was proceeding fairly well.

Information had, however, reached me of the defeat and retreat of the 3rd French Army, and the continued falling back of Lanrezac. I judged also, by the method and direction of the attack, that strenuous attempts were being made to turn our left flank and press me back on Maubeuge. The force opposed to me was growing in size, and I judged it to be more than double my numbers. As subsequent information proved, we were actually opposed by four corps and at least two cavalry divisions.

Early in the afternoon it was clear to me that further definite decisions must be taken. We could not stand on the line towards which the troops were now retiring.

The fortress of Maubeuge lay close on my right rear. It was well fortified and provisioned. It is impossible for anyone, who has not been situated as I was, to realise the terrible temptation which such a place offers to an army seeking shelter against overpowering odds.

For a short time on this fateful afternoon I debated within

myself whether or not I should yield to this temptation; but I did not hesitate long, because there were two considerations which forced themselves prominently upon my mind.

In the first place, I had an instinctive feeling that this was exactly what the enemy was trying to make me do; and, in the second place, I had the example of Bazaine and Metz in 1870 present in my mind, and the words of Sir Edward Hamley's able comment upon the decision of the French Marshal came upon me with overwhelming force. Hamley described it as "The anxiety of the temporising mind which prefers postponement of a crisis to vigorous enterprise." Of Bazaine he says, "In clinging to Metz he acted like one who, when the ship is foundering, should lay hold of the anchor."

I therefore abandoned all such ideas, and issued orders at about 3 p.m. directing the retreat some miles further back to the line Le Cateau—Cambrai.

The pressure of the enemy on our left flank became greater towards night. All reports and reconnaissances indicated a determined attempt to outflank us and cut across our line of retreat, but Allenby's cavalry was splendidly disposed and handled. The German columns were kept at bay, and the troops bivouacked generally on a line somewhat south of that towards which they had been ordered to retreat in the morning. There was some confusion in the retirement of the 2nd Corps. The 5th Division crossed the rear of the 3rd near Bavai, got to the east of them and somewhat on the line of the retreat of the 1st Corps, whose movement was thus hampered and delayed.

I got back to Headquarters at Le Cateau late in the evening, where a budget of reports awaited me. The most important news was contained in a telephone message received at 9.40 p.m. from Major Clive of the Grenadier Guards, who was my liaison officer at French Headquarters. This ran as follows:

> The 4th Army, fighting against an enemy estimated at three Corps, has fallen back to the line Virton—Spincourt. Three Reserve Divisions made a counter-attack this afternoon from the south against the enemy's left flank. The 3rd Army, fighting in difficult country, has fallen back to

better ground this side of the Meuse, about Mézières and Stenai. The enemy have been unable to cross the Meuse. The 3rd Army is waiting for sufficient strength to make a counter-attack from its right. The 1st Corps of the 5th Army found that the Germans had crossed the Meuse behind them south of Dinant; they therefore fell back to the neighbourhood of Givet and Philippeville.

Murray followed me to Headquarters about 3 a.m., and reported that all orders had been carried out effectually and that the move was proceeding satisfactorily. All the troops were very tired and had suffered severely from the heat. Our losses in the fighting of the last two days were considerable, but not excessive, having regard to the nature of the operations.

In the early hours of the 25th the retreat was continued, again covered skilfully by Allenby's cavalry.

During the night the 4th Division had nearly completed their detrainment, and were taking up the position assigned to them towards Cambrai. In the course of the morning of the 25th I visited Snow, who commanded this Division, and went over the ground with him.

The only action of importance during the day occurred at Solesmes, when the rearguard of the 3rd Division under McCracken was heavily attacked. Allenby, with the 2nd Cavalry Brigade (4th Dragoon Guards, 9th Lancers, and 18th Hussars), came to his assistance and enabled him to continue his retreat. He did not, however, arrive at his appointed destination till late in the evening, and then it was with very tired men.

The reports received up till noon of the 25th showed that the French were retiring all along the line, and there was no longer any doubt in my mind as to the strength and intention of the enemy in our own immediate front. Three Corps and a Cavalry Division were concentrating against us, whilst a fourth Corps and another Cavalry Division were trying to turn our western flank.

I had now to consider the position most carefully and again come to a momentous decision. Was I to stand and fight on the line to which the Army was now retiring (Le Cateau—Cambrai) or continue the retreat at daybreak?

To hold the Le Cateau position in view of the heavy threat on my front and western flank was a decision which could only be justified if I were sure of the absolute determination of the French Commander to hold on all along the line with the utmost tenacity; but our Allies were already a day's march in rear of us, and every report indicated continual retreat. At least one Army Corps and two Cavalry Divisions of the enemy were engaged in an outflanking movement on my left, in which they had already made some progress, and the only help I could depend upon in that quarter was from two French Reserve Divisions spread out on an enormous front towards Dunkirk, and very hastily and indifferently entrenched. It was unlikely that they would be able to oppose any effective resistance to the enemy's flank movement.

If this flank attack were successful, my communications with Havre would be practically gone.

There had been neither time nor labour available to make the Le Cateau position strong enough to withstand a serious onslaught by the superior numbers which were advancing against my front, and the British troops, which had been almost continuously marching and fighting since Sunday morning, stood in much need of rest, which could only be secured by placing some serious obstacle, such as a river line, between my troops and the enemy.

After long and anxious deliberation, it seemed clear to me that every consideration pointed to the necessity of resuming our march in retreat at daybreak on the 26th, and orders to that effect were accordingly issued.

I determined to direct the march on St. Quentin and Noyon. The troops were to be held so concentrated as to enable me to take immediate advantage of any change in the situation which might check the retreat and offer favourable opportunities for taking the offensive. Failing such developments, my idea was to concentrate behind the Somme or the Oise. Behind such a barrier I should be able to rest the troops, fill up casualties and deficiencies in material, and remain ready to act effectively with the Allies in whatever direction circumstances might dictate.

The retreat had been resumed at daybreak, and at 6 p.m. all the troops of the 2nd Corps were on the Le Cateau line except McCracken's Brigade, which, as before described, had been obliged to stand and fight at Solesmes. The 1st Corps, however, was delayed in starting for several hours, and was only able to reach the neighbourhood of Landrecies; so that at the conclusion of the day's march a somewhat dangerous gap existed between the 1st and 2nd Corps, which caused me considerable anxiety in the small hours of the morning of the 26th.

When darkness fell on the 25th, the enemy had sent forward advance troops in motors and lorries through the Forêt de Mormal in pursuit of the 1st Corps. This culminated in a violent attack on Landrecies, which, however, was splendidly driven off with heavy loss to the enemy, chiefly by the 4th (Guards) Brigade under Brigadier-General Scott-Kerr.

With reference to this action, the following is an extract from a letter which I despatched to Lord Kitchener on August 27th:

> The 4th Brigade were fighting in the early morning in the streets of Landrecies. A German infantry column, about the strength of a brigade, emerged from the wood north of the town and advanced south in the closest order, filling up the narrow street.
>
> Two or three of our machine guns were brought to bear on this magnificent target from the other end of the town. The head of the column was checked and stopped, a frightful panic ensued, and it is estimated that, in a very few minutes, no less than 800 to 900 dead and wounded Germans were lying in the streets.

Sir Douglas Haig, although his troops were very tired and handicapped also by heavy rearguard fighting, still proceeded to carry out the instructions he had received, and the retirement of the 1st Corps was continued in excellent order and with complete efficiency.

Things did not go so well with the 2nd Corps. General Allenby, who had been most ably covering the retreat of the Army with his cavalry, had already materially assisted the rearguard of the 3rd Division to surmount their difficulties at Solesmes. McCracken's Brigade (7th) (3rd Batt. Worcester Regt., 2nd Batt. S. Lancs Regt., 1st Batt. Wilts Regt., and 2nd Batt. R. Irish Rifles) did not reach the Le Cateau position until 10 or 11 p.m. on the 25th. His men were, of course, nearly done up, and he had suffered severe losses.

Colonel Ansell, Commanding the 5th Dragoon Guards, one of the finest cavalry leaders in the Army, who fell at the head of his regiment a few days later, gave information to General Allenby at about 2 a.m. regarding the nature of the German advance. This seemed of such great importance that the latter at once sought out Sir Horace Smith-Dorrien and warned him that, unless he was prepared to continue his march at daybreak, he would most probably be pinned down to his position and would be unable to get away. Sir Horace asked General Allenby what, in his opinion, were the chances he had if he remained and held the position, adding that he felt convinced his troops were so exhausted as to preclude the possibility of removing them for some hours to come. Allenby's reply was that he thought, unless the commander of the 2nd Corps made up his mind to move at daybreak, the enemy probably would succeed in surrounding him.

Nevertheless, Sir Horace determined to fight. As to this decision, a commander on the spot, and in close touch with his Divisions and Brigades, is in the best position to judge of what his men can do.

I had, late on the evening of the 25th, before leaving for my Headquarters at St. Quentin, visited several units of the 2nd Corps in their bivouacs and, though tired indeed, they had not struck me as being worn out troops.

By the break of day on the 26th the 5th Division on the right had secured several hours' rest. The same may be said of the 8th and 9th Brigades, which came next in the line. The 7th Brigade had only just arrived at cantonments at 10 p.m. or 11 p.m. on the 25th, after a heavy day's march and some severe fighting, but they could in such an emergency have marched at dawn. The 4th Division on the left of the 2nd Corps was comparatively fresh.

I visited in particular one Artillery Brigade, some of whose guns had been saved from capture on the previous day by the cavalry. The Brigade Commander broke down with emotion as he recounted to me the glorious bravery displayed by Francis Grenfell and the 9th Lancers.

This Brigade fought magnificently for several hours next day on the Le Cateau position.

All reconnaissance and intelligence reports received up to midnight on the 25th concur in saying that Cambrai was then still in the possession of the French, and that the position there was not yet seriously threatened; further, that whilst there were clear signs of the outflanking movement in progress, no considerable bodies of the enemy had yet crossed the line Valenciennes—Douai, and that, after their repulse at Solesmes by McCracken and Allenby, the enemy was not in strength south of the line Valenciennes—Maubeuge.

This estimate of the situation was confirmed by a German wireless message, intercepted towards the evening of the 26th, which stated that the outflanking German Corps was only at that time *moving towards* Cambrai, and that the remaining Corps, which were engaged in the frontal attack, were only then "moving on" towards Cattenières, Walincourt and Le Cateau respectively.

The 1st Corps had, as we know, experienced a much harder day's march on the 25th, and was attacked at Landrecies and its neighbourhood before it could get any rest at all. Sir Douglas correctly appreciated the strength of the enemy on his immediate front and gauged the situation, namely, the German design to impose on us the idea that he was in great strength, and to pin our troops to the ground whilst his flanking movement became effective.

For this purpose the enemy had hurried forward a large force of Artillery, composed of guns and howitzers of all calibres, escorted and protected by four Cavalry Divisions and a limited number of *jäger* battalions.

These troops were pushed forward against the 2nd Corps at Le Cateau as they had been against the 1st Corps at Landrecies, and with a precisely similar purpose.

The superb gallantry of the troops, and the skilful leading by Divisional and Brigade and Battalion Commanders, helped very materially by the support given by Allenby and, as I afterwards learned, by Sordet and d'Amade, saved the 2nd Corps, which otherwise would assuredly have been pinned to their ground and then surrounded. The cavalry might have made good their retreat, but three out of five Divisions of the British Army with the 7th Brigade must have been lost.

The enemy, flushed by this primary victory, would have pressed in on the flanks of the 1st Corps, cut off their retreat, and, continuing his combined front and flank attack, would have almost certainly pushed the whole Allied Army off their line of retreat, and a stupendous repetition of Sedan might well have resulted.

The magnificent fight put up by these glorious troops saved disaster; but the actual result was a total loss of at least 14,000 officers and men, about 80 guns, numbers of machine guns, as well as quantities of ammunition, war material and baggage, whilst the enemy gained time to close up his infantry columns marching down from the north-east, at the cost of losses not greater than, if as great, as our own, but which were, in view of the immense superiority he possessed in numbers and fighting power, infinitely less important to him.

The effect upon the British Army was to render the subsequent conduct of the retreat more difficult and arduous.

The hope of making a stand behind the Somme or the Oise, or any other favourable position north of the Marne, had now to be abandoned owing to the shattered condition of the Army, and the far-reaching effect of our losses at the Battle of Le Cateau was felt seriously even throughout the subsequent Battle of the Marne and during the early operations on the Aisne. It was not possible to replace our lost guns and machine guns until nearly the end of September.

In my dispatch, written in September, 1914, I refer eulogistically to the Battle of Le Cateau. I had been, together with my staff, directing the movements of the British Army day and night up to the time of the Battle of the Marne—in the course of which battle I received an urgent demand from the Government that a dispatch should be forwarded.

It was completed, of necessity, very hurriedly, and before

there had been time or opportunity to give thorough study to the reports immediately preceding and covering the period of that battle, by which alone the full details could be disclosed.

It was, indeed, impossible, until much later on, to appreciate in all its details the actual situation on the morning of August 26th.

At the time the dispatch was written, indeed, I was entirely ignorant of the material support which was rendered throughout the day by Generals Sordet and d'Amade, and I accepted without question the estimate made by the commander of the 2nd Corps as to the nature of the threat against him and the position of the German forces opposed to him.

It is very difficult for the uninitiated to realise the concentration which the direction of an Army carrying out a vigorous offensive like that of the Marne, demands from the brain of the Commander-in-Chief, if he is to make the best use of the forces under his command.

In the surroundings and under the conditions of a great battle, the preparation of material for and the compilation of any dispatch is a matter of great difficulty. It is very easy to say: "Why not employ others?" I have always held that it is only the General who conducts an operation of any magnitude who can, or should, sum up and describe it. No one else can know what was passing in his mind, or how his judgment was directed and formed by the swiftly moving procession of events.

Nor can *exact* information become available for weeks or months, sometimes, indeed, even for years, after the conclusion of a particular series of operations.

In more than one of the accounts of the retreat from Mons, it is alleged that some tacit consent at least was given at Headquarters at St. Quentin to the decision arrived at by the commander of the 2nd Corps. I owe it to the able and devoted officers of my Staff to say that there is not a semblance of truth in this statement.

CHAPTER 5

Further Course of the Retreat

General Joffre had arranged for a conference at my Headquarters at St. Quentin with Lanrezac and myself, to take place early on the 26th. I had reached St. Quentin at about 8 a.m. on the 25th. There had been little sleep during the night for any of us. In the earlier hours continual reports came in regarding the dangerous position of the 1st Corps. In addition to the unfortunate but inevitable delay in commencing their march in the morning, the troops were further greatly embarrassed and worried by the retirement of the French from the Sambre, and their convergence on our own line of march.

The enemy's cavalry, supported by guns, *Jäger*, and detachments of Infantry carried on motor cars and lorries, closely pressed our columns through the Forêt de Mormal. The result of this was to make it imperative that the 2nd Division should make a firm stand at Landrecies and Maroilles before the 1st Corps could reach the line assigned to it in the morning. A gap of some eight miles existed between the right of the 2nd Corps at Le Cateau and the left of the 1st Corps at Landrecies.

The moment this news reached me I summoned Huguet, and through him dispatched an urgent request to two French Reserve Divisions (which formed part of the 5th French Army and were nearest to the British) to move up and assist Haig.

They readily responded, and the effect of the diversion enabled Haig to extricate his Corps from this most dangerous situation, which he did with great skill and judgment, whilst inflicting severe loss on the enemy.

Towards morning it was reported to me that the enemy had drawn off, and at dawn the retreat was resumed by the whole of the 1st Corps as ordered. The fighting of the 1st Corps through this night, combined with its skilful and efficient withdrawal in the morning, was one of the most brilliant episodes of the whole retreat.

No sooner was my mind made easier by this happy deliverance of the 1st Corps when the trouble related in the last chapter commenced with the 2nd Corps.

It was not until 8 a.m. on the 26th that I knew the left wing of the Army was actually committed to the fight. At this time I was anxiously awaiting the arrival of Joffre and Lanrezac.

Staff Officers were sent to General Smith-Dorrien, carrying peremptory orders to break off the action and to continue the retreat forthwith.

Shortly afterwards the French Commander-in-Chief arrived with his Chief of Staff. He was followed by the Commander of the 5th French Army, and we proceeded to discuss the situation.

I narrated the events of the previous two days, and pointed out the isolated situation in which the British Army had been placed by the very sudden change of plan and headlong retirement of the 5th French Army on my right.

Lanrezac appeared to treat the whole affair as quite normal, and merely incidental to the common exigencies of war. He offered no explanation, and gave no reason for the very unexpected moves he had made. The discussion was apparently distasteful to him, for he remained only a short time at my Headquarters, and left before any satisfactory understanding as to further plans and dispositions had been arrived at.

Joffre remained with me some considerable time. I gathered that he was by no means satisfied with the action and conduct of his subordinate General. No very definite plans were then decided upon, the understanding, as the French Commander-in-Chief left, being that the retreat was to be continued as slowly and deliberately as possible, until we found ourselves in a favourable position to make a firm stand and take the offensive. The Commander-in-Chief urged me to maintain my position in the line, which I told him I hoped, in spite of the heavy losses which we had suffered, to be able to do.

Immediately Joffre left I set out for Sir Horace Smith-Dorrien's Headquarters, as I could get no satisfactory report from that General. For the first few miles we were able to make fair progress, but as we went on, the road got worse and worse, and sometimes we were absolutely blocked for several minutes together.

The whole country-side was covered with refugees and their belongings, whilst our own transport were endeavouring to make all the haste they could to convey much needed food, ammunition and material to the Divisions in front.

Several messages reached me on the road, and at last I got information that Smith-Dorrien had broken off the action and that his columns were once more on the march. He was only just in time, for subsequent reports reached me during this motor journey of considerable Uhlan patrols in the neighbourhood, and towards evening St. Quentin itself was threatened by hostile cavalry, which, however, did not succeed in entering the town.

On reaching Headquarters I found that more or less detailed reports had arrived, which showed the shattered condition of the troops which had fought at Le Cateau.

All idea of making any prolonged stand on the Somme south of St. Quentin, which had during the day seriously entered my mind as a possibility, was definitely abandoned.

The first necessity was to rally and collect the troops, which had become mixed up and scattered by the trying experiences of the previous days and nights. The great essential was to recover order, restore confidence, and infuse fresh spirit with a clear aim in view. To enable all this to be brought about we had first to look to the cavalry. Orders were at once sent to Allenby to make such dispositions as would effectually cover our rear and western flank. I told him he was to enlist the co-operation of the French cavalry under Sordet. The Corps Commanders were ordered to move towards the line La Fère—Noyon.

On the evening of the 26th, Headquarters were moved to Noyon, where I arrived late at night to consider the possibilities of making a stand behind the Oise.

On the 27th the orders issued for the efficient conduct of the retreat began to take effect, and the cavalry kept the enemy well at bay.

Smith-Dorrien reported himself in the early hours of the morning, and later Major Dawnay (2nd Life Guards)—the recollection of whose splendid and invaluable services until he fell at the head of his regiment will for ever remain with me—brought news of Haig's progress, whilst Shea of the Indian cavalry—afterwards a renowned leader of a Division at the front—told me of the valuable role which was being so efficiently performed by the Cavalry.

In a telegram, which I communicated to the troops, General Joffre very handsomely acknowledged what he described as the "invaluable" services rendered to the Allied cause by the British Army throughout the past few days.

It was a sincere gratification to the Army to see the generous terms in which the French Commander-in-Chief expressed his appreciation.

I spent the early hours of the 27th in personally reconnoitring the country bordering the south bank of the Oise, in the neighbourhood of Noyon.

The one idea which now possessed my mind was the possibility of making a stand with the object of obtaining the necessary time for rest, and to make good equipment and bring up reinforcements.

At first sight it appeared to me that the line of the Oise and its tributary canalised waters offered such an opportunity.

The cursory examination of the ground which I was able to make on the morning of the 27th satisfied me that it possessed decided capabilities for a defence which was not intended to be prolonged, and I thought, also, that the tortuous course of the river afforded some alternative features, by availing ourselves of which a powerful offensive might be commenced at the right time.

During the day I had another interview with Joffre, which took place before I had time to estimate the actual fighting capabilities of the 2nd Corps and the 4th Division.

I was not even then fully aware of the terrible extent to which we had suffered at Le Cateau. That these losses were heavy I never doubted, but I had no idea, until many hours later, that they were such as must paralyse for several days any movement in the direction of taking the offensive.

My early morning deliberations were very much in accord with the view of the French Commander-in-Chief. The proposal Joffre then communicated to me was that the Allied Armies should fall back on a line, roughly, from Rheims on the east to Amiens on the west, which would bring the British Forces into the zone of country south of the Oise, whose course I had already reconnoitred. We discussed the situation thoroughly, and Joffre was most sympathetic and "understanding" in reference to our special position. He promised that the 5th French Army should be directed to take energetic action to relieve us from undue pressure by the enemy, and told me of his projects for the formation of the 6th French Army on our left.

We parted without coming to any actual decision: for my part I could give no promise until I knew exactly what I had to rely upon; whilst energetic pursuit by the enemy might well prevent Joffre rendering me that support on both flanks which the situation imperatively demanded.

As a matter of fact, no more was heard of this project, and the idea of standing on the above-mentioned line was abandoned.

On the morning of the 28th, General Headquarters moved to Compiègne, where we remained till the morning of the 31st.

It was during Friday the 28th that I fully realised the heavy losses we had incurred. Since Sunday the 23rd this had reached, in officers and men, the total of upwards of 15,000. The deficiency in armament and equipment were equally serious. Roughly, some 80 guns and a large proportion of our machine guns, besides innumerable articles of necessary equipment and a large quantity of transport, had fallen into the enemy's hands.

It became quite clear to me that no effective stand could be made until we were able to improve our condition.

It was on this day that I received the assurance, the most welcome to a commander in retreat, that the cavalry under Allenby's skilful direction was effectively holding off the enemy's pursuit.

Gough with the 3rd Cavalry Brigade at St. Quentin, and Chetwode with the 5th at Cérizy, vigorously attacked the leading troops of the German cavalry at both these places, and threw them back in confusion and with heavy loss on to their main bodies.

On our left, d'Amade with the two French Reserve Divisions, and Sordet with his Corps of cavalry, attacked the Germans in and around Péronne.

Allenby's Headquarters were then at Cressy (north-west of Noyon), and Sordet called upon him for support in this enterprise.

Before arrangements could be made for such assistance the French were driven back.

Although this attack failed to drive the Germans north, it was most valuable and effective in checking the pursuit, and by their vigorous action the troops of d'Amade and Sordet showed the stuff of which the embryo 6th Army was being formed: that Army which a few days later covered itself with imperishable glory on the Marne and Ourcq.

On our right there still appeared little encouragement to hope for an early effective stand. The 5th French Army was in full retreat, the Reserve Divisions, after fighting at Urvillers, were retiring on the Oise, whilst the 18th Corps on their right was thrown back from Itancourt to the Oise by a violent German attack.

I spent several hours of the 28th in going the round of the troops, as it was possible to intercept various columns on the march or at their temporary halts. I was able to get the men together on the roadside, to thank them for the splendid work they had done, to tell them of the gratitude of the French Commander-in-Chief, and the immense value of the service they had rendered to the Allied cause. I charged them to repeat all this to their comrades, and to spread it throughout the units to which they belonged. There was neither time nor opportunity for any formal inspection or set parade. The enemy was on our heels, and there was little time to spare, but it touched me to the quick to realise how, in the face of all the terrible demand made upon their courage, strength and endurance, these glorious British soldiers listened to the few words I was able to say to them with the spirit of heroes and the confidence of children. It afforded me gratifying evidence of the wonderful instinctive sympathy which has always existed between the British soldier and his officer. These men had seen how they had been *led*, they *knew* the far greater proportionate loss suffered by their officers, they *felt* that they trusted them and were ready to follow them anywhere. It is this wonderful understanding between "leaders" and "led" which has constituted the great strength and glory of the British Army throughout all ages.

In all these roadside talks and confidences never did I hear one word of complaint or breath of criticism. The spirit of discipline was as palpably shown amongst these scattered groups of unkempt, overstrained, tired soldiers, as on any King's Birthday Review ever held on the Horse Guards Parade. Their one repeated question was: "When shall we turn round and face them again?" And they would add: "We can drive them to hell."

It was distressing, indeed, to look at some battalions, which I had seen near Mons only some three or four days earlier in all their fresh glory and strength, now brought down to a handful of men and two or three officers; but the glorious spirit I saw animating the men gave me the keenest pleasure, and inspired a confidence which was of the utmost help.

On this day I inspected a large proportion of the transport of both Army Corps, which I found in a much better condition than could have been thought possible.

I did not reach my Headquarters at Compiègne until five. I found Huguet waiting for me with a Staff Officer of the 7th French Army Corps, which was to form part of the new 6th French Army. It was from the talk I had with them that I learnt how Joffre was forming the new 6th Army.

Huguet informed me that a considerable force was being railed round from Verdun to Amiens, and that the new Army would be commanded by General Maunoury. I knew nothing then of the French Commander-in-Chief's ultimate plans, and I doubt if at that moment he had been able to formulate any decided line of action. At this particular time I think the unprepared condition of Paris loomed largely in his mind, and that his original intention with regard to the 6th Army was most probably to make further provision for the protection of the capital.

Joffre had particularly asked me to undertake the Air reconnaissance on the western flank of the Allied forces.

Our Intelligence Service had been admirably organised, and was working most effectively under the able direction of Brigadier-General Macdonogh. I cannot speak too highly of the skill and ability displayed by this distinguished officer throughout the whole time during which we served together. His service was invaluable; his ingenuity and resource in obtaining and collecting information, his indefatigable brain, and the unfailing versatility and insight with which he sifted every statement and circumstance were beyond all praise. He trained an excellent Staff who valued his leadership, for he had an extraordinary power of getting the most and best work out of everyone. His information as to the enemy's movements were remarkably accurate, and placed me throughout in the best position to interpret the enemy's probable intentions.

During my stay at Compiègne all appreciations of the situation pointed to the immediate investment of Paris by the right wing of the German Army as being the enemy's first objective.

It is fairly certain that the concentration of an important new Army on the western flank of the British, to the north of Paris, was quite unknown to the Germans, and did not enter into their calculations until some days later.

We had also the best reason for believing that the German Higher Command regarded the British Forces as shattered and almost useless, at any rate so far as any effort which we could make for the defence of Paris was concerned. In fact, believing the capital to be practically at its mercy, the right wing of the German Army was blindly marching into a veritable hornet's nest, in spite of the backward condition of the Paris defence.

On the 29th a very brilliant and successful attack by the French 5th Army at Guise heavily defeated three German Army Corps and threw them back with severe loss. This had a great effect in assisting the retreat, for it not only enabled the 5th Army to hold its own for some time on the Oise, between Guise and La Fère, but it considerably relieved hostile pressure on the British and on the French troops on our left.

From Roye on the west, Montdidier, Noyon, La Fère, Guise, up to Hirson on the east, the heads of the Allied columns were established, well covered by their advanced cavalry.

Throughout this day reports often contradictory and conflicting reached me. It was quite clear that our position on the Oise was being dangerously threatened by superior forces, and I felt it to be impossible to stand on that line even until we could make good some of our heavy losses, and I could not hope to get anything up for several days to come.

With great reluctance I ordered the retreat to be continued to the line of the Aisne from Compiègne to Soissons, but in view of the knock given to the enemy at Guise by the 5th French Army, and the desire expressed by General Joffre that the Allied forces should hold their ground as long as possible and only retire when necessary, I directed commanders to carry out their marches with all deliberation, and to take advantage of every opportunity to check the enemy's advance.

It now became known to the Allied Command that the enemy had detached a considerable force to his eastern frontier, where he was being seriously threatened by the Russians. Joffre's natural desire to profit by this, coupled with his fears for the safety of Paris, made him very anxious to take the offensive at the earliest possible moment. He came to see me on the afternoon of the 29th August at Compiègne, and urged these views upon me. I remained firm in my absolute conviction that the British forces could not effectively fulfil their share in such action for some days, and that, so far as we were concerned, a further retreat was inevitable. I assured the French Commander-in-Chief that no serious gap should be made in his line by any premature or hasty retirement, but I imperatively demanded the necessary time to refit and obtain reinforcements.

I strongly represented to Joffre the advantage of drawing the German armies on still further from their base, even although we had to move south of the Marne. Indeed, the ideas which

I afterwards expressed at the British Embassy in Paris to M. Millerand, the French Minister of War, in the presence of Lord Kitchener, were the same which I had in my mind during this interview with Joffre, namely, that our stand should be made on some line between the Marne and the Seine.

The French Army was still in full retreat. The 6th French Army on our left was not yet formed, and the Commander-in-Chief had put no definite plan of attack before me, with an assigned role which he desired me to fulfil. All he asked me to do was to remain in the line and fill up the gap between the 5th and 6th Armies. This I had every intention of doing.

I am bound to say that I had to make this decision in the face of resistance from some of my subordinate commanders, who took a depressed view as to the condition of their troops. When I discussed the situation at a meeting of British commanders held at Compiègne, Sir Horace Smith-Dorrien expressed it as his opinion that the only course open to us was to retire to our base, thoroughly refit, re-embark and try to land at some favourable point on the coast-line. I refused to listen to what was the equivalent of a counsel of despair.

Our communications with Havre being now dangerously threatened, it became necessary to effect a change of base and establish a fresh line. St. Nazaire and Nantes were fixed upon, with Le Mans as advanced base.

The morning of the 30th found our cavalry with two brigades to the north-west of Compiègne, one to the north and one to the north-east. The 5th, under Chetwode, covered the retirement of the 1st Corps. Our line that night was through Nampiel on the west to Coucy-le-Château.

Huguet today communicated to me Joffre's new dispositions. He was retiring the 5th French Army to the line of the Serre, their left on La Fère; their right on the left of the 4th French Army towards Rethel. The 6th French Army was to fall back to the line Compiègne—Clermont. Sordet's Cavalry Corps was to be on the left of the line.

Joffre sent an urgent request to me to destroy the bridges over the Oise between Compiègne and La Fère.

Huguet once more pressed upon me Joffre's urgent desire that I should remain and fill the gap between Compiègne and La Fère. In reply I again repeated emphatically what I had previously stated, namely, that I could be in no condition to stand and fight for several days, and therefore I could not consent to fill any portion of a fighting line. I was fully prepared to continue the retreat slowly and deliberately, retaining my present position between the 5th and 6th Armies.

Now, as before, the view I took of my responsibilities, in accordance with my interpretation of the special instructions given me, guided my deliberations in these difficult days.

I could not forget that the 5th French Army had commenced to retreat from the Sambre at least 24 hours before I had been given any official intimation that Joffre's offensive plan had been abandoned. I knew that it was alone due to the vast superiority of our cavalry over that of the enemy, and to the splendid tenacity and the superior marching and fighting powers of our troops, that we had been saved from overwhelming disaster. My duty to my country demanded that I should risk no recurrence of such a situation, and I determined that our needs and the interests of our Empire must be duly weighed and balanced in the councils of the Supreme Headquarters Staff.

I despatched a letter to Lord Kitchener on this day, in which the following passage occurs:

> I feel very seriously the absolute necessity for retaining in my hands complete independence of action and power to retire towards my base should circumstances render it necessary.

On this day Pulteney arrived, and the formation of the 3rd Army Corps under his command was commenced forthwith. It was composed of the 4th Division and the 19th Brigade, with some mounted troops temporarily attached, pending the arrival of the 6th Division, which had now been ordered to France.

On the morning of the 31st, Headquarters were moved to Dammartin. After riding round to see whatever troops I could, we reached there early in the afternoon. Huguet was waiting for me with more information and messages from Joffre. The demand that we should stand and fight was not only urgently repeated, but was actually backed by imperative messages from the French President, and from Lord Kitchener and the British Government, yet at this very moment Lanrezac was actually throwing back the left flank of the 5th Army and widening the gap between us. At the same time Lord Kitchener was assuring the Home Government that our losses were comparatively small, and that all deficiencies had been made good.

I retain the most profound belief that, had I yielded to these violent solicitations, the whole Allied Army would have been thrown back in disorder over the Marne, and Paris would have fallen an easy prey into the hands of the Germans.

It is impossible to exaggerate the danger of the situation as it existed. Neither on this day nor for several subsequent days did one man, horse, gun, or machine gun reach me to make good deficiencies.

I refused. This brought Lord Kitchener to Paris, where I met him on September 1st at the British Embassy. I went there with my Chief of Staff at his urgent request, regarding him as a representative of His Majesty's Government.

I deeply resented being called away from my Headquarters at so critical a time. Two important actions were fought by considerable detachments of the Army under my command during this day, over which there was no one to exercise any co-ordinating control. Either might have easily brought on a general engagement.

The interview had one important result. M. Millerand (the War Minister) and M. Viviani (the Prime Minister) were present at the Conference, and before them all I was able to give a clear exposition of my views as to the future conduct of the Allied operations.

M. Millerand undertook to lay this document before General Joffre at once. This great statesman and invaluable servant of his country occupied the post of War Minister during most of the time I was in France. His invariable kindness and courtesy, coupled with his skilful and astute appreciation of the military situation throughout all its difficult and varying periods, will always be gratefully remembered by me.

The result of my proposals will be the better understood if I quote General Joffre's reply to the War Minister, and a personal letter which I received from the Commander-in-Chief on the same subject.

> Grand Quartier Général des Armées de l'Est
> Au G.Q.G. le 2 septembre 1914
> Le Général Commandant-en-Chef à
>   M. le Ministre de la Guerre
>
> J'ai reçu les propositions du Maréchal French que vous avez voulu me communiquer; elles tendent à organiser sur la Marne une ligne de défense qui serait tenue par des effectifs suffisamment denses en profondeur et particulièrement renforcés derrière le flanc gauche.
>
> Les emplacements actuels de la Ve Armée ne permettent pas de réaliser le programme tracé par le Maréchal French et d'assurer à l'Armée Anglaise, en temps voulu, une aide efficace sur la droite.
>
> Par contre, l'appui de l'Armée du Général Maunoury qui doit se porter à la défense des fronts Nord-Est de Paris est toujours assuré à l'Armée Anglaise sur la gauche; celle-ci pourrait, dans ces conditions, tenir sur la Marne pendant quelque temps, puis se retirer sur la rive gauche de la Seine qu'elle tiendrait de Melun à Juvisy; les forces Anglaises participeraient ainsi à la défense de la capitale et leur présence serait pour les troupes du camp retranché un précieux réconfort.
>
> Je dois ajouter que des instructions viennent d'être données aux Armées en vue de coordonner leurs mouvements, et qu'il pourrait être désavantageux de modifier ces instructions. Elles tendent à placer nos troupes dans un dispositif leur permettant de prendre l'offensive dans un délai assez rapproché. Le date de leur mouvement en avant sera communiqué au Maréchal French afin de permettre à l'Armée Anglaise de participer à l'offensive générale.

Grand Quartier Général des Armées de l'Est État Major
Au G.Q.G. le 2 septembre 1914
Le Général Commandant-en-Chef à M. le Maréchal French
Commandant-en-Chef les Forces Anglaises
Monsieur le Maréchal,
J'ai l'honneur de vous addresser mes remerciements pour les propositions que vous avez bien voulu soumettre au Gouvernement de la République, relatives à la co-opération de l'Armée Anglaise et qui m'ont été communiquées.
La situation actuelle de la 5e Armée ne permet pas à cette Armée d'assurer à l'Armée Anglaise un appui suffisamment efficace sur la droite.
En raison des événements qui se sont passés depuis deux heures, je ne crois pas possible actuellement d'envisager une manoeuvre d'ensemble sur la Marne avec la totalité de nos forces. Mais j'estime que la co-opération de l'Armée Anglaise à la défense de Paris est la seule qui puisse donner un résultat avantageux dans les conditions exposées par la lettre ci-jointe que j'adresse à M. le Ministre de la Guerre et dont j'ai l'honneur de vous faire parvenir la copie.
Veuillez agréer, Monsieur le Maréchal, l'expression de ma haute considération et mes sentiments de cordiale camaraderie.

I replied as follows:

Mortcerf
September 3rd, 1914, 12 noon
To the Commandant-en-Chef
From Field Marshal Sir John French
Commander-in-Chief, British Forces
Dear General,
I have the honour to acknowledge the receipt of your very kind and cordial letter of September 2nd (3332).
I felt some considerable hesitation in putting forward my views as to the general trend of the future operations, and I am much indebted to you for the kind and friendly support which you have accorded to my expression of opinion.

I have now received your 'Instruction No. 4' and your 'Note pour les Commandants d'Armée' of September 2nd, and I completely and clearly understand your plans and the part you desire me to take in carrying them out. You may rely on my most cordial co-operation in every respect.

My troops have very much appreciated the kind consideration you have shown them in sending so many decorations for distribution.

French

I touch with some diffidence on less agreeable features of this memorable discussion in Paris.

Lord Kitchener arrived on this occasion in the uniform of a Field Marshal, and from the outset of his conversation assumed the air of a Commander-in-Chief, and announced his intention of taking the field and inspecting the troops.

On hearing this, the British Ambassador (Sir Francis, now Lord, Bertie) at once emphatically objected, and drafted a telegram to the Foreign Secretary stating clearly and unmistakably his views, and demanding instructions. He gave this despatch to Lord Kitchener to read. The latter then asked for my opinion, and I said my views on the subject coincided entirely with those of the Ambassador.

After some discussion, the Secretary of State decided to abandon his intention, and the telegram to Sir Edward Grey was not sent. In the conversation which followed between us all, Lord Kitchener appeared to take grave exception to certain views which I expressed as to the expediency of leaving the direction of the operations in the field in the hands of the military chiefs in command in the field.

He abruptly closed the discussion and requested me to accompany him for a private interview in another room.

When we were alone he commenced by entering a strong objection to the tone I assumed. Upon this I told him all that was in my mind. I said that the command of the British Forces in France had been entrusted to me by His Majesty's Government; that I alone was responsible to them for whatever happened, and that on French soil my authority as regards the British Army must be supreme until I was legally superseded by the same authority which had put that responsibility upon me. I further remarked that Lord Kitchener's presence in France in the character of a soldier could have no other effect than to weaken and prejudice my position in the eyes of the French and my own countrymen alike. I reminded him of our service in the field together some 13 years before, and told him that I valued highly his advice and assistance, which I would gladly accept as such, but that I would not tolerate any interference with my executive command and authority so long as His Majesty's Government chose to retain me in my present position. I think he began to realise my difficulties, and we finally came to an amicable understanding.

Important telegrams and messages were then brought me, and I told Lord Kitchener that it was impossible for me to absent myself any longer from my Headquarters, whither I at once repaired with all possible speed.

It is very difficult for any but soldiers to understand the real bearing and significance of this Paris incident. If the confidence of the troops in their commander is shaken in the least degree, or if his influence, power and authority are prejudiced by any display of distrust in his ability to conduct operations, however slight the indications of such distrust may be, the effect reacts instantly throughout the whole Army.

This is more than ever true with troops which, as at the moment in question, were being subjected to great and severe demands upon their courage, endurance, and, above all, *faith in their leaders*. Then again there was the effect which might have been produced on the French. Ministers and Generals were present and witnessed Lord Kitchener's apparent assertion of his right to exercise the power and authority of a Commander-in-Chief in the Field.

Fortunately, the incident terminated in a manner which led to no regrettable publicity. Lord Kitchener realised his mistake and left Paris that night.

I did not reach my Headquarters at Dammartin until about 7 in the evening of September 1st. Two important rearguard actions had been fought during the day, one at Néry—where

Captain Bradbury was killed, whilst "L" battery fought heroically against overwhelming odds—and the other at Villers-Cotterets.

The proximity of the enemy, and the close presence of detachments of hostile cavalry with guns, which had broken through our line, required the retirement of my Headquarters to Lagny on the Marne. As it was necessary to move with precaution, this place was not reached until 1 a.m. on the 2nd.

I have already reproduced the communications from General Joffre under date September 2nd, in connection with the Paris interview on the 1st. Although I did not receive these documents until late on the 2nd, they indicated the ideas which occupied my own mind on that day, namely, the defence of the Marne with a view to a subsequent offensive.

On this day I also received a letter from the Governor of Paris which, with my reply, run as follows:

Gouvernement Militaire de Paris,
Le Gouverneur
Paris, le 2 septembre 1914
Le Général Gallieni
Gouverneur Militaire de Paris et
    Commandant-en-Chef des Armées de Paris
Monsieur le Maréchal French
Commandant-en-Chef des Armées Anglaises
Monsieur le Maréchal,
J'ai appris ce matin, dans la tournée que j'ai faite dans nos régions N.E. de Paris, que vous veniez d'arriver à Dammartin. Comme Gouverneur de Paris et Commandant-en-Chef des Armées de Paris, je m'empresse de vous souhaiter le bienvenu et de vous dire combien je suis heureux de savoir que les braves troupes anglaises qui se sont conduites si vaillamment ces derniers jours, se trouvent à la proximité de Paris. Vous pouvez compter sur le concours absolu que nous devons à nos courageux compagnons d'arme.
Personnellement, j'ajouterai que votre nom ne m'est pas inconnu, étant moi-même un colonial ayant fait de nombreuses campagnes, et notamment m'étant trouvé à Madagascar lorsque vous commandiez l'expédition anglaise contre les Bo-

ers. Je suis donc sûr d'avance que je puis fermement compter sur l'entière collaboration d'un chef tel que vous.

Vous savez que le Général Commandant-en-Chef vient de faire placer Paris dans la zone de ses opérations. Je vous envoie donc les dispositions que je viens de prendre, afin que vous soyez bien orienté à ce sujet, pour couvrir les fronts N. et E. de Paris qui paraissent les plus exposés et d'autre part, pour attirer sur nous les corps qui menacent le flanc gauche de notre armée.

Je vous serais reconnaissant de vouloir bien me tenir au courant de vos intentions et des dispositions que vous prendrez.

Veuillez agréer, Monsieur le Maréchal, l'assurance de ma haute considération et de mes sentiments profondément dévouées.

Gallieni

Mortcerf
September 3rd, 1914, 12 noon
My dear General,
I have received your very kind letter (with enclosures) for which I beg to offer you my most sincere thanks.

A French officer attached to my Staff is now going into Paris, and will explain the situation of the British Forces and their intentions fully to you.

You may rely upon my most cordial and energetic co-operation with the French Forces on my right and left.

I have duly received Gen. Joffre's 'Instruction No. 4' and his *'Notes pour les Commandants d'Armée'* of September 2nd, and I fully understand the Commander-in-Chief's plans and intentions.

May I say what a keen pleasure and satisfaction it is to me and the Army under my command to be fighting side by side with the Grand Army of France!

Believe me, My dear General,
Yours most sincerely
French
Field Marshal
Commander-in-Chief, British Forces

From these documents it will be seen that the safety of the capital was the paramount thought in the minds of the French Generals.

On September 2nd, the 5th French Army on my right and the 6th on my left were retiring on Chateau-Thiérry and Paris respectively, whilst our own troops reached the line of the Marne towards Lagny and Meaux. The 4th Division was, however, delayed by a small rearguard action and passed the night south of Dammartin.

I had spent the greater part of the day in carefully reconnoitring the best defensive positions south of the Marne, and to these points the British forces were directed to move on the following day, destroying the bridges after they had passed.

By early morning of September 3rd, General Joffre's letter (quoted above) had reached me, by which I judged that, whilst generally agreeing in my views, the General did not think it advisable to attempt a deliberate defence of the Marne. On this, the orders given to the British troops on the night of the 2nd were modified, and they were directed to continue their march to the line Montry—Crécy—Coulommiers.

Reinforcements of all kinds were ordered up to these points and were well on their way, but the railways were badly blocked and there was much delay.

I must now turn to the discussion of important information which began to reach us on the afternoon of the 3rd regarding the movements of the enemy.

It appeared that a direct advance on Paris by the German right wing was no longer intended. They were reported to be moving in large columns south-east and east. A few regiments were said to be moving east by train. Later on, further reports arrived that the country in our front for several miles north of the Marne was clear of the enemy. No less than four German Corps were said to be concentrating on Chateau-Thiérry and to the east along the Marne, and it was reported that they had begun an attack on the 5th French Army. The latest information told us that Chateau-Thiérry was in the hands of the enemy, and that the 5th French Army was retiring south to the Seine.

The ideas underlying this concentration on their centre by the enemy look as if it was based on a totally wrong appreciation of our situation. The Germans were ignorant of the real strength which was gathering north of Paris in the formation of the 6th French Army. They regarded the British Army as practically crushed, and almost useless as a fighting force.

Relying upon this, they had no hesitation in leaving what they thought were the remnants of the Allied forces immediately north and east of the Paris fortifications to be dealt with by such of their own forces as were operating through Amiens and on their extreme right. The German Higher Command then decided to strike with overwhelming force at the Allied centre south of the Marne and to cut our Armies in two.

The first necessity for the enemy was a quick decision by a great victory to be achieved at once. They were out-marching their supplies; there was Russia to be crushed and their eastern frontier to be secured; and, further, a prolonged campaign was what they desired to avoid at all costs. The desperate attempt was no sooner fairly launched than the fatal error of over-confidence and the folly of under-rating one's enemy stared them in the face with all its stupendous consequences, as west of the Ourcq the country was seen to blaze along its whole length with the fire of the French 75's, whilst the British and 5th French Armies, now at bay, threw the enemy back in confusion over the Marne.

With their usual arrogance and pomposity the Germans, ignoring the fact that it was their own negligence which had led them into a most dangerous situation, claim that General von Kluck showed unusual skill in extricating the 1st German Army from the toils.

After considering the subject very carefully, and with a thorough knowledge of the situation and the ground, I have formed the opinion that von Kluck manifested considerable hesitation and want of energy.

The rear section of the British General Staff had been established during this day at Melun, on the Seine. The leading section remained with me at Mortcerf, which became my advanced Headquarters.

Information which arrived during the 4th confirmed all our anticipations of the previous day, and, in the evening at Melun, messages reached me from Joffre that he was formulating his new plan.

I had spent most of the day at advanced Headquarters, and had passed some time with Haig near Coulommiers. It seemed likely, by the direction of the German advance, that the 1st Corps might be attacked, and Haig had retired his 2nd Division in line with the 1st and was preparing for any eventuality. I conversed with him for a considerable time on the state of his troops, about which he expressed some anxiety. He said they stood in urgent need of rest and refitment, but as usual he was full of fight and ready to meet any emergency.

Whilst I was with Haig, Smith-Dorrien arrived.

The British Army had, indeed, suffered severely, and had performed an herculean task in reaching its present position in such fighting form, and its moral had withstood the ordeal.

I think the Germans were probably justified in doubting our offensive powers, but the thing they forgot was the nation from which we spring.

On my return to Melun on this night (September 4th) I found that Murray had received a visit from General Gallieni, Governor of Paris, who had communicated Joffre's plans for my consideration.

He wished the 6th French Army to recross the Marne between Lagny and Meaux on Sunday the 6th, and then to take up a position facing east towards the Ourcq. He asked me to fill up the space between the right of the 6th Army (on the Marne) and the left of the 5th Army (near Provins). He then intended the whole of the Allied Armies to advance east, north-east, and north, and endeavour to crush the German Corps operating between us.

General Franchet d'Esperey had now superseded Lanrezac in command of the 5th Army. I had sent Wilson (Sub-Chief of the General Staff) to him on the previous day, and tonight he returned and told me that d'Esperey was making similar plans.

I must say a word here with regard to Henry Wilson. I have

known him for many years. He possesses a striking personality. In appearance very tall and spare, his frame is surmounted by a face in which one sees great intelligence and power, combined with a very kindly and humorous expression. In looking at him it is impossible not to realise the strength of will and character which he undoubtedly possesses. His appearance does not belie him, he is all that he looks. Not one of his many friends has had a more thorough experience of him than I, both in "Sunshine and Shadow." However dark the surroundings, however desperate the situation, however gloomy the prospect, his fine humour, splendid courage and high spirit are always the same.

In those many weary, anxious days we passed together during my term of command in France, I cherish a most grateful remembrance of his unfailing and invaluable help, as well as of his sincere, loyal, and wholehearted support. Of iron nerve and frame, nothing seemed to tire him. Having passed through the Staff College early in life with high honours, he was marked out for the most important Staff work; and after filling many important minor positions with distinction he became Commandant of the Staff College, where his great talents were employed in reforming and much improving that institution. His *magnum opus* in peace time was done when he was Director of Military Operations at the War Office during the four years preceding the War. His countrymen have never realised, and probably may never know, the vital importance and invaluable results of the work he did there, not only in regard to the share he took in the preparation of the Expeditionary Force, but also in establishing those happy relations with the French Army which have proved of such help to Allied operations throughout the War.

Fearing no man, it was the very essence of his nature to speak his mind openly on all occasions, and when the great Irish crisis in the spring of 1914 was at its height, he sided openly with his native Ulster. He accompanied me to France as Sub-Chief of the General Staff, and when Murray's health broke down, in January 1915, I selected Wilson as his successor; but, owing to his candid expression of opinion in the Irish *embroglio*, he had many enemies, and his appointment was vetoed. It was this bad luck alone which prevented his valuable services then being used for his country's benefit in the best direction, and in a position for which he was better qualified than anyone else.

But to return to my story.

I somewhat feared the gap which existed between my right and d'Esperey's left, although the cavalry under Allenby at Garatin were on this flank. Because of this, and also because the Germans were exercising some pressure on Haig on this night (September 4th), I ordered the British Forces to retire a few miles further south.

This facilitated the movements of reinforcements, supplies and material, which were coming up fast.

I have now brought the story down to September 5th, the last day of the great German advance. The British forces had halted on the previous night on a line facing nearly east and extending from Villers-sur-Morin on the north to Fontenay on the south. The 5th French Army lay east of my right flank on an east and west line through Provins, facing north. The 6th Army was on my left, preparing to recross the Marne between Lagny and Meaux.

I was at Melun early in the morning. Huguet had arrived in the night with despatches and a Staff Officer from Joffre, with whom I held a long conference.

It appeared that the 6th Army had already crossed the Marne, and would be in position west of the Ourcq at 9 a.m. on the 6th, on which day the French Commander-in-Chief proposed that the whole Allied Army should advance to the attack.

Shortly afterwards General Maunoury, commanding the 6th French Army, arrived, and we proceeded to discuss the situation fully. He described in detail what he intended doing, which was almost exactly as I have explained above. He thought that very few of the enemy still remained north of Paris, his cavalry having reconnoitred for some distance north and north-west. He expressed it as his intention to attack most vigorously (*au fond*), and asked for my best support, which I promised to give.

I despatched Murray at once to visit the Corps and Cavalry Commanders and ascertain exactly the condition of their troops.

He returned later in the day with very favourable reports. All were in excellent spirits and eager for the advance. They were having some much-needed rest; whilst reinforcements both of men and material were beginning to arrive.

Reports received during the day confirmed all we had previously heard. The enemy's concentration against the centre of our line was complete. They had crossed the Marne at several points, and their advanced troops had been engaged during the past night and this day with our cavalry and 1st Army Corps on our right, and along the entire front of the 5th French Army.

Later in the day Joffre came to Melun, and I had a long conference with him. We again went over all plans, and it was definitely arranged that the attack was to commence all along the line next day, the 6th.

Joffre was full of enthusiasm, and very hopeful of success if we all fulfilled our respective roles and attacked *au fond*.

Thus ended the "Great Retreat."

* * * * * * * *

In these pages I have avoided as far as possible any detailed account of the many splendid engagements which have added new and undying laurels to the battle rolls of all the distinguished regiments which fought them.

I repeat that the main cause of the success, which prepared this vast battle ground and opened the way for the decisive battle of the Marne, is to be found in the able dispositions made by the leaders; the magnificent example set by officers and non-commissioned officers; and in the wonderful spirit, courage, and endurance which was displayed by the rank and file of the Army.

My main object in writing this record is to explain as clearly as possible to my countrymen the line of thought which was in my own mind, the objects I set out to attain, and the reasons why I directed the troops as I did and came to the decisions at which I arrived at each successive phase of the operations.

In concluding this chapter I am anxious to lay particular stress on a principle which seems to me of the utmost importance, namely, the danger of undue interference by the Government at home with the Commander of an Army in the field. Stanton's interference with McClellan in the American Civil War should have been a sufficient warning.

I have referred to the natural anxiety which was deeply felt by the French President, Government, and Generals for the safety of Paris.

The utmost pressure was brought to bear upon me to alter my dispositions so as to make a dangerous stand on lines and in places which, in my judgment, would have exposed the British Army to the greatest danger of annihilation.

The shattered condition of my troops was not realised, but perhaps in view of the situation such pressure was natural and inevitable.

I had the power, in accordance with the instructions which I had received before coming to France, to use my full discretion in agreeing to or resisting such demands, and in all my happy experience of them, never did I find my French comrades resentful of such resistance when they realised the true reason for it.

But when, in spite of my earnest representation of the true condition of affairs, the Secretary of State for War himself and the Government with him, brought still greater pressure to bear, backed by the authority they possessed, to enforce their views, I was placed in a position of the utmost difficulty.

Lord Kitchener came to Paris with no other object than to insist upon my arresting the retreat, although no sign of a halt appeared at any part of the Allied line.

He was ignorant of the condition of the Army as I knew it, and was mistaken in his assertion that reinforcements of men and material had already reached me. The impression conveyed by his visit was that I had greatly magnified the losses which had occurred, and exaggerated the condition of the troops. It was difficult to resist such pressure.

Fortunately I was able to do so.

Chapter 6

The Battle of the Marne

When day dawned on the ever memorable morning of September 6th, 1914, some ray of the great hopes in which I had indulged during the first two or three days at my Headquarters at Le Cateau seemed to revive. Taught now by a bitter experience, I felt more than ever the necessity of being prepared for anything. There was much, however, to inspire confidence. Great changes had been made amongst the higher commanders in the army of our Allies. The finest military leaders of France were now heading the splendid soldiers of that truly martial nation, and we had all learnt most valuable and practical lessons in the hard school of adversity.

The latest reports showed that French and British soldiers alike were animated by the highest spirit and meant to "do or die." As regards the British Army, reinforcements had arrived, deficiencies in armament and material had been partially made good, and, most important of all, the promise of an immediate advance against the enemy had sent a thrill of exultation and enthusiasm throughout the whole force. A modicum of rest had also been secured.

As I have said before, it is not my purpose in these pages to write a history. Many volumes have been published with this object. They have appeared in many countries and in many languages. A few have seemed to me to be wonderfully accurate accounts, considering the great difficulty of arriving at the truth long before the time when full and authentic material can possibly be available.

All I have had in my mind in writing this book is to explain, so far as I can, my own part throughout these great events in carrying out the responsible task entrusted to me by my country; the aspect in which the situation presented itself in my mind from day to day; and my reasons for the decisions which guided the action of the troops under my command.

My desire here is to recall exactly what was in my mind on the morning of the 6th September, which saw the opening of the Battle of the Marne, and to describe the *view* which presented itself to me of the situation on both sides; in other words, the basis for the orders which were issued to the troops.

These orders were necessarily founded upon my own personal appreciation of the situation as it appeared to me at the moment. It was impossible for me to know that situation accurately in all its details. For instance, I could not then know, as I know now, that the Germans had abandoned their vigorous offensive 24 hours earlier than this, nor should I have conceived it possible that they could have done so.

Reverting, then, to my general view of things on the morning of the 6th; in the first place, my personal conference with Joffre on the night of the 5th had put me in full possession of his exact plans and all that was in his mind.

His intention was to attack at all points *au fond*, to inflict a crushing defeat on the whole German Army on our front by assailing its flank with the 6th French and British Armies attacking from a line running roughly from Le Plessis-Belleville on the north through Cuisy—Iverny—Neufmontiers—Meaux, across the Marne to Villers-sur-Morin—Rozoy—la Chapelle Iger to Gastins on the south.

At the same time the 5th French Army was to advance north from its present position and, with all the French Armies to its right, Franchet d'Esperey was to make a simultaneous frontal attack. The following were General Joffre's orders of September 4th:

> 1. Advantage must be taken of the risky situation of the German 1st Army to concentrate against it the efforts of the Allied Armies on our extreme left. All preparations must be made during the 5th for an attack on the 6th September.

2. The following general arrangements are to be carried out by the evening of September 5th:—

(a) All the available forces of the 6th Army north-east of Meaux are to be ready to cross the Ourcq between Lizy and May-en-Multien, in the general direction of Château-Thiérry. The available portions of the 1st Cavalry Corps which are close at hand are to be handed over to General Maunoury for this operation.

(b) The British Army is to establish itself on the line Changis—Coulommiers, facing east, ready to attack in the general direction of Montmirail.

(c) The 5th Army will close slightly on its left and take up the general line Courtaçon—Esternay—Sézanne, ready to attack, generally speaking, from south to north. The 2nd Cavalry Corps will ensure connection between the British Army and the 5th Army.

(d) The 9th Army will cover the right of the 5th Army by holding the southern outlets of the St. Gond marshes and by placing part of its forces on the tableland north of Sézanne.

3. These different armies are to attack on the morning of September 6th.

The 8th Division of the 4th French Corps was to arrive south of Meaux during the early morning and maintain connection with the British 3rd Corps about Villers-sur-Morin, whence the British line following the points named above was facing nearly due east.

My own view of the enemy's situation and intentions was fairly in accordance with the Germans' actual positions, although I did not know at that time that a retreat had really set in, or how the various Corps and Divisions were placed. Judging from the Air and Cavalry reconnaissances and from Intelligence Reports, I thought that a large part of von Kluck's 1st Army was now south of the Grand Morin River, and that the enemy's western columns had crossed the Marne about Meaux and Trilport, although one or two Divisions were still north of that river and west of the Ourcq. From the fact that the rearguards of both my 1st and 2nd Corps in their retirement on the day previous were slightly engaged, whilst a few outpost affairs were reported as having occurred in the night, I judged the enemy to have got some distance south of the Grand Morin River. The appearance of hostile cavalry detachments on the previous evening indicated the presence of that arm.

Whilst it appeared to me that our dispositions promised great things, I also realised fully that the situation demanded the utmost care and watchfulness, as everything depended on the timing of our movements, the utmost measure of mutual support, and the most vigorous and continuous attacks.

The area in which the British Army operated in the Battle of the Marne may be described as the country enclosed between the tributaries of the Marne, the Ourcq on the north and the Grand Morin on the south, between which boundaries it is intersected by the Marne itself, and a third tributary, the Petit Morin.

This area forms the western portion of the Plateau de la Brie, which rises to a height of 400 to 500 feet above the plain of Champagne. The general slope of the ground is from east to west. The plateau is of rock formation, and the rivers, which were formerly of greater volume than at present, have worn away deep channels, with the result that the ground falls very steeply to the river-beds. A certain amount of alluvial deposit has been brought down by the rivers and streams, in the immediate vicinity of which are to be found marshy pools and swamps. With the exception of the Forêt de Crécy, to the south-west of the area under consideration, there are no extensive woods, the higher ground being covered with small copses of thick undergrowth with a sprinkling of oak.

The country generally is open, and presents no obstacles to the passage of troops of all arms. The steep cliffs rising abruptly from the river-beds afford good defensive positions suitable for rearguard actions, obliging an advancing force to concentrate at defiles.

The roads and railways follow generally the course of the rivers. The chief roads are—(a) Paris—Meaux—La Ferté-sous-Jouarre, where one branch continues through Montmirail to Châlons, and the other bends slightly north through Château-

Thiérry and Dormans to Rheims and Epernay. (b) Paris—Lagny—Coulommiers—La Ferté-Gaucher—Esternay. (c) Soissons—Villers-Cotterets—Meaux, and thence through the Forêt de Crécy to Melun.

The chief railways are—(1) Paris—Nanteuil—Crépy-en-Valois, thence to Compiègne and Soissons. (2) Paris—Meaux—Rheims (following the Ourcq). (3) Paris—Meaux—Château-Thiérry—Epernay (following the Marne). (4) Paris—Tournan, through the Forêt de Crécy to Coulommiers, and thence to Esternay (following the Grand Morin).

In addition to the roads mentioned above, which are *routes nationales*, there are numerous smaller roads (*routes départementales*) which are practicable for all arms and transport. In places the gradients are steep where the roads cross the deep beds of the rivers.

The march of the Army on the morning of the 6th was ordered in a direction bearing generally about east-north-east, and I did not then expect to reach the Grand Morin River the same evening, as heavy fighting was most probable.

I joined Haig about 9.30 a.m. He was then engaged all along his front against detachments of the enemy, which appeared to be advanced guards with some supporting cavalry. The fighting had commenced about 7.30 a.m. by a move of hostile infantry on Rozoy. They were attacked and thrown back by the 4th Guards Brigade.

Although the German artillery was in action early in the day, close observation, combined with constant reports, showed us before noon that this advance was not being pushed with much vigour, and later (the right of the 1st Division being thrust forward towards Vaudoy, the left of the 2nd Division at Ormeaux), as we attempted to close with them, it was discovered that a general retreat was in progress, covered by rearguards.

A visit which I paid to the 2nd Corps on Haig's left confirmed this impression.

On this I gave orders that the enemy was to be closely pressed, and that, if possible, the line of the Grand Morin River was to be made good before night.

As a matter of fact, this was not done till the next day, but a considerable further advance was made. Our cavalry from Gastins drove the enemy back north of Dagny.

On the morning of September 7th, the 2nd Cavalry Brigade was acting as left flank guard to the Cavalry Division, with the 9th Lancers as advanced guard to the Brigade.

On reaching Frétoy, the village of Moncel was found to be occupied by a patrol of Germans, and was taken at a gallop by the leading troop, followed by the one remaining machine gun of the regiment. About a troop and a half, accompanied by the Commanding Officer, Lieutenant-Colonel D. Campbell and Major Beale-Browne, moved up on the left of the village. Shortly afterwards two squadrons of the 1st Garde Dragoner charged the village and drove out the troop of the 9th Lancers after a little street fighting. A third Dragoner squadron then came up to the village from the north in support. The troop and a half of the 9th Lancers, led by the Commanding Officer and 2nd in Command, attacked this squadron in perfect order, charged the left half of the German squadron and pierced it with loss, both sides facing the charge; the Germans at a 15-mile rate and the 9th Lancers at speed.

Swinging round after the charge, the 9th Lancers gained the village and rallied on the south of it. At the same time, the 18th Hussars, who had been sent up in support, drove off the Germans by fire from the wood on the left of the village. In this charge by the 9th Lancers Lieutenant-Colonel Campbell was wounded in the arm by a lance and in the leg by a bullet, both wounds, however, being slight. The adjutant, Captain G. F. Reynolds, was severely wounded in the shoulder by a lance. Lieutenant Alfrey, the machine-gun officer, who must have gone to his assistance from the village, was killed whilst extracting the lance from Captain Reynolds. Our casualties were slight—one officer (Lieutenant Alfrey) killed, two men killed; two officers (Lieutenant-Colonel Campbell and Captain Reynolds) wounded and five men wounded. The number of Germans left on the ground was considerable.

Shortly afterwards, "I" Battery, R.H.A., was moved to the

north of the village, and the 18th Hussars were sent to Faujus and to a line of trees to the south of that village.

"B" Squadron, 18th Hussars, under Major Leveson, took up a position by this line of trees, dismounting in the corn stooks, and was immediately charged by a German squadron in perfect order, in line at close order. The 18th Hussars squadron met the charge with well-directed fire at close range, and the German squadron was almost annihilated. A few passed through the firing line and were shot by the horse holders. Thirty-two dead and wounded Germans were counted on the ground in front of the squadron, and of the 60 or 70 which charged not more than a dozen escaped. A second charge was attempted shortly afterwards, but did not approach closer than 400 yards.

Aircraft at night reported the German 2nd Corps (which had been moving north nearly all day) to have entered a large forest from which we supposed them to be debouching through Lizy north of the wood.

The 3rd Corps were practically in reserve, but moved up during the day a little on our left rear.

On this day I saw most of the troops and found them in excellent spirits.

The 6th French Army on our left was opposed chiefly by the German 4th Reserve Corps, which, however, was reinforced by a considerable part of the retiring 2nd Corps. The 4th German Corps had also been directed towards this part of the battlefield.

The 5th French Army on our right, after a heavy day's desperate fighting, reached the line Courtaçon—Esternay—La Villeneuve-les-Charleville. At the close of the advance and fighting on the 6th, I returned to Melun to receive reports and ascertain the general situation of the Allied Forces. It was perfectly clear now that the enemy had abandoned the offensive and was in full retreat towards the Marne. I sent a despatch to General Joffre, telling him of our work during the day and the points we had reached, and requested instructions from him for the 7th.

Very late at night I got his reply, telling me that the 5th Army had made good progress, which had been materially helped by the pressure of the British Forces east of the enemy's right flank.

He asked me to continue the move tomorrow, but in a rather more northerly direction.

During the night of the 6th-7th it became necessary to study the situation with great care. Joffre's original plan presupposed a continued German advance to the south and south-east, culminating in a great attack on the 5th and 9th French Armies. His directions to me on the 5th were to move *east*, and attack this advance in flank.

It was to attain that object that the moves of the 6th were ordered, and, as a matter of fact, the 1st Corps under Haig did move almost due east. The troops which opposed him were on that day supposed to be the flank guard of the enemy which was attacking the 5th French Army.

As stated above, I spent some time in the morning of the 6th with the 1st Corps, but it was not before noon that the possibility of a German retirement began to take shape in my mind. The conviction that such a retirement was actually taking place was increased as the day wore on and after my visits to the 2nd and 3rd Corps.

It was on my return to Melun late in the evening of this day that Air and Intelligence Reports, combined with the impression which my own observations had made upon me, left no doubt in my mind that the German retreat had really been in full progress for many hours, and that the British Army must be immediately moved in a direction which would bring it in close contact with the enemy.

Orders were therefore issued directing the march on the Grand Morin River, which was to be forced and passed with all possible speed on the 7th.

Joffre's request to me to move in a rather more northerly direction pointed to some such conclusion; but I do not think that his information during the day had impressed him to the same extent with the drastic change in the situation, and the fact that the Germans had so soon taken the alarm and been overtaken by a veritable "panic."

My intention to close at all speed with the enemy had to be tempered by consideration for the French Armies on my flank, both of which were opposed by much larger forces.

It was necessary to keep close touch with Franchet d'Esperey on my right, and to direct the movements of the 3rd Corps on my left so as to bring the best possible support to the hard-pressed right of the 6th Army, who were fighting there so gallantly and well.

The cavalry acted with great vigour in advance of the Army throughout the 7th, and on that day the Grand Morin River was forced and positions were taken up well to the north-east of it.

The 5th and 6th French Armies were both heavily engaged throughout the 7th. The left of the 5th Army on my right reached La Ferté—Gaucher at nightfall.

The position of the British Army at daybreak on the 8th was, roughly:

3rd Corps	La Haute Maison
2nd Corps	Aulnoy and neighbourhood
1st Corps	Chailly and Jouy-sur-Morin

The problem before me on the night of the 7th-8th may be stated thus:

I knew that the 5th Army on my right had been heavily opposed on the 7th, and that powerful forces of the enemy were still in front of it. The 6th Army was fighting hard west of the Ourcq, opposed to nearly all the German 1st Army. I gathered at this time that the enemy forces opposing our own immediate advance consisted chiefly of cavalry with a strong artillery supporting, backed up by some infantry detachments.

I have referred before in this book to a visit I paid to Germany in 1911. On that occasion I saw a great deal of German cavalry in manoeuvre, and the knowledge I thus acquired enabled me to estimate the value of the forces which were now opposing me.

For years the German cavalry have been trained in rearguard action such as the work they were now doing. They carry a large quantity of machine guns, which they are trained to handle very efficiently. To each brigade of cavalry there is attached a regiment of *jäger*, picked riflemen, chosen for their skill in shooting and in taking advantage of ground. These troops are specially valuable for the defence of river lines and positions which are intended to cause delay to an advancing enemy.

There was little doubt in my mind that the Petit Morin and Grand Morin rivers could be forced with comparative ease, but I knew that good troops would be required, and the chief question to be considered at that moment was how the hardly-pressed 6th French Army could best be assisted whilst effective connection with the 5th French Army on the right was safeguarded.

There was the certainty that the passages of the Marne opposite my left flank, between Changis and La Ferté-sous-Jouarre, would be strongly guarded, and that our advance at this point would be very difficult. A large force of German heavy artillery was reported to be in the loop of the river near Varreddes.

After considering alternatives of action, *e.g.*, the possibility of sending round direct help to Maunoury, or the advisability of strengthening my left flank to ensure a quicker passage there, I decided that the best help I could bring to the 6th Army was to effect a speedy passage of the Grand Morin, Petit Morin, and Marne rivers.

The course of the Marne at the point to be passed from left to right was generally north-east, and the British Army after passing would be facing north-west, which would bring it almost directly upon the line of retreat of the 1st German Army, which was in close contact with Maunoury across the Ourcq. The adoption of any other method of action which I had considered must have meant delay and a weakening of my front. What was wanted was a speedy decision of the critical situation on the left.

I had also to remember the necessity of keeping up close connection with d'Esperey on my right. Orders were accordingly issued for a general attack on the Petit Morin River, to begin early on the 8th.

On that morning I found Haig at La Trétoire (north of Rebais), near where the 4th Guards Brigade of the 2nd Division (2nd Batt. Grenadier Guards, 2nd and 3rd Batts. Coldstream Guards, 1st Batt. Irish Guards), supported by some field batteries, were forcing the passage of the Petit Morin.

I can well recall the scene. We were on some high ground which was intersected by rocky ravines and sandhills. Just below where we stood was the village, into which the enemy were putting a good many shells, and beyond it lay the line of the Petit Morin stream with its wooded, shelving banks, upon which the enemy was holding a strong rearguard position on the further bank.

The 5th Brigade was brought up in support of the 4th, and the heavy artillery were got into action. The crossing of the river at this point was stoutly opposed for a considerable time; but the passage of it, when secured, was much assisted by the cavalry and the 1st Division, which had effected a crossing some way higher up.

The detailed story of this great fight is worth the telling. Approaching the river on a fairly wide front, on the right of the 1st Corps was the 1st Guards Brigade with a troop of the 15th Hussars, some cyclists, the 23rd Field Co., R.E., and the 26th Brigade, R.F.A., which, under General Maxse, formed the advance guard to the 1st Division in its advance from Jouy-sur-Morin to Bassevelle. A French Cavalry Division was operating on our right and front, covered by our Cavalry Division.

At 9.15 a.m. a French cavalry officer reported to Maxse that French cavalry was in occupation of the heights to the north of Bellot. At 9.30 a.m. the 1st Batt. Black Watch and one battery of the 26th Brigade, R.F.A., had reached Bellot village, and the main guard was approaching the village through a ravine, when a battery of the enemy's horse artillery opened fire on the column from high ground near Fontaine St. Robert. The fire was quickly silenced by French horse artillery guns which cooperated with our 26th Brigade. The casualties were remarkably low considering the circumstances.

An alarming report reached General Maxse that a brigade of French cavalry was cooped up in Bellot exposed to artillery fire, and that a large force of German infantry was advancing southwards through the woods to attack them. This somewhat delayed the further advance of our troops.

It was 10.40 a.m. when Colonel Grant Duff advanced to seize and picket the heights north of the valley of the Petit Morin and to safeguard the advance of the column down the valley to Sablonnières. This main guard crossed the Petit Morin at 11 a.m., and shortly afterwards the advance guard was in contact with some 250 of the enemy's *jäger* of the Guard in the thick woods north of the ravine.

Some close fighting ensued, during which the Black Watch and Cameron Highlanders suffered casualties. The enemy lost some 50 killed and 50 wounded. Subsequently the advance was continued northwards on Hondevilliers, the 1st Guards Brigade advancing on the east and the 3rd Brigade on the west of the ravine. Advanced troops reached Bassevelle. The 43rd Howitzer Brigade and 26th Heavy Battery were engaged in supporting the advance of the 2nd Division during the day.

On the left the 4th (Guards) Brigade and the 41st Brigade, R.F.A., under Lieutenant-Colonel Lushington, R.F.A., formed the advanced guard to the 2nd Division moving from St. Simeon *via* Rebais and La Trétoire.

When the vanguard of the 3rd Coldstream Guards had just passed La Trétoire, shell fire was opened on them from the high ground round Boitron.

The enemy's guns did not remain long in action; but the crossing was held by the enemy, who had a machine-gun battery. The valley is closely wooded, and the machine guns were so well placed that, whenever our infantry came into action, they were met by a heavy fire from these guns. The other battalions were brought up one by one to support the 3rd Coldstream Guards; two guns were placed at the bend in the road just north of La Trétoire, and howitzers were also brought up north of that village.

At 12 noon the Worcestershire Regt. was sent to assist the 4th (Guards) Brigade, and moved *via* La Trétoire—Launoy—N. of Ruine—Moulin Neuf, to force the passage of the river at Le Gravier, and to work up stream to assist the Guards Brigade.

By 1.30 p.m. the bridge had been seized by the Worcestershire Regt., who captured about 30 prisoners in the farm by the bridge. The 2nd Grenadier Guards also managed to cross at La Forge.

The enemy retired, leaving a good many dead and two machine guns in our hands.

An advance was then made to the north of Boitron church, where the Divisional Artillery came into action.

The Connaught Rangers were despatched to work down the right bank to assist the passage of the 3rd Division. They encountered some opposition at Le Moulin du Pont, but pushed on to near Orly, where they found the 3rd Division already across the river.

At 2.30 p.m. the Grenadiers and 2nd Batt. Coldstream Guards were sent northwards to protect the front, whilst the Highland Light Infantry were sent towards Bussières to endeavour to cut off the enemy's retreat.

The remainder of the 5th Infantry Brigade were engaged with small bodies of the enemy in the woods north-east of the Bécherelle—Maison Neuve road, but the Brigadier-General withdrew his three battalions, fearing they would fire on the 4th Brigade and Highland Light Infantry, and they reached Boitron about 5 p.m., except one company of the Connaught Rangers, which worked through the woods and emerged at Le Cas Rouge, and claimed to have headed off some German stragglers. Meanwhile, at about 4.30 p.m. the enemy made a counter-attack with machine guns against our gun position from the woods north-west of Boitron church. This was dealt with by the Guards Brigade. The 3rd Coldstream Guards and Irish Guards made a direct attack, whilst the 2nd Coldstream Guards swung round against the enemy. The whole machine-gun battery of five guns surrendered with 100 personnel.

I then went to Smith-Dorrien, whose Headquarters were at Doué. His corps had then forced the passage of the river, but had encountered severe opposition in doing so.

I found the 3rd Corps on the left advancing well at all points, driving the enemy before them and inflicting considerable loss all along the line. Pulteney was in touch with the 8th French Division on his left; and Gough, with the 3rd Cavalry Brigade (4th Hussars, 5th Lancers, and 16th Lancers), was successfully engaged all the morning on the left flank. There appeared to be a considerable force of the enemy in the woods lying to the south of Lizy, north of the Marne, and later reports stated that some 90 German guns were deployed there against the right flank of the 6th French Army.

I impressed on Pulteney the necessity for pushing on to the utmost of his ability in aid of the 6th Army. It looked as if he would have considerable opposition at Changis and La Ferté-sous-Jouarre. The Germans retiring over the Marne at the latter place occupied the town in strength and blew up the bridge.

Although the 3rd Corps were not able to pass the Marne till daybreak on the 10th, there could be no doubt that the vigour of Pulteney's attack took considerable pressure off the right of the 6th French Army. The British troops fought all along the line with splendid spirit, energy, and determination, and they were skilfully handled and led.

From what I could observe, however, it seemed to me that the infantry were not in a wide enough formation, and perhaps in some cases the field artillery were not pushed far enough forward. I called attention to these points in the following Memorandum, which was issued on the 10th:

> The latest experiences have shown that the enemy never neglects an opportunity to use all his available artillery in forward positions under cover of cavalry and other mobile troops.
>
> Our cavalry is now organised in two Divisions, the first of three, the second of two Brigades, each with a Brigade of Horse Artillery. During the present phase of the operations—which consist of as rapid a pursuit and pressure of the enemy as possible in his retreat—two Corps will generally be in first line. A Cavalry Division will be directed to work on the front and flank of either Corps and well in advance. The Commander of the cavalry will remain in the closest concert with the Corps Commanders on the flank on which he is working.
>
> The Corps Commanders will send forward with the cavalry as much of their field artillery as can be usefully employed in harassing the enemy's retirement. They will place them under the direction of the Cavalry Commander for the day, the latter officer being responsible for their safety. When, owing to the approach of darkness, the field artillery can no longer find useful targets, they will be with-

drawn from the cavalry back to the Division to which they belong. Should the enemy make any decided stand during such operations and a general action arise or become imminent, the field artillery in the front will either fall back or retain their position, at the discretion of the Corps Commander, and again come under their Divisional Commander.

The withdrawal from under the supervision of the Cavalry Commander will always remain at the discretion of the Corps Commander.

I wish to call the attention of Corps Commanders to the necessity of warning their infantry against what is known as 'bunching up.' Losses and delay in overcoming rearguards resistance during the present phase of the operations have undoubtedly been caused by this.

Instances have also occurred when undue delay in effecting the passage of a river has been caused by a failure to realise the nature of the problem from the purely local standpoint.

Small flanking parties, crossing at unguarded points by hastily improvised means, will dislodge hostile infantry and Maxims much more quickly and effectively than by frontal attacks, however powerfully supported by artillery.

On the night of the 9th and 10th, the 3rd Corps occupied La Ferté-sous-Jouarre and the left bank of the Marne, but were unable to cross, and our left ran roughly eastward through Bussières and Boitron to Hondevilliers.

In all the villages which the enemy had so hastily occupied and evacuated, there was evidence of violent damage and looting.

At La Ferté-sous-Jouarre, Doué, and Rebais, there were signs of great disorder and lack of discipline.

At daybreak on the 9th the advance on the Marne was continued. My Headquarters were now at Coulommiers, where a number of Air reports were received early in the day. They seemed to show that the powerful German battery of 90 guns which had been located on the previous day in Lizy had been withdrawn, and that the enemy in front of the 5th French Army was somewhat reduced. The front of the 5th French Army was apparently clear up to the Marne.

A considerable concentration of Germans was said to be between Chateau-Thiérry and Marigny, but as the large columns in the rear were seen to be marching north, this looked only like a strong rearguard.

The following orders were issued to the troops at 7-30 p.m. on the 8th:

General Headquarters
September 8th, 1914

1. The enemy are continuing their retreat northwards and our Army has been successfully engaged during the day with their rearguards on the Petit Morin, thereby materially assisting the progress of the French Armies on our right and left, which the enemy have been making great efforts to oppose.

2. The Army will continue the advance north tomorrow at 5 a.m., attacking rearguards of the enemy wherever met. The Cavalry Division will act in close association with the 1st Corps and gain touch with the 5th French Army on the right. Gen. Gough, with the 3rd and 5th Cavalry Brigades, will act in close association with the 2nd Corps and gain touch with the 6th French Army on the left.

3. Roads are allotted as follows:
1st Corps—Eastern road, Sablonnières—Hondevilliers—Nogent—l'Artaud—Saulchéry, eastern side of Charly-sur-Marne. Western road: La Trétoire—Boitron—Pavant—western side of Charly—Villiers-sur-Marne—Domptin—Coupru; both inclusive.

2nd Corps—Western road: St. Ouen—Saacy—Méry—Montreuil inclusive, and all roads between this and western road of 1st Corps exclusive.

3rd Corps—Western road: La Ferté-sous-Jouarre—Dhuisy; western road of 2nd Corps exclusive.

Supply Railheads for September 9th, 1914.
Cavalry Division Chaumes. Brig.-Gen. Gough's Brigades Chaumes. 1st Corps Coulommiers. 2nd Corps Cou-

lommiers. 3rd Corps Mortcerf. L. of C. (line of communications) Chaumes. G.H.Q. (General Headquarters) Chaumes. R.F.C. (Royal Flying Corps) Chaumes. Ammunition railroad Verneuil.

Reports to Melun till 9 a.m., after that hour to Coulommiers.

A. J. Murray
Lieut.-General
Chief of the General Staff

Allenby, with the cavalry, seized the bridges at Charly-sur-Marne and Saulchéry and, advancing rapidly to the high ground north about Fontaine Fauvel, covered the rapid passage of the 1st Corps over these bridges. Clearing the ground of the enemy and making many captures, the 1st Army Corps reached Domptin, and the cavalry the heights about Montgivrault, some miles further north.

The 3rd Division of the 2nd Corps, to the left, seized and crossed the bridge at Nanteuil early in the day. The 5th Division (2nd Corps) crossed at Méry, but was then held up for some time by German artillery said to be in the neighbourhood of La Sablonnière. It was essential to my general plan that the 2nd Corps should not get too far north until the 1st and 3rd Corps were completely established on the further bank of the Marne. Smith-Dorrien was instructed accordingly.

As the fight progressed during the day, our 3rd Corps at La Ferté-sous-Jouarre and the 8th French Division at Changis found difficulty in crossing the river. I then instructed Smith-Dorrien to send one Division towards Dhuisy to menace the rear of the troops opposing these crossings. The 5th Division was directed there, but as they were unable to overcome the enemy's resistance they only succeeded in reaching Montreuil, 2 miles S.E. of Dhuisy, very late at night.

I found Pulteney south of La Ferté early in the morning, and heavy fighting going on to gain the passage of the river which the enemy was still vigorously disputing. It was a remarkable scene. The banks of the Marne at this point are somewhat steep, and there is high commanding ground on either side of the river. The old town of La Ferté, so famous in Napoleon's campaign of 1814, presented a picturesque appearance with its ancient church and buildings. Surrounded and held by the enemy, it seemed to frown down on the broken bridge, forbidding all approach. The enemy was vigorously defending the passage, strongly supported by artillery from the high ground north of the town.

The 4th Division in two columns attempted to advance on the bridge with a view to repairing it and then to close and establish a bridgehead on the northern bank, but all their attempts were frustrated by the German guns. Just after dark, however, Hunter Weston's 11th Brigade (1st Batt. Somersetshire Light Infantry, 1st Batt. East Lancashire Regt., 1st Batt. Hampshire Regt., and 1st Batt. Rifle Brigade) was able to reach the southern bank, where a number of boats were seized. In these the brigade was pushed across, and by 10 p.m. had established an effective footing on the northern bank, under cover of which a pontoon bridge was constructed by the Royal Engineers of the 4th Division under very heavy fire. It was a very fine piece of work, to which the Commander of the 3rd Corps particularly drew my attention. During this operation Colonel Le Marchant was killed.

Another detachment also effected a crossing further up the river in the neighbourhood of Chamigny, but the main body of the 3rd Corps crossed by the pontoon bridge in the early hours of the 10th.

I found Smith-Dorrien at Pulteney's Headquarters.

The 3rd and 5th Cavalry Brigades were operating between the 3rd and 2nd Corps, filling up the gap, which, however, in view of the enemy's hurried retirement, never caused me any apprehension.

It has been stated that on the 8th I called upon General Maunoury for assistance in forcing the river, and that this was the reason why the French 8th Division was not taken away.

I can only say that no such request was ever made by me or my Headquarters Staff, nor had any other commander my sanction for such a demand. I felt throughout the battle that my principal role was to bring assistance in the best manner and in the most effective direction to the 6th Army, for I fully appreciated the much greater difficulty of the task which they were undertaking. On the other hand my diary shows that on the 9th I received two urgent messages from Maunoury begging me to take the pressure of the enemy's 3rd Corps off him, and I think the action of the British Army on the 9th had this effect.

In the afternoon I rode across the Marne at Nogent and met several units of the 1st Army Corps moving up the heights of the north side of the river. I was tremendously struck by their general appearance and attitude. They were full of spirit and fired with enthusiasm. They had upon them that war-worn look which we all know so well, but one felt, as one rode beside them, that here were troops whom nothing could stop, who asked only to be led forward, and who were enveloped in an atmosphere of confidence and victory.

They were very tired, however; how tired was not brought fully home to me until I came to the 5th Cavalry Brigade (the Scots Greys, 12th Lancers, and 20th Hussars).

The whole brigade was dismounted behind some woods on the heights. Every man of them, except a small proportion of horse holders, was lying fast asleep on the ground.

Accompanied by the Brigadier (Chetwode), I rode into the midst of the sleeping mass, my horse picking his way through the recumbent figures. They hardly stirred.

I was anxious to say a few words to the men, and the Brigadier asked me if he should call them up to attention. I said, "No, let them rest," adding that I would talk to them for anyone to hear who happened to be awake and not too done up to listen. I thanked them, as they lay there on the ground, for all they had done; I told them of the situation and of our hopes of complete victory. A few men tried to struggle up; others, half awake, leaned on their elbows and drowsily listened. I hardly realised that they had heard anything of what I had said. This particular regiment was the Scots Greys, commanded by Lieutenant-Colonel Bulkeley Johnson, who afterwards fell so gallantly at the head of his brigade on the Ancre. Bulkeley Johnson subsequently told me that every word I had spoken on that occasion was published afterwards in the local papers all over Scotland. From the Greys I went on to the other two regiments of the brigade and the horse batteries, where I witnessed similar scenes.

On my return to Headquarters I received the welcome news that the 5th French Army on my right was across the river and in close touch with the British; and that the 6th French Army, after desperate fighting, had practically got possession of the lower bridges of the Ourcq, to which river the enemy was only clinging on his northern flank in order, apparently, to cover his retreat. In short, since noon the Germans had given up resistance and were now, at nightfall, in full retreat.

During this day we made large captures in prisoners and war material, and our position at night was (roughly) along the line La Ferté—Bezu—Domptin, with the cavalry well forward.

In my dispatches of September 17th, 1914, I estimated that the Battle of the Marne reached its conclusion on the night of September 10th, and I see no reason to think otherwise now.

On that night the British forces reached the line La Ferté—Milon—Neuilly—St. Front—Rocourt.

The 6th French Army had been wheeling up their right into line with us, and the 5th French Army was nearly in line on our right. The enemy were in full retreat to the north and northeast. During the day, the cavalry, the 1st Army Corps, and the 2nd Army Corps had fought numerous engagements with the enemy's rearguard, and had made large captures. Allenby, as usual, had handled his cavalry with great vigour and skill, nor had his detachments of the 3rd and 5th Brigades on the left under General Gough been less energetic. The bridging of the Marne at La Ferté-sous-Jouarre by engineers of the 3rd Corps was a fine piece of work. Our casualties were heavy, but, having regard to the results attained, by no means excessive.

I was able to visit some of the hospital trains on the 10th. Although there had been no chance yet of fully developing the organisation of the wounded transport service, I think the best was done with the means available at the moment. Much has been written to recount the story of this great battle, and, doubtless for the next century, controversy will rage over the event and its results.

At the opening of the battle, on the morning of September 6th, the Allied forces had to turn from the task of arranging defensive positions on the Seine. The 5th French Army and the British Army had already fallen back close to that river in accordance with the general plan, and the rear echelons of transport, etc. rested to the south of it.

Between September 6th and 12th the German Army was driven back pell-mell from the Seine to the Marne, a distance of 65 miles, whilst the front extended from Paris to Verdun. Their losses in officers, men, prisoners, guns, machine guns, and war material were enormous. Most desperate battles were fought all along the line.

Many different views have been put forward regarding the initial foundation upon which the Germans built up their strategic scheme for the invasion of France. It is not my purpose here to discuss them or to speculate upon what was actually in the minds of the Great General Staff when they set out upon this gigantic enterprise. Whatever the original conception may have been, I claim for the Allies that its fulfilment was crushed for ever and a day at the Battle of the Marne.

Splendidly, however, as the Allied Armies fought, skilfully as each of the various corps and armies which were engaged supported one another; it was the Germans themselves who deliberately threw away whatever chance they ever had of securing a decisive victory. We have seen that so late as the morning of September 6th, Joffre and I were still so certain that the German thrust was in full career that an advance by the British Army in an almost easterly direction was ordered and partially undertaken.

Yet at that time von Kluck's great "advance" had for some hours become a counter-march in hurried "retreat."

Why this sudden change?

Because he then discovered that his communications were about to be threatened on the Ourcq. Surely the most inexperienced of generals might have anticipated some such threat, and, further, might have realised that the line of the River Ourcq afforded him the most convenient and efficient means of securing flank protection. It has been said by critics of the battle that, had Maunoury delayed his movement on the Ourcq, von Kluck would not have taken alarm. But when the German General first ordered the counter-march the French General had hardly recrossed the Marne.

The fact probably is that von Kluck and his Staff never really liked the role which was forced upon them by the Great General Staff, and that they undertook their part in the battle with wavering minds and with their heads half turned round.

When the Allied Armies look back to this great battle and realise what was accomplished, they cannot fail to remember with a thrill of pride that they fought and badly defeated an army not only flushed with the knowledge that it had effected a tremendous inroad into the enemy's territory, but which also enjoyed one other incalculable advantage; it was commanded and led by a Sovereign who possessed absolute authority—military and civil. Its Emperor and Commander-in-Chief was served by a Great General Staff which had been steadily and vigorously preparing for this tremendous trial of strength for a period of over forty years.

This great collision of nations in arms had been kept steadfastly in view. In the preparation of the German Army for this supreme moment not a chance had been thrown away. In man power, armament, training, and equipment; in the instruction of leaders and officers; on the choice of commanders and every other element which makes for efficiency in an army, the most laborious thought and care had been expended.

Compare with this the conditions in which the French and British Armies had been brought up to this fateful hour—systems, staffs, military policy, even money grants, all undergoing constant and drastic change year after year with every fresh wave of popular opinion and every fresh clamour, whilst the intrigues which run riot in all branches of the public service when "votes" rule everything, exercised their usual baneful influence.

As regards the tactical aspect of the Battle of the Marne, I believe that the name of Marshal Joffre will descend to posterity with that battle as one of the greatest military commanders in history; I believe that the battles fought and won throughout the great length of the line over which they took place by the Armies of France under their splendid leaders, will outshine for valour and skill even those glorious deeds of the past, the memorials of which deck their colours with imperishable laurels.

For the British Army I claim that we carried out the role assigned to us, and that our rapid passages of the various river lines in face of great opposition, and our unexpected appearance on the lines of retreat of the forces opposing the 5th and 6th Armies, were practically decisive of the great result.

CHAPTER 7

The Battle of the Aisne

I am throwing my thoughts back, and endeavouring to recall the mental atmosphere which surrounded me during the two days of pursuit following the fighting on the Marne, and during the early days of the Battle of the Aisne, which I am now about to recount. I know that the predominant sentiments which ruled my mind were decidedly optimistic.

As I pointed out in the opening pages of this book, we had not *even then* grasped the true effect and bearing of the many new elements which had entered into the practice of modern war. We fully believed we were driving the Germans back to the Meuse if not to the Rhine, and all my correspondence and communications at this time with Joffre and the French Generals most closely associated with me, breathed the same spirit.

This will be better understood if I quote an order which was issued from French General Headquarters, at Chatillon, dated September 10th, the day which practically saw the close of the Marne battle:

> The German forces are giving way on the Marne and in Champagne before the Allied Armies of the centre and left wing.
>
> To confirm and take advantage of this success, it is necessary to follow up this movement with energy so as to allow the enemy no rest.
>
> The offensive movement will, therefore, be continued along the whole front in a general N.N.E. direction.

(a) The 6th Army will continue to rest its right on the Ourcq at the Sapières stream and on to the line Longpont—Chaudun—Courmelles—Soissons (inclusive). Bridoux's Cavalry Corps will gain ground on the outer wing and will endeavour to disturb the enemy's line of communication and retreat.

(b) The British forces should follow up their victorious advance between the above-mentioned line and the road Rocourt—Fère-en-Tardenois—Mont Notre Dame—Bazoches, which will be at their disposal.

(c) The 5th Army east of the latter line will turn the forest S. and N. of Epernay on the west, covering itself against hostile troops which may be found there, and ready to act in an easterly direction towards Rheims against the columns which are retiring before 9th Army. The 10th Corps will move from about Vertus in the direction of Epernay—Rheims, securing connection between the 5th and 9th Armies and ready to support the latter at any time.

Subsequent to the issue of the above orders, Joffre and I held several consultations with reference to marches through the wooded country (Forêt de St. Gobain and other places) lying to the north of the Aisne.

In these first few days of this period of the war we were decidedly encouraged by reports from other theatres. The Belgian Army appeared to be well established in Antwerp, and a fine sortie, directed by the King of the Belgians, had considerable effect in scattering the German forces operating there, and certainly delayed the movement of reinforcements which had been ordered south.

The news from Russia was also not unfavourable.

However, we were destined to undergo another terrible disappointment. The lessons of war as it is today had to be rubbed in by another dearly bought experience, and in a hard and bitter school.

The first surprise came when the "Jack Johnsons" began to fall. This was a nickname given by the men ("Black Marias" was another) to a high-explosive shell fired from 8-in. howitzers, which had been brought down from the fortress of Maubeuge to support the German defensive position on the Aisne. They were our first experience of an artillery much heavier than our own. Although these guns caused considerable damage and many bad casualties, they never had any very demoralising effect upon the troops.

As day by day the trench fighting developed and I came to realise more and more the much greater relative power which modern weapons have given to the defence; as new methods were adopted in the defensive use of machine guns; and as unfamiliar weapons in the shape of "trench mortars" and "bombs," hand grenades, etc. began to appear on the battlefield, so, day by day, I began dimly to apprehend what the future might have in store for us.

This drastic process of education went steadily on, but still reports came periodically from our aircraft, from our trenches, and from the French on either flank, that the enemy in front of us was "weakening," that (phantom!) columns had been seen marching north, etc.—and so the small still voice of truth and reality, trying to speak within me, remained faint and almost unheard.

Presently came Maunoury's great effort to turn the German right flank. I witnessed one day of this fighting myself with General Maunoury and came back hopeful: alas! these hopes were not fulfilled. Afterwards we witnessed the stupendous efforts of de Castelnau and Foch, but all ended in the same trench! trench! trench!

I finished my part in the Battle of the Aisne, however, unconverted, and it required the further and more bitter lesson of my own failure in the north to pass the Lys River, during the last days of October, to bring home to my mind a principle in warfare of today which I have held ever since, namely, that given forces fairly equally matched, you can "bend" but you cannot "break" your enemy's trench line.

Everything which has happened in the war has borne out the truth of this view, and from the moment I grasped this great truth I never failed to proclaim it, although eventually I suffered heavily for holding such opinions.

The great feature of the pursuit on the 11th was the capture by the 3rd French Army of all the artillery of a German corps.

On the 12th my Headquarters were moved to Fère-en-Tardenois. Early in the day I joined Pulteney at some cross-roads two miles south of Buzancy (S.E. of Soissons). The enemy was opposing the passage of the Aisne to the 6th French Army all along its line westwards from Soissons, and the 4th Division held a position on the bridges south-east of Soissons to assist it.

The banks of the Aisne are very precipitous, and our position on the heights gave us a wonderful view of the fighting. What astonished me was the volume of the fire. Between Soissons and Compiègne the river seemed ablaze, so intense was the artillery fire on both sides.

I watched the action till about 1.30 p.m., when the German artillery, which had been very active all the morning at Montagne de Paris (south of Soissons) and other important points, withdrew north of the river. We saw large masses of transport and troops moving in a N.E. direction.

At nightfall our 3rd Corps was close to the Aisne, the bridges of which were destroyed.

On my return to Headquarters at night the reporting officer informed me that the 6th French Army had reached the Aisne after some opposition, and that the French cavalry on the left were working round by Compiègne and moving N.E. to threaten the German communications.

The 5th French Army on our right was on the line Cormicy—Rheims—Verzy, the 18th Corps being thrown back on its left flank in touch with our right.

A message from Joffre informed me that the 9th and 4th French Armies had both made considerable progress and driven back the enemy.

The cavalry under Allenby did very good work on this day. They cleared the town of Braine and the high ground beyond it of strong hostile detachments. They bivouacked this night at Dhuizel. Allenby reported to me some excellent work done in the neighbourhood of Braine by the Queen's Bays assisted by Shaw's 9th Brigade of the 3rd Division (1st Batt. Northumberland Fusiliers, 4th Batt. Royal Fusiliers, 1st Batt. Lincolnshire Regt., and 1st Batt. Royal Scots Fusiliers). The 1st Corps reached Vauxcéré and the 2nd Corps Braine and neighbourhood. Gough, with the 2nd Cavalry Division, was at Chermizy.

Thus, on the morning of September 13th, the day on which the Battle of the Aisne really opened, the British Army was in position south of that river in its course between Soissons on the west and Bourg on the east, with outposts on the river.

Now as to the ground over which the British Army fought. The Aisne valley runs generally east and west, and consists of a flat-bottomed depression, of width varying from half a mile to two miles, down which the river follows a winding course to the west, at some points near the southern slopes of the valley and at others near the northern. The high ground, both on the north and south of the river, is approximately 400 ft. above the bottom of the valley itself, which is broken into numerous rounded spurs and re-entrants. The most prominent of the former are the Chivres spur on the right bank and the Sermoise spur on the left.

Near the latter place the general plateau on the south is divided by a subsidiary valley of much the same character, down which the small river Vesle flows to the main stream near Sermoise. The slopes of the plateau overlooking the Aisne on the north and south are of varying steepness, and are covered with numerous patches of wood, which also stretch upwards and backwards over the edge on to the top of the high ground. There are several small towns and villages dotted about in the valley itself and along its sides, the chief of which is the town of Soissons.

The Aisne is a sluggish stream of some 170 ft. in breadth, but, being 15 ft. deep in the centre, it is unfordable. Between Soissons on the west and Villers on the east (the part of the river attacked and secured by the British forces) there are eleven road bridges across it. On the north bank a narrow-gauge railway runs from Soissons to Vailly, where it crosses the river and continues eastward along the south bank. From Soissons to Sermoise a double line of railway runs along the south bank, turning at the latter place up the Vesle valley towards Bazoches.

The position held by the enemy was a very strong one, either for a delaying action or for a defensive battle. One of its chief military characteristics is that, from the high ground, on neither side can the top of the plateau on the other side be seen, except for small stretches. This is chiefly due to the woods on the edges of the slopes. Another important point is that all the bridges are under either direct or high-angle artillery fire.

The general lay and contour of the ground in the region over which the British Army fought at the Battle of the Aisne are deeply impressed on my memory.

Rolling downs of considerable altitude characterise the country over which the approaches to the river from the south lead, whilst the banks of the river itself, especially at the south, are wooded, precipitate and rocky. Thus was I able to secure many posts of observation which enabled me to compass a much greater personal survey of the fighting than in any other terrain over which we fought.

During the early phases of the Battle of Ypres, the high ground north of the River Lys presented some similar features; just as Kemmel Hill, and the height overlooking Lens and, further south, the rolling plains west of the Somme, were also good for observation; but these all differed from the Aisne as affording a distant view, whereas, by avoiding observation and creeping through woods and undergrowth, it was possible to reach points of vantage on the southern bank of the Aisne, whence a close observation of the fighting line could be maintained.

I can remember sitting for hours at the mouth of a great cave which lay high up the southern bank of the river, within about 400 yards of the village of Missy and to the eastern flank of it, from which point I saw some of the first effects of the 6-in. siege howitzers which were sent to us at that time. Missy lay along the bed of the stream on both banks, and the Germans occupied a curiously shaped, high, conical hill which was called "Condé Fort." This was situated about 600 yards north of Missy, and reached by a steep ascent from the banks of the river. The hill completely dominated the village.

On the day of which I am writing (September 24th), it was very interesting to witness the clearance of this hill by our high-explosive shells. We could see the Germans flying in all directions to the rear, and we subsequently got reliable information that their losses on this occasion were very heavy.

Although this relieved the pressure on the 5th Division, which was holding Missy and the entrenchments to the north of it, I have always thought it very creditable to Sir Charles Fergusson and his command that he retained his hold on Missy to the last in face of the threatening situation on his front.

He was no doubt much helped by the superior power of observation obtained by his artillery owing to the configuration of the ground all along the south bank, and this, in fact, was most helpful to the British Army throughout the battle.

Missy is another instance in proof of the principle which all recent fighting has clearly established, namely, that command of ground is of value chiefly with regard to the power of observation it affords.

On another occasion I well remember spending a long time lying on the top of a rick, covered by hay for concealment. From this point very valuable artillery observation was secured, and an excellent view of all Haig's positions was afforded.

Poor Wing, the C.R.A. of the 1st Corps, took me to this place, and was beside me all the time. He was afterwards killed at the Battle of Loos whilst in command of the 12th Division. He was beloved by all who served with him; his gallantry, skill, and dash were spoken of by every one, and his loss was deeply felt.

In the early hours of the 13th, we attacked the river line all along our front. The enemy artillery made a vigorous defence, employing many heavy and other kinds of guns. The German infantry was not very energetic in defence, but the bombardment continued heavily all day on both sides. At nightfall all passages except that at Condé were secured and held, our advance line running from Bucy-le-Long on the west through spurs N. and N.E. of Celles to Bourg on the east.

On this afternoon I went to see the bridge which the 3rd Corps had thrown over the Aisne at Venizel. The task had to be done under fire of heavy guns with high-explosive shell, and it was a fine piece of work.

After leaving there, I went to the Headquarters of the 5th Division at Serches, where I met Fergusson. Here I learnt that up to then they had been unable to approach the crossing at Missy, as the enemy had infantry and machine guns on the opposite bank, supported by artillery in rear. Throughout the battle this particular point was a locality of great interest.

Early on the 14th I got news that the 6th Division, which had been sent out to me from England, was now concentrated south of the Marne, and was beginning its march to join us.

During the night of the 13th all three Corps had constructed bridges on their fronts for crossing, and in the early morning of the 14th, the remainder of the 1st Corps crossed at Bourg, the 2nd at Vailly and Missy, and the 3rd Corps at Venizel. On the 14th I spent some time with Haig, who was very successful, and made an excellent advance considering the strong opposition which confronted him.

Early in the morning, Lomax, with the 1st Division, surprised the enemy at Vendresse, capturing 600 prisoners and 12 guns. This distinguished Divisional Commander died a few months later from the effect of wounds received during the first Battle of Ypres.

From the opening of the campaign up to the day he was wounded his services were invaluable. The Division he commanded was always in the hottest of the fighting, and he commanded it throughout with consummate skill and dash. His personality gained for him the esteem and affection of all who served with him, and his loss was badly felt throughout the Army.

On this day (14th) the 2nd Division also made good progress, and in the evening its left held the Ostel Spur, an important point of vantage.

The centre and left of the Army were not so successful. The 3rd Division, after crossing at Vailly, had nearly reached Aizy (about 2½ miles north of the river) when they were driven back by a powerful counter-attack supported by a strong force of heavy artillery. At nightfall, however, they were still one mile north of the river. The enemy's artillery position north of Aizy was a very strong one.

The 5th Division was unable to advance beyond the northern edge of the Chivres plateau. Here also a considerable force of heavy artillery was concentrated against them.

The 4th Division retained during the 14th the position they had taken the day before north of Bucy-le-Long.

The 6th French Army pushed up its left flank, and the 4th French Corps was advancing east in support of the 7th Corps, which was holding the enemy from the north.

The French position about Soissons was well held all day.

The 18th Corps (5th French Army) had its left flank close to the right of our 1st Corps on the heights of Craonne. The remainder of the 5th Army was heavily engaged the whole day all along its line as far as Rheims.

On the night of the 14th I began to think that the enemy was really making a determined stand on the Aisne.

Our situation on this night was as follows:

1st Corps and Cavalry Division holding line Troyon—S. of Chivy—S. of Beaulne—Soupir, with 1st and 2nd Cavalry Brigades on the left, all in close touch with the enemy.

1st Corps Headquarters: Courcelles (afterwards Dhuizel).

2nd Corps: 3rd Division holding circle round Vailly, 5th Division holding south of Chivres plateau to Ste. Marguerite and Missy, both in close touch with the enemy; guns on south bank of river.

3rd Corps: 4th Division holding south end of Spurs from Le Moncel to Crouy (French on north of Crouy ridge), also in close touch with enemy; 19th Brigade in reserve at Venizel Bridge.

Gough's 3rd and 5th Cavalry Brigades: Chassemy.

On this day our casualties were heavy, amounting to between 1,500 and 2,000, including three Commanding Officers.

On the 15th my impression of the previous day, namely, that the enemy was making a firm stand in his actual position, was confirmed also by an intercepted German wireless message. It seemed probable that we had the whole of the German 1st Army in front of us.

This being my appreciation of the situation, I was not satisfied with my own position in two important respects. In the first place, our losses were heavily accumulating, and I had not sufficient reserves to reinforce dangerous points; the enemy had a great artillery superiority, and at this time and for some days afterwards I badly felt the want of the guns and machine guns which had been lost at Le Cateau and were not yet made good. In the second place, I was most anxious to get the 2nd and 3rd Corps forward and more in line with the 1st Corps on the right.

The 6th Division had now crossed the Marne, moving north, and orders were sent to its Commander, General Keir, to come up as quickly as possible. My idea was that the 6th Division should go to Haig, and that, with this reinforcement, he should advance west and take the pressure off the 2nd and 3rd Corps.

The 1st Corps was heavily counter-attacked on several occasions throughout the 15th, and, although the enemy was most gallantly repulsed everywhere, our losses were very severe.

Towards evening a retirement of both German infantry and cavalry took place, and my hopes were revived of the continuance of the enemy's retreat. On this I directed the 6th Division to join its own 3rd Corps on the left.

However, the enemy showing no further signs of leaving the position, my hopes for a further advance at last began to be founded altogether upon the probability of a successful attack by the 6th French Army.

On the 16th I went to see General Maunoury at his Headquarters. I found him watching an attack of the 61st and 62nd Divisions on the village of Nouvron and the plateau above it. The General and his Staff were standing on a kind of grassy tableland on the edge of a wood. I remember that a French Staff Officer who was there spoke English fluently. I threw myself down on my face on the grass and watched the battle taking place on the other side of the river. I spent an hour or two with the General at this spot and discussed the situation with him. From all I could see the French appeared to be getting on very well.

On my way back I visited the Corps Commanders again, and they all expressed the utmost confidence in their ability to hold their positions.

After my return to Headquarters in the evening, Colonel C.

B. Thompson (liaison officer with the 6th French Army) reported to me. His accounts were disappointing after my experience during the day with Maunoury. He said that the 13th French Corps had been checked south-west of Noyon by a night-attack of troops from the 9th Reserve German Corps, which was said to have reached Noyon from Belgium. Here was another incident in that continual "flanking" and "outflanking" manoeuvre which was only to cease at the sea. Again, the 4th French Corps arriving east had been arrested on finding the German force entrenched on its left (northern) flank.

It is from this particular evening of 16th September that I date the origin of a grave anxiety which then began to possess me.

In the years which preceded the war, discussions on various subjects which had come before the Imperial Committee of Defence, of which I was a member, had imbued my mind with a sense of the vital importance it was to Great Britain that the Channel ports should be held by a power in absolute friendship with us.

I venture here to quote some extracts from a paper which I wrote very shortly before the war, for circulation amongst the members of the Committee of Imperial Defence:

> .... I think it will be allowed that, in a war between ourselves and a great Continental Power which is in possession of the Eastern Channel coast-line between Dunkirk and Boulogne, submarines, assisted by aircraft, would effectually deny the passage of the Straits of Dover to any war or other vessel which was not submersible. In fact, the command of the sea, in so far as this part of the Channel is concerned, would not depend upon the relative strength of the opposing Navies, but would remain in dispute until one side or other effected practical destruction of its adversary's aircraft and submarines.
>
> The way would then lie open to the Power which had gained this advantage to move an invading force of any size in comparative safety across the Straits at any part of the coast between (say) Ramsgate and Dungeness on the one side and Dunkirk and Boulogne on the other.

The command of these Straits would be a contest between submarines and aeroplanes.....

If the Continental Powers secured the command they would possess the great advantage of menacing us with a twentieth century edition of the stroke Napoleon intended to deal against us from Boulogne in 1805.

To put the matter briefly; I hold that the Straits of Dover, regarded as a military obstacle to the invasion of this country, will, in the not far distant future, altogether lose their maritime character, and the problem of their successful passage by an invading force will present features somewhat resembling those involving the attack and defence of great river lines or operations on the great lakes in a war between Canada and the United States.

The main object to be attained in trying to secure the passage of a great river line is to gain possession of the opposite bank and establish a strong bridgehead.

In accordance with the views enunciated in this paper, I apply the same principle to the Straits of Dover, and hold that the only reliable defence against a powerful attack by hostile aircraft and submarines in vastly superior numbers, is to possess a strong bridgehead on the French coast with an effective means of passing and repassing across the Straits which would only be secured by the projected Channel Tunnel.

The bearing of all this upon the subject of the present chapter is apparent. So long as the Germans were being driven back, whether by frontal or flank attack, the Channel ports might be considered comparatively safe; but on the particular night of which I am speaking (September 16th) I had arrived at the conclusion that a frontal attack was hopeless, whilst it began to appear that any threat against the German flank would be effectually countered if not turned against ourselves.

This, then, was my great fear. What was there to prevent the enemy launching a powerful movement for the purpose of securing the Channel ports, whilst the main forces were engaged in practically neutralising one another?

From this time I sent constant and urgent warnings to London by wire and by letter to look out for the safety of these same ports.

It was just about now that I began to conceive the idea of disengaging from the Aisne and moving to a position in the north, for the main purpose of defending the Channel ports and, as a secondary reason, to be in a better position to concert combined action and co-operation with the Navy.

At the moment of which I am speaking, and for many days afterwards, there was no serious thought or belief that Antwerp was in danger. My fear for the Channel ports, which then began to lay a strong hold upon my thoughts, in all probability influenced my mind, and, perhaps, affected my dispositions throughout the rest of the time during which I took my part in the Battle of the Aisne. I remember on the same day (September 16th) visiting some hospital trains which were taking the wounded away. It was gratifying to mark the great improvement in their organisation and equipment.

On the 17th the 1st Corps was heavily attacked, but repulsed the enemy with great loss. Craonne was lost by the 18th French Corps, but a strong position was still maintained by them on the Chemin des Dames.

Our operations on the Aisne were at this time much hampered by heavy rain.

On this day (September 17th) a French Reserve Division captured two complete battalions of Prussian Guards in Berry-au-Bac, and a French Cavalry Corps made a splendid raid on the German communications, operating from Roye and moving east as far as the neighbourhood of Ham and St. Quentin. In this raid General Bridoux, commanding the Cavalry Corps, was killed in his motor, and his papers were captured.

I detached the 6th Division from Pulteney's command (3rd Corps) to form an Army Reserve, but gave him the use of the divisional artillery.

An entrenched position was now selected and laid out, and work begun on it south of the Aisne in view of a possible retreat to the south of the river.

The 1st Corps continuing to be subject to heavy and constant attacks, I reinforced Haig on the 18th with a brigade of the 6th Division, and moved the remainder of that Division into a more central position. My anxiety as to reserves caused me also to move Gough's Cavalry Division from the 2nd Corps to take up that duty.

The prominent feature of this day's dispositions was the issue of an order from Joffre by which the 6th French Army assumed a defensive role, occupying the line Soissons—Vic-sur-Aisne—Tracy-le-Val—Bailly, pending the formation of another Army to consist of four Corps (4th, 14th, 13th, and 20th French) with two Cavalry Corps.

This Army was to concentrate at once to the N.W. of Noyon; it was intended that it should operate in an easterly direction against the enemy's flank, and it was placed under the command of de Castelnau.

I had enjoyed the great advantage and privilege of a close acquaintance with this distinguished French commander for some years before the war, and in that time I had learnt enough of his splendid, soldierlike character, and great capabilities as a leader, to experience no surprise when actual war revealed his ability.

Although de Castelnau and the Army he commanded were not successful in actually turning the enemy's flank and compelling his retreat, I believe that history will assign to this great General the honour of commanding the Army which drove the first big nail into the German coffin, for it was the Army which struck the blow that changed the line of battle from east and west to north and south. De Castelnau, by the fine leading of that Army, built the first section of the great besieging wall, which was destined to form an impenetrable barrier between Germany and her main objectives.

In directing this great movement as he did, Marshal Joffre must once again be credited with one of those flashes of military genius which have never been surpassed in the annals of war.

A somewhat significant and rather amusing example of Haig's power of resource was shown on the 19th, when he arranged with the Zouaves on his right to give them 10,000 rations of bully beef in exchange for the loan of two heavy guns.

It was estimated that the enemy's attacks against the 1st Corps up to this time had cost him at least 7,000 men. The dead were lying thick in front of our trenches.

The fighting on the 19th September will always remain memorable to the French, because on this day the Germans practically destroyed Rheims Cathedral by artillery fire.

On the 20th I had a long conference with Haig at his Headquarters, and afterwards visited both his Divisional Commanders (Lomax and Munro) and also some of the Brigadiers.

The 1st Corps was indeed hard pressed, but was gallantly repulsing all attacks. Nevertheless, it was suffering heavy losses and badly needed rest. I told Haig he could call upon the remaining two brigades of the 6th Division (he already had the 18th Brigade in his trenches) for reinforcement, if necessary.

Later in the day a violent attack on the 3rd Division (2nd Corps) obliged me to place the 16th Brigade (1st Batt. the Buffs, 1st Batt. Leicester Regt., 1st Batt. Shropshire L.I., and 2nd Batt. York and Lancs. Regt.) at Smith-Dorrien's disposal. This left only the 17th Brigade and Gough's cavalry in general reserve.

I told Haig he could call upon them if absolutely necessary, but asked him to do without them if possible. Although he was heavily pressed he finished the day without the aid of these troops.

The position of the three Reserve Divisions on the left of the 6th French Army gave cause for great anxiety on this evening, as the development of de Castelnau's movements to the north could not make itself felt for some two or three days.

On the 21st I was able to effect a much needed relief of the troops holding the trenches. The 16th Infantry Brigade of the 6th Division relieved the 7th Infantry Brigade (3rd Batt. Worcester Regt., 2nd Batt. S. Lancs. Regt., 1st Batt. Wilts Regt., and 2nd Batt. R. Irish Rifles) of the 3rd Division, the 7th Brigade joining the 6th Division in general reserve at Couvrelles. The 17th Infantry Brigade (1st Batt. R. Fusiliers, 1st Batt. N. Staffs Regt., 2nd Batt. Leinster Regt., and 3rd Batt. Rifle Brigade) relieved the 5th Infantry Brigade (2nd Batt. Worcester Regt., 2nd Batt. Oxford and Bucks L.I., 2nd Batt. H.L.I., and 2nd Batt. Connaught Rangers) of the 2nd Division, the latter joining the 6th Division as general reserve at Dhuizel.

A significant result of our recent experience was that the cavalry were calling out loudly for *bayonets*.

On this day Sir Henry Rawlinson arrived and reported himself. General Snow having met with a severe accident owing to his horse falling, I placed General Rawlinson in temporary command of the 4th Division.

General Maxwell, the newly appointed Inspector-General of Lines of Communication, also reported his arrival.

On the afternoon of the 22nd I went out with Allenby to the extreme right of Haig's position, where the cavalry were working, and made a close reconnaissance of the ground over which the 1st Army Corps was fighting.

We ascended the heights north of the Aisne leading to the plateau which lies to the south of the Chemin des Dames, now so famous a locality. The ground was thickly wooded up to the edge of the plateau, and the winding narrow road led through small groups of rough houses and buildings which seemed as if they had been hewn out of the rock. The enemy's "Black Marias" constantly searched those roads in close proximity; indeed, actually within the boundaries of these locations, but still tiny children were to be seen playing beside the road all unconscious of any danger.

Near the top of the ascent was an enormous crater or valley, apparently of volcanic origin, which furnished covering and concealment to a large force of Moroccan troops in reserve, who completely filled it. They, like the children, seemed to be perfectly oblivious of the high-explosive shell which often fell amongst them. Lying about in their light blue and silver uniforms they presented a very picturesque appearance.

On the night of the 22nd I got a letter from Maunoury telling me that the enemy was most certainly going away from his front, and that he intended to advance and attack at 4 a.m. on the 23rd, and he asked me to support him. I learned also that the 5th French Army on my right was also planning an attack.

I arranged to co-operate accordingly, but by the night of the 23rd very little progress had been effected.

After this I think all our eyes were turned eagerly towards the north and to de Castelnau, whilst, as to myself, I was more determined than ever that my proper sphere of action was clearly on the Belgian frontier in the north.

The 2nd French Army made decided progress up to the end of September, but their action did not compel the enemy to evacuate his positions on the Aisne, nor did it seriously turn his flank.

On the 26th, de Castelnau was heavily engaged, and was on that evening roughly on the line Ribécourt—Roye—Chaulnes—Bray-sur-Somme, with one Cavalry Division north of the Somme. On the 26th it was clear that the flanking movement of the 2nd (French) Army had for the moment failed, as the 2nd Bavarian Corps was on its left north of Péronne.

By the 30th, de Castelnau was practically thrown on the defensive, and another Army was composed of units drawn from the east. This Army was intended to effect a turning movement pivoting on de Castelnau's left.

There are a few salient points in the history of these last few days of the month which materially affected the course of the campaign.

On the 26th, Sir Charles Haddon, Master General of the Ordnance, arrived at my Headquarters to discuss the question of armament and ammunition. I took this opportunity to impress upon him how terribly deficient we were in heavy artillery as compared with the Germans, and urged as strongly as I possibly could that the manufacture of this class of ordnance, as well as an abundance of ammunition, should be put in hand at once.

My official correspondence with the War Office on this vital subject dates back to this time, and continued right up to June, 1915, when at last Mr. Lloyd George came to the rescue and entered upon his career of patriotic salvation. Britons all over the world will ever remember this distinguished statesman with the utmost gratitude as one of the greatest of their Empire's sons.

Only those who were in any degree associated with Mr. Lloyd George in this time of trial can fully realise the awful responsibility which rested upon him, and the difficult nature of the problem he had to solve. His work was done in face of a dead weight of senseless but powerful opposition, all of which he had to undermine and overcome.

In later pages of this volume I shall refer again to the subject of deficiencies in armament and ammunition. I have mentioned it here because I am firmly convinced that, had my advice with regard to it been listened to and acted upon at the time, the War would have finished long before it did, and untold suffering would have been saved to the civilised world.

I think it was on September 24th that a few 6-inch siege howitzers arrived and proved of great help to me.

As I am about to recount the *pourparlers* with Joffre which led up to our move north, I am reminded that it was during these latter days of September that my friend, Winston Churchill, paid me a visit. I think of him in connection with this subject—quite apart from any question of Antwerp, which was not then in danger—because it was at that time that we first discussed together the advisability of joint action by the Army and Navy. It was then that we sketched out plans for an offensive with one flank towards the sea, which, although the subsequent fall of Antwerp effected a drastic change in the conditions, were the same in principle as those which took substantial shape and form in the early days of 1915, and which will be recounted in their proper place.

I cannot adequately express my sense of the valuable help which I received throughout the War from Winston Churchill's assistance and constant sympathy. Not only have I always indignantly repudiated the shameful attacks which his countrymen have so often made upon him, but it rejoices me to know that I have been able to do so—having a full knowledge of all the facts—with a deep and true sense of the horrible injustice of the charges brought against him. I shall have more to say on this subject later.

On September 29th I addressed to the French Commander-in-Chief the following note which was conveyed to him that evening by General Wilson:

> Ever since our position in the French line was altered by the advance of General Maunoury's 6th Army to the River

Ourcq, I have been anxious to regain my original position on the left flank of the French Armies. On several occasions I have thought of suggesting this move, but the strategical and tactical situation from day to day has made the proposal inopportune. Now, however, that the position of affairs has become clearly defined, and that the immediate future can be forecasted with some confidence, I wish to press the proposal with all the power and insistence which are at my disposal. The moment for the execution of such a move appears to me to be singularly opportune.

In the first place, the position of my force on the right bank of the River Aisne has now been thoroughly well entrenched.

In the second place, I have carefully reconnoitred an alternative position on the left bank of the River Aisne, and have had this position entrenched from end to end, and it is now ready for occupation.

The strategical advantages of the proposed move are much greater. I am expecting to be reinforced by the 7th Division from England early next week.

Following closely on this reinforcement will come the 3rd Cavalry Division from home, and then the 8th Division from home, and simultaneously with this last reinforcement will come two Indian Divisions and an Indian Cavalry Division.

In other words my present force of six Divisions and two Cavalry Divisions will, within three or four weeks from now, be increased by four Divisions and two Cavalry Divisions, making a total British force of ten Divisions (five Corps) and four Cavalry Divisions.

All through the present campaign I have been much restricted both in initiative and in movement by the smallness of my Army in face of the enormous numbers of the enemy.

With an Army of five Corps and four Cavalry Divisions my freedom of action, field of operation and power of initiative will be increased out of all proportion to the numerical increase in Corps, more especially as almost half my total force will then consist of fresh troops and will be opposed by an enemy already much worn by the severity of the previous fighting.

Another reason of a strategical nature for changing my position in the line is the great advantage which my forces will gain by a shortened line of communication, an advantage which falls almost equally on your railways.

It appears to me, therefore, that both from strategical reasons and from tactical reasons it is desirable that the British Army should regain its position on the left of the line.

There remains the question of *when* this move should take place. I submit that *now* is the time.

We are all sedentary armies, and movements and changes are easily made. Once the forward movement has been commenced, it will be more difficult to pull out my Army from the line of advance, and a further delay in the transfer of my force from its present position will lead to great confusion both at the front and on the L. of C., and a great loss of power and efficiency in the coming campaign.

It is for these reasons that I advocate the transfer of my force from its present position to the extreme left of the line, and I advocate that the change should be made now.

On the 30th, I received the following reply from Joffre:

Great General Headquarters Staff
3rd Bureau
September 30th, 1914.
Note by General Joffre, Commander-in-Chief, to Marshal French, Commanding British Army.

His Excellency, Marshal French, has been good enough to draw the attention of the Commander-in-Chief to the particular interest attaching to the proposal that the British Army should reoccupy the position which it originally held on the left of the French Armies.

In view of the ever-increasing strength of the British Forces, this position would offer great advantages in lightening the work of the French railways and diminishing the length of the British line of communication, and, above all, in giving to Marshal French's Army a liberty of action and of power very superior to those it now possesses.

The increase of strength which will shortly accrue to the British Army by the arrival of the 7th and 8th Divisions and a Division of Cavalry, and the two Indian Divisions and one Cavalry Division from India entirely justifies the Marshal's request. The Commander-in-Chief shares this view, and is persuaded that if this movement had been possible it would have been very advantageous for the Allied Armies; but so far the general situation has not admitted of this being carried out.

Is it possible at this moment to contemplate its realisation in the future? His Excellency, Marshal French thinks that the present moment is particularly favourable to his project. In front of the British line, as also in front of the 6th, 9th, and 4th Armies, the situation is, so to speak, unchanged. For nearly 15 days the Armies of the centre have been *accrochées* to the ground without making any real advance. There have been violent attacks and periods of calm, but the Commander-in-Chief wishes to point out that this is far from being the case on the wings.

As a matter of fact, on the right, the 3rd Army and a portion of the 1st Army for several days in the neighbourhood of St. Mihiel have been fighting an obstinate battle, the issue of which is not in doubt, but the results of which have not yet made themselves felt. On the left, the 2nd Army, which today forms the extreme flank of the line has for three days past been the object of furious attacks, which show how important it is for the enemy to crush our wing.

Will this Army always form the left of the French forces? We cannot think so, because the fact that today the Army there has been subdivided will doubtless lead the Commander-in-Chief to form a new Army there; the transport of troops necessitated by the creation of this Army, formed from elements taken away from the front without leaving a gap in our line, must of necessity render our situation somewhat delicate for some days.

If the Commander-in-Chief has contemplated the possibility of withdrawing a certain number of Corps without modifying his front, he has never thought of transporting an entire Army, the removal of which would create a gap impossible to fill.

The battle has been going on since September 13th. It is necessary that during this period of crisis, which will have considerable influence on the subsequent operations, everyone should maintain his position without thinking of modifying it, so as to be ready for all eventualities.

Now, the movement contemplated by His Excellency Marshal French would inevitably entail complications, not only in the position of troops but also in those of supply trains, etc. It might possibly create confusion in the general dispositions of our Armies, the extent of which it would be difficult to measure.

For the above reasons the Commander-in-Chief cannot share the view of Marshal French as to the time at which this movement should be carried out; on the other hand, it appears that it might be possible to begin it from to-day onwards by making certain dispositions, the detail of which is given below:—

1. The British Army might operate like the French Army. It is today strongly entrenched in the positions which it occupies. While maintaining the integrity of its front, it might doubtless be possible for it to withdraw a certain number of divisions (to begin with one Corps), which might in succession be transported to the left.

2. The British Cavalry Division is at the present moment unemployed on the front; it might, similarly to the 11th and 10th Corps and 8th Division of Cavalry, move by rail or by march route to the extreme left to act as a communicating link between the Belgian Army and the French troops.

3. The 7th and 8th Divisions, which will shortly arrive, could be disembarked in the neighbourhood of Dunkirk. They would subsequently operate in the direction of Lille. Their action would immediately make itself felt on

the right flank of the German Army, which daily receives fresh reinforcements. These divisions would be joined to the divisions withdrawn from the front.

4 The Indian Divisions, as soon as they are able to take the field, would move by rail to join the English formations assembled in the northern region, and would form the nucleus with which would be united the other British Divisions as soon as they should be removed.

5. As soon as the advance can be resumed, the front will be narrowed; it would then be possible for the English to halt and slip behind with a view to moving the left of the line while the 6th and 5th Armies close in towards each other. The fewer units remaining to be moved, the easier would be the operation.

To sum up, the Commander-in-Chief shares Marshal French's view that it is desirable for the whole British Army to be on the left of the French Armies, but cannot be entirely of the same opinion as to the time at which this movement should be carried out. The Commander-in-Chief would be grateful to His Excellency, Marshal French, if the latter would let him know whether he shares his views as to the proposals indicated above.

On the same date, I replied to the Commander-in-Chief as follows:

September 30th, 1914

Note by the Field Marshal Commander-in-Chief, British Forces, to His Excellency the Commander-in-Chief.

The Field-Marshal Commander-in-Chief, British Forces, has received the note which His Excellency the Commander-in-Chief has been kind enough to address to him, in reply to his Memorandum of the 29th instant.

Sir John French entirely agrees with the views expressed, and will give effect to them at once in the following manner:

1. The 2nd Cavalry Division, consisting of two Brigades under the command of Major-General Gough, which is now located in rear of the left of the line held by the

British Forces, will hold itself in readiness to proceed to whatever point on the railway His Excellency the Commander-in-Chief may decide upon, to be moved thence to Lille, if that place should be decided upon as the point upon which the British Forces should first concentrate on reaching the left of the Allied line.

2. As soon as trains are available, the Field-Marshal Commanding-in-Chief will disengage the 2nd British Corps which now occupies the centre of the British line. This Corps will concentrate in rear and be ready to move by the same route and for the same destination as the 2nd Cavalry Division.

3. In like manner, the 19th Infantry Brigade will be held in readiness to move immediately after the 2nd Corps.

4. The position in the centre of the British line, held now by the two Divisions of the 2nd Corps, will be divided between the 1st Corps, now occupying the left of the British line, in such a manner as to unite the inward flanks of the two Corps; whilst the 1st Cavalry Division will be held as a reserve south of the river.

5. The Field Marshal understands that, as soon as a forward move by the whole line becomes feasible, these two corps and the 1st Cavalry Division will remain behind, their places being filled up by closing in the 5th and 6th French Armies on their inward flanks.

6. The Field Marshal will immediately inform the British Secretary of State for War of these arrangements, and will ask that the 7th and 8th Divisions may be moved as soon as practicable *via* Boulogne or Havre to join the British forces concentrating at Lille.

7. The Indian Division will be directed to move in accordance with the views expressed in the note of September 30th.

Sir John French hopes that these proposals will meet with the approval of His Excellency the Commander-in-Chief.

The following was General Joffre's reply:

October 1st, 1914

The Commander-in-Chief of the French Forces has the

honour to acknowledge receipt of the letter of His Excellency the Field Marshal Commanding the British Army, dated September 30th, referring to the future movements which are to be carried out by this Army.

He is happy to be able to comply with the wishes expressed by the Field Marshal and to state, once more, the entire unanimity of views which exists between the Commanders of the Allied Armies. At the same time, owing to the necessities of the railway service, it is not possible to commence entraining before the afternoon of October 5th.

Referring to the points touched on in the letter of September 30th, and in accordance with the views given by the Field Marshal, it is suggested that the following instructions might be given:

1. The 2nd Cavalry Division (two brigades under the command of Gen. Gough) should move by road, owing to the lateness of the date on which entrainment becomes possible. They should move in rear of the 6th and 2nd Armies, by Villers-Cotterets—La Croix—St. Ouen—Amiens—St. Pol—Lille (similarly to the 8th and 10th French Divisions).

2. The 2nd Corps should march to the area Longueil—Pont St. Maxence, by October 5th, to be moved by rail to the Lille district, its place on the front held by the British to be taken as arranged by the Field Marshal in his letter of September 30th.

3. The 19th Infantry Brigade to be in readiness to follow the 2nd Corps.

4. As regards the two Corps and the Cavalry Division remaining at the front, it would appear inconvenient to leave them halted there when the general advance of the whole line becomes possible.

Apart from the unfairness of depriving the British troops of the satisfaction of advancing after their valiant fighting, it will be more convenient to halt them successively, as the closing in of the inner flank of the 5th and 6th Armies shortens the front allotted to the British Army.

It would be advisable for the Commander-in-Chief and

the Field Marshal to arrange mutually, at some convenient date, the conditions under which the transport of these troops by rail should be made.

5. Referring to the disembarkation of the 7th and 8th Divisions, the Commander-in-Chief is most anxious that these two Divisions should proceed as soon as possible to Boulogne. Their arrival at Lille, where they are to join the British Forces pushed to the front, would then be more rapid than if they were disembarked at Havre and the arrangements would be simpler. Their movement from the port of landing could be carried out by road with the assistance of the railway for marching troops.

6. The Indian Divisions should be moved to the neighbourhood of Lille as soon as the Field Marshal reports that they are ready.

The G.O.C.-in-C. hopes that these proposals are in accordance with the views expressed by the Field Marshal in his letter of September 30th, and he would be glad to be assured of this as soon as possible in order that steps may be taken to execute them.

J. Joffre

I acknowledged the above in these terms:

October 1st, 1914

The Field Marshal Commanding-in-Chief the British Forces has duly received the note dated October 1st, 1914, from His Excellency the Commander-in-Chief. He is extremely glad to find that the proposals contained in his last note meet with the approval of the Commander-in-Chief. Such modifications as are suggested in the present note are perfectly feasible, and Sir John French will give immediate effect to them.

The necessary orders were issued today, and the preliminary movements are now in progress.

The Field Marshal hopes that the 2nd Cavalry Division will commence its march towards Lille on the morning of October 3rd.

CHAPTER 8

The Siege and Fall of Antwerp

In our appreciation of the situation at British Headquarters on October 1st it was considered that the reduction of Antwerp was at this moment the great objective of the enemy. Personally, I had no reason to think that Antwerp was in any immediate danger, and therefore a message which I received from the Secretary of State on October 2nd came as a most disagreeable surprise.

I was informed that a serious situation had been created at Antwerp, which was in grave danger of falling in a short time.

Further information reached me at 3 a.m. on the 3rd from London that the Belgian Government, acting on the advice unanimously given by the Superior Council of War in the presence of the King, had decided to leave at once for Ostend. It was further stated that the King, with the Field Army, would withdraw from Antwerp in the direction of Ghent to protect the coast-line and in the hope of being able to co-operate with the Allied Armies. The message added that the town could hold out for five or six days, and that the decision to evacuate was taken very seriously as a result of the increasingly critical situation.

It is needless to say that I was perturbed on receipt of this news, It was difficult to understand why the Belgians, who had fought so well at Liége, were unable to do more in defence of a fortress which was much stronger, and situated, moreover, in a position where it could be supported by the British Fleet.

I fully realised the consequence of the capture and occupation of Antwerp by the Germans. It was impossible to say how much of the coast-line the captured terrain would include, but there could be no doubt that the Channel ports would be gravely imperilled.

Operating from such a base, there would appear to be no insuperable obstacle to an immediate German advance on Dunkirk, Calais, and Boulogne. The Belgian Army was in no condition to resist such an advance. The occupation of these places and the formation of a defensive line which would include the whole of the Pas-de-Calais, might become a *fait accompli* before the troops could arrive from the main theatres to prevent it.

But here, again, we have an example of the over-confidence which for ever possessed that army which set out for world conquest. As on the Marne, so at Antwerp, they were not prepared to seize the psychological moment and to play boldly for the great stake.

It is seldom that fortune offers another chance to a military leader who has once failed to gather the rich harvest which she has put into his grasp. Yet the German Emperor presents, together with his great General Staff, one of the few instances in history of a Commander-in-Chief so soon being given a splendid opportunity to retrieve such mistakes as those of September 5th and 6th.

With all these tragic possibilities in my mind in these early October days, I redoubled my endeavours to effect a speedy move of the British forces to the north. Added to the other cogent reasons to which I referred in the last chapter was now the most vital of all—the relief of Antwerp.

Lord Kitchener did not make things easy for me.

Keenly desirous to influence the course of operations, his telegrams followed one after another each containing "directions" regarding a local situation of which, in London, he could know very little.

For instance, in one message he told me he was communicating with General Joffre and the French Government, but, as he did not do so through me, I was quite unaware of what was passing between them, yet all the time he was urging me to make what I knew to be impracticable suggestions to General Joffre. This could only lead to misunderstandings and confusion of ideas, and I must repudiate any responsibility whatever for what happened in the north during the first ten days of October. I was explicitly told by the Secretary of State for War that the British troops operating there were not under my command, as the following telegram shows:

> Have already given Rawlinson temporary rank. I am sending him instructions regarding his action Antwerp. The troops employed there will not for the present be considered part of your force.

Rawlinson, I may remark, had been sent for to meet the 7th Division at Ostend and take command of it.

Had I been left to exercise my full functions as Commander-in-Chief of the British Army in France, I should certainly have made different dispositions with regard to the disposal of these troops. I regret that I must record my deliberate opinion that the best which could have been done throughout this critical situation was *not* done, owing entirely to Lord Kitchener's endeavour to unite in himself the separate and distinct roles of a Cabinet Minister in London and a Commander-in-Chief in France. I feel it only right and in the interest of my country, with a view to any war we may be engaged in in the future, to make this plain statement of fact. The calamity at Sedan was due in part to interference from Paris with the Army in the field, and the American Civil War was more than probably prolonged by the repeated interference on the part of the Secretary of State with the Commanders in the field.

As to the method of employing the 7th Infantry and 3rd Cavalry Divisions, the following telegram will show that the French Commander-in-Chief completely concurred in my views:

> General Commanding-in-Chief to Col. Huguet
> October 8th, 8.45 a.m.:
> The Commander-in-Chief has the honour to inform Marshal French that he entirely agrees with the ideas on the subject of employing the whole of the British Forces united.
> He estimates that, in the actual situation of Antwerp, the

reinforcement of the garrison by the 7th English Division will not have any effect on the fate of the place.

In these conditions he believes on the contrary that it is very advantageous that this English Division should unite as early as possible with the main body of the British Forces in the northern zone.

Will the Marshal be kind enough to inform Lord Kitchener of the Commander-in-Chief's views of the situation? He will ask the President of the Republic to confirm these views to the British War Minister.

As to the confusion of ideas to which I have referred, the following telegram which I found it necessary to address to the Commander of the 7th Division, Sir Henry Rawlinson, will show that it existed up to the 11th instant:

> Your message No. 19, addressed to Lord Kitchener and repeated to me, received. I really do not understand whether you regard yourself as under my orders or not; but if you do, please be good enough to explain your situation clearly without delay, as I have no knowledge of any necessity for your re-embarkation or of your intention to do so. Hazebrouck will be in occupation of the 3rd Corps tomorrow morning. Be good enough to answer me by some means at once, as my own and General Joffre's plans are much put out and perhaps compromised by all this misunderstanding.

To this Rawlinson replied that he was under my orders, and proceeded to give me the information I requested.

Such, then, was the general atmosphere of doubt and uncertainty in which I had to work after the fall of Antwerp until towards the 10th of the month (October), when at length the Secretary of State for War consented to allow me full liberty of action to direct the movements of all British Forces in France.

Some 3,000 marines had been landed in Dunkirk towards the end of September and, when Antwerp was threatened, Lord Kitchener—saying nothing of it to me—arranged with General Joffre that the latter should send one or two French Territorial Divisions to join them and act with them.

The first intimation I had of this was a wire from Lord Kitchener, received late at night on October 3rd, which ran as follows:

> I do not know when the two Divisions promised by the French Government from Havre will be able to start. Could you ascertain this and let me know your views on the situation and how you contemplate acting?

To this I replied in the early hours of the 4th:

> I do not know what has passed direct between English and French Governments, but French General Headquarters told me positively in answer to repeated enquiry that they are only sending one Territorial Division from Havre to Ostend, which they say is to start at once by sea.
> With reference to the last sentence in your message 1315, please refer to my message F272 dispatched last night at 7.30. I shall get report from officer I sent yesterday to Bruges and Antwerp directly and will wire again.

That part of my message F272 (referred to above), which bears on the subject, runs as follows:

> French wish us to use Boulogne for 7th Division and Cavalry to disembark..... I am strongly averse to sending any troops inside the fortress (of Antwerp) even if they could be got there.

General Joffre's telegram for me of October 8th has already been quoted, and I had previously been in constant communication with him on this subject. When I dispatched telegram F272 I knew that Joffre's views accorded with my own.

That the wishes of the Allied Commanders were ignored in London is further shown by the following message received by me from the Secretary of State for War at 2.30 p.m. on October 4th:

> I am embarking 7th Division and portion of Cavalry Division today, but I cannot get report from Antwerp on the military situation from which I can decide where they should be disembarked.
> My present opinion is Zeebrugge, where there are good

landing facilities. Can you send Rawlinson by motor to Antwerp to take charge and study the situation before the troops arrive?

This message was amplified by the following message which was sent later in the day:

> I am arranging following Expeditionary Force for relief Antwerp:
> British Force: 7th Division, under Gen. Capper, 18,000 men, 63 guns; Cavalry Division, under Gen. Byng, 4,000 men, 12 guns. To arrive at Zeebrugge October 6th and October 7th.
> Naval detachments under Gen. Alston, 8,000 men, already there; also naval and military heavy guns and detachments already sent. Headquarters Staff will be subsequently notified.
> French Force: Territorial Division, Gen. Roy, 15,000 men, proper complement guns and two squadrons to arrive Ostend October 6th to October 9th; Fusiliers Marins Brigade under Rear-Admiral Ronarch, 8,000 men; grand total, 53,000 men. Numbers are approximately correct.

In order to summarise the situation as it was reflected in my mind at this time, I will quote two more telegrams. Lord Kitchener wired on the early morning of the 6th:

> Please let me have a telegraphic appreciation of the situation of the Allied Forces for information of the Government.

To which the following reply was sent:

> Allied line extends from La Bassée, about 14 miles southwest of Lille on the left, through Arras, east of Albert, Bray-sur-Somme, west of Roye, Ribécourt, Nampcelle, Nouvron, Soissons, north of Braye-en-Laonnois, Craonnelle, Berry-au-Bac, then south of Rheims, then east to Verdun, then south to St. Mihiel, then east to Thiaucourt. On the extreme left is the 21st French Corps, with two Cavalry Corps operating between Carvin and Lens.
> Hard fighting north of the Oise, where strength of French

Force equivalent to 12 Corps and six Cavalry Divisions. Comparative quiet on the Aisne; British forces in progress of evacuating positions and moving north of the Somme near Abbeville; move should be completed by the 20th instant.

The German line extends from about Lille, roughly parallel to the Allies, west of Bapaume, Chaulnes, Roye, south of Noyon, thence along the hills north of the Aisne to Craonne, Brimont, Nogent-l'Abbesse, Somme Py, northeast of Verdun, where it turns south to Fresnes-en-Woevre, then to near St. Mihiel, Thiaucourt, and east of Thiaucourt. The strength of the Germans north of the Oise is probably 11 Corps and nine Cavalry Divisions in position. In addition to the above forces, one Brigade was detraining at Cambrai yesterday, and reserve troops are holding entrenched positions about Mons and Valenciennes, numbers variously reported from 50,000 to 70,000.

The object of the Allies is to bring about a retirement of the Germans from their present line by turning their north flank, and at the same time to hold in this theatre of operations as many German Corps as possible. French General Headquarters anticipated that the northern turning movement would have been facilitated by the close co-operation of the Belgian Field Army.

So far as I am able to have an object apart from the general French view of the situation, I place the relief of Antwerp as of first importance as regards forces under my command.

Lord Kitchener had dispatched these troops *en route* to Antwerp itself before he even asked me for an appreciation of the general situation.

The history of the rapid investment and fall of Antwerp, the evacuation of Ostend and Zeebrugge and the retreat of the Belgians to the Yser, is very well known now, and it is not my intention to go over the ground again here; but I feel sure that, had the views of the Commanders in the field (Joffre and myself) been accepted, a much better and easier situation would have been created.

It is perfectly clear that the operations for the relief of Antwerp should never have been directed from London.

It should have been left entirely in the hands of the French Commander-in-Chief (or in mine acting with him) to decide upon the dispositions and destination of the troops immediately they left British shores. We alone were in a position to judge as to the best methods by which to co-ordinate the objectives and distribute the troops between the northern and southern theatres.

As things actually turned out, the troops which were landed at Ostend and Zeebrugge had (to quote from General Joffre's wire to Huguet on October 8th) no influence on the fate of the fortress, and what help they were in protecting the retreat of the Belgians and saving that Army from destruction might have been equally well rendered from a safer and more effective direction. This would not have necessitated that dangerous and exhausting flank march, costing such terrible loss, by which alone they were able eventually to unite with the main British forces.

Dispatched from England on October 5th or 6th, and disembarking at Calais or Boulogne (Dunkirk could have been used if the Belgian Army had required more help), they would have deployed six or seven days later in the valley of the Lys south of the 3rd Corps, and Lille might have been saved.

It is quite possible also to conceive a situation starting from these preliminary dispositions, which would have resulted in saving Ostend, even Zeebrugge and that line of coast, the possession of which by the enemy, dating from October, 1914, was a source of such infinite trouble to us.

Although I was given no voice in these Antwerp dispositions, and was left in partial ignorance of what was going on, which, in my position as Commander-in-Chief, was deplorable—I took what steps I could to keep in close touch with the progress of events.

Colonel Bridges of the 4th Dragoon Guards was with his regiment in the Cavalry Division. He had formerly been Military Attaché in Brussels and understood the Belgians well. He had already greatly distinguished himself in earlier battles, and I sent for him.

Bridges commenced the War as a squadron commander, and it will always be a matter of deep gratification to me that I was enabled to see him in command of a Division before I gave up the Army in France.

Of tall and spare figure, his face has always struck me as that of an ideal leader of men. He has an absolute contempt of any personal danger, and was constantly putting himself in the most exposed positions, so that I was often in dread of losing him. I know he was hit slightly once or twice and said nothing about it, but on another occasion he was so severely wounded that for a day or two his life was in danger. He was calm, quiet and very deliberate in all situations, and his reports were of the utmost value. He never appeared to want anything in the way of personal comfort, was quite indifferent in any weather as to whether he slept on a bed or on the ground, and had a happy knack of seeming delighted to start on any mission however difficult and dangerous, or for any place however distant, with nothing but the clothes he stood up in.

I wish I could describe Tom Bridges better. He is a typical fighting soldier and leader, and I have entertained the deepest regard for him ever since we first met many years ago. I certainly had hoped ere this to have seen him in command of an Army Corps.

In accordance with my instructions he arrived at my Headquarters during the night of October 3rd–4th. I dispatched him at 5 a.m. on the 4th by motor to Brussels, instructing him to get into immediate communication with the Belgian General Staff and endeavour to persuade them to hang on to Antwerp, promising support from us so soon as we could possibly get to them.

Colonel Sykes was at that time second to Sir David Henderson in command of the Royal Flying Corps. I sent him by aeroplane in the same direction, telling him to find out all he could and bring me back a report from Bridges.

I directed Sir David Henderson to establish air reconnaissances towards Antwerp, which he did.

Finally, I did my utmost to expedite the move of all the British Forces to the northern theatre. It appeared likely that there might be considerable delay in relieving the 1st Corps. I therefore dispatched Henry Wilson to General Joffre with the following note, dated October 4th, 1914:

> With reference to Sir John French's note and the importance, therein dwelt upon, of the earliest possible relief of

the 1st Corps from its present position, he suggests to His Excellency the Commander-in-Chief the possibility of an extension by the 18th Corps of its line to the left, as far as the point where the Aisne Canal passes through the line of entrenchment occupied by the 1st Corps in the neighbourhood of Braye.

In this connection Sir John French would particularly bring to the notice of His Excellency the greatly increased strength of the entrenchment by reason of the work which has been carried out during the long time it has been under occupation by the 1st Corps. He would also point out that the enemy is now much weaker than before, and that such feeble attempts as he makes on the line of entrenchment are entirely in the nature of reconnaissances, with a view to discover whether the entrenchment is still held or not. Another consideration of importance is that the line now held by the 18th Corps and French troops attached to it is much less in extent than that occupied by the British 1st Corps.

In these circumstances Sir John French trusts that His Excellency the Commander-in-Chief will be able to give such orders as will ensure the troops occupying the portion of the line extending from the right of the British entrenchment to the canal being relieved by troops from the 18th Corps, the change to be carried out on the night of 6th-7th October.

To this General Joffre replied as follows:

General Wilson has been good enough to convey the desire expressed by His Excellency Marshal French to see the whole of the British Army follow the move of the 2nd Army Corps to the left wing of the Allies line.

The Commander-in-Chief has the honour to state that he will endeavour to satisfy this request, but as already stated in Note No. 159 of October 1st the movement of the British troops can only be carried out in succession. The heavy task with which the railway service is at present burdened, and the difficulty of immediately replacing on the front all the British units employed there, render it impossible to contemplate the simultaneous withdrawal of all the British forces.

A French Division will arrive tomorrow in the area of Soissons. Its billeting area is fixed by the G.O.C. 6th Army and it is intended to relieve the 3rd Army Corps. When this Corps has been withdrawn from the front it will march to the area Compiègne—Longueil—Pont Ste. Maxence, where it will entrain in its turn. The route to be followed can be decided upon by agreement with the G.O.C. 6th Army. Admitting that the relief can be carried out on the night, October 5th-6th, the 3rd Corps, taking three days to march to the neighbourhood of Pont Ste. Maxence, will be ready to entrain on October 9th.

With regard to the movement of the 1st Army Corps it is impossible at present to decide the date at which its withdrawal can be carried out. Indeed, its withdrawal will depend on the general situation, the difficulty of bringing up other troops to be taken from the front to replace the 1st Army Corps, and finally on the tasks imposed on the railway service, but the Commander-in-Chief begs once more to assure Marshal French that he will make the greatest efforts to concentrate the whole of the British Army in the north. He takes note that the Commander of the British troops wishes to see his forces concentrated with all speed. The 1st Cavalry Division will move by march route as has already been done by Gen. Gough's Division.

Regarding the detrainment area, Lille was first of all regarded as the centre, but in view of existing circumstances it appears difficult to determine as yet in what area the 2nd Corps now in course of transport can be detrained. This Corps will have finished detraining on the 8th and will be ready to act on the 9th. The most favourable area for detraining appears to be that of St. Omer-Hazebrouck.

The 3rd Corps, having been withdrawn from the front on the 6th and entraining on the 9th, will be detrained on the

12th in the same area. It will be ready to act on the 13th. Lastly, the Commander-in-Chief reiterates the request already made in the note of October 1st that the 7th British Division may be disembarked at Boulogne with the least possible delay. As soon as this Division has been assembled, it will move by march route to join the 2nd and 3rd Corps. No precise indications can be given as to the date on which this junction will be effected, as it will depend on the date of arrival in France of the 7th Division, which date the Commander-in-Chief is not in a position to decide.

The Indian Divisions will join the British Army as soon as desired by Marshal French.

In order to strengthen the forces in this part of the theatre of operations the request made to the French Government by His Excellency Lord Kitchener has been responded to by sending to Dunkirk two Territorial Divisions, one going from Havre by sea and the other railed from Paris without in any way retarding the movement of the British Army.

These are the dispositions that have been made with regard to the movements to be carried out in the immediate future. The Commander-in-Chief, however, wishes to lay particular stress on the following considerations. The operations in progress necessitate the constant reinforcement of our left wing by troops taken away from different portions of the front. The movements carried out at Marshal French's request, which can only be effected in succession will result—

Firstly.—In temporarily dividing the British Army in two.

Secondly.—In preventing for nearly ten days all movement of French troops to the north and, in consequence, creating a serious delay in the realisation of the operations contemplated.

Now it is of capital importance for the success of the operations that all movements made to the north, either English or French, should immediately contribute to the same object, viz., to arrest and outflank the German right wing. The result will certainly not be achieved should His Excellency Marshal French propose to defer his action until all his forces are concentrated. It would be advantageous to have time enough to complete the English movement so that the British Army could be engaged all at once, but it appears certain that events will decide otherwise.

The Commander-in-Chief may be forced to ask Marshal French to co-operate with British Divisions as they detrain and without waiting for the whole of the detrainment to be carried out. He would be obliged to consider the case of the retreat of the left wing, the extent of which he would not be in a position to limit, if with the object of carrying out a concentration which, though certainly advantageous, is not indispensable, some Divisions remained inactive at the time when the fate of the campaign was being decided; moreover, it is to be noted that the enemy on his side engages as he detrains; we cannot act differently.

The Commander-in-Chief feels sure that His Excellency Marshal French will be good enough to examine this question of capital importance with all the attention it deserves, and will take the necessary action without which the gravest consequences must be faced.

To sum up, the Commander-in-Chief has the honour to submit to His Excellency Marshal French the following points on which he begs His Excellency may be good enough to give a prompt reply:

1. Transport of the 2nd Army Corps to the same area, Hazebrouck, completed the 9th.
2. Transport of the 3rd Corps to the same area, completed the 13th.
3. Lastly, and this is the essential point, without which the fate of the campaign may be compromised, the possibility of engaging the British Divisions in the north as they arrive, without waiting for the British Army to be concentrated.

The task of the British Army now in the general operations should, therefore, be constantly to prolong the general line as it detrains, in order to outflank the enemy and thus to join hands with the Belgian Army.

The support of our Cavalry Corps operating in the northern area will always be given.

I answered thus:

Sir John French has duly received His Excellency's note 791 for which he begs to offer him his best thanks.

The arrangements therein proposed are perfectly satisfactory, and the role which the British Army can fulfil on the left flank of the Allied Force will, Sir John French hopes and believes, tend best to the efficient progress of the campaign.

He can assure His Excellency of the very best support of the British Army at all times; and, should necessity arise, the various units, as they arrive in the new area, will on no account be held back to await a general concentration, if and when their immediate action is demanded by the exigencies of the campaign.

Sir John French would like to point out particularly to His Excellency that the possibility of his having to engage his forces, unit by unit, before the entire force is concentrated, offers another great reason why it is most essential that the relief of the 1st Army Corps from its present position should be effected with the least possible delay.

Whilst feeling quite assured that His Excellency the Commander-in-Chief will do his utmost to effect this, Sir John French feels that it is most necessary to insist upon the vast importance of the presence of all the British Forces on the left flank at the earliest possible moment.

His Majesty's Government feel great anxiety as to the condition of the Fortress of Antwerp, the fall of which stronghold would have far-reaching consequences, political, material and moral.

Sir John French is now in close daily communication with the Belgian Commandant of the Fortress, and if he can daily assure him that there is no delay in a movement which must have the ultimate effect of relieving the situation at Antwerp, so long as that place is able to hold out, it should prove a great encouragement to the garrison.

Sir John French will address another note later on to His Excellency on the subject of the Indian Divisions.

Sir John French wishes to call His Excellency's attention to the fact that the 2nd Corps will not complete its detrainment until the evening of the 9th instant, and therefore will not be ready to act until the 10th instant. In his memorandum His Excellency the Commander-in-Chief states as follows, referring to the 2nd Corps: This Corps will have finished detraining on the 8th and will be ready to act on the 9th.

Antwerp fell on the 9th October and was followed by the retirement of the Belgian Army to the line of the Yser.

The 7th Infantry and 3rd Cavalry Divisions were not placed under my orders until October 10th. From that date, however, I will commence to chronicle their doings.

CHAPTER 9

The Aisne and Northwards

I spent some hours on October 1st closely examining the centre of the enemy's position on the Aisne, and arrived at the conclusion that troops had certainly been withdrawn and that the Germans were weaker in strength. I was not, moreover, apprehensive of any great difficulty in effecting our withdrawal from the Aisne front, and I prepared at once to carry out the arrangements made with Joffre.

Operation orders were issued ordering the 2nd Corps (less the 16th Infantry Brigade) to withdraw during the nights of October 1st-2nd and 2nd-3rd, and assemble in the area Cuiry—Houssé—Oulchy-le-Château with a view to moving to Pont Ste. Maxence (12 miles south-west of Compiègne), there to entrain for the left flank; the 1st and 3rd Corps and 1st Cavalry Division to be withdrawn when opportunity occurred; the 2nd Cavalry Division and 19th Infantry Brigade to follow the 2nd Corps; the 1st Corps and 16th Infantry Brigade to take over positions at the moment held by the 3rd Division; the 3rd Corps to take over those held by the 5th Division.

I certainly entertained sanguine hopes at this time, in spite of the bad news received as to the condition of Antwerp, and although such hopes were never realised I still think they were justified. These optimistic anticipations were grounded entirely upon the advance which the Russians were then making through Galicia, and the splendid fights they had put up in East Prussia and Poland. We estimated that they were not far from Cracow, and if that fortress were taken, and the Russians maintained their position, I looked forward to a great reduction of the German forces opposed to us on the Western front.

The Grand Duke Nicholas had proved himself to be a commander of high courage, energy and skill, and we all hoped for great things from his leadership.

At this time we never had the faintest idea of the actual political situation in Russia, and knew nothing of the terrible dissensions and intrigues which were destined to nullify all the magnificent self-sacrifice displayed by the Russian troops, and to ruin every attempt made by these great armies of the East to assist and support the Allied operations.

I feel sure that the British Army officers and men alike will ever hold these Russian soldiers and their loyal leaders in honour and grateful memory and admiration. Their prompt invasion of Eastern Prussia did much to make the victory of the Marne possible.

As a matter of fact, however, in depending upon our Eastern Allies to the extent that we subsequently did, we showed as limited a mental prevision in the *political* as we did in the *military* outlook.

Just as we had failed during the past to read accurately the lessons as regards the fighting of the future, which modern science and invention should have taught us, so we had never foreseen how unstable and unreliable a country must be whose ruler and Government are absolutely despotic, and in no sense representative of the will of the people. Worse than this, the governing classes in Russia were saturated with disloyalty and intrigue in the most corrupt form. But for their black treachery the war would have ended successfully at the latest in the spring of 1917.

How could such a people successfully withstand the strain of so mighty a clash of arms, especially when the immense foreign loans and the placing of enormous contracts brought grist to the mills of that corrupt mass of financiers whose business in life was only to fatten on the misfortunes of their fellow creatures?

But to proceed with my narrative. Gough's Cavalry Division was moving up towards the north next day. I saw him and discussed the situation fully. I explained the desperate nature of the situation at Antwerp and told him how necessary it was that he should expedite his movements to the utmost, adding that he must, therefore, avoid being drawn *en route* into any local encounter in which French troops might be engaged.

The situation will be clearer if I state the actual position of the troops on the night of 2nd October.

1st Corps and 16th Infantry Brigade and 32nd R.F.A. Brigade holding former positions and, in addition, the trenches round Vailly formerly held by 3rd Division. 3rd Corps holding former positions and, in addition, the trenches round Missy formerly held by the 5th Division. 1st Cavalry Division as before, but 1st Cavalry Brigade holding trenches covering Condé Bridge. 2nd Cavalry Division moved to area Silly-sur-Ourcq—Hartennes—Ambrief. 2nd Corps. 3rd Division in area Oulchy-le-Château—Grand Rozoy, with 7th Brigade at Cerseuil; two battalions 9th Brigade still in trenches at Vailly to be withdrawn this night (October 2nd). 5th Division in area Couvrelles—Ciry—Nampteuil-sous-Muret.

On the 3rd, General Sir James Willcocks, commanding the Indian contingent, arrived and reported himself. Of the Indian troops, one cavalry regiment (15th Lancers), one brigade of artillery and two brigades of infantry had reached Orleans, which was the Indian advance base. I fully discussed the situation with him.

Much has been said and written about the work of the Indian troops in France, and various opinions have been expressed. For my part I can only say that, from first to last, so long as they were under my command, they maintained and probably surpassed even the magnificent traditions of the Indian Army. In a country and climate to which they were totally unaccustomed, the exigencies of the moment required that they should be thrown into action successively by smaller or greater units before they could be properly concentrated.

I shall always gratefully remember the invaluable assistance they and their Commander, Sir James Willcocks, rendered under these difficult conditions in the most critical hours of the First Battle of Ypres, especially the Lahore Division, commanded by General Watkins.

Just after the appearance of the Indian troops in our trenches, we intercepted a German wireless message sent to the enemy commanders on the Indians' front, directing them to take prisoner as many unwounded Indians as possible, to treat them with all possible courtesy and consideration and send them in to Headquarters. It was a cunning attempt to undermine the loyalty of the Indian contingents, but it never met with the slightest success.

I received news on this day that the 21st French Corps had commenced to detrain 3 miles west of Lille. This Corps formed the left of the French Army under de Maud'huy, which was concentrating to the north of de Castelnau, in order to carry on the great attempted outflanking movement.

The Armies under de Castelnau and de Maud'huy, with some cavalry divisions, formed a group under the supreme command of General Foch, who was directed also to exercise general control over all the French Armies operating in the northern theatre.

No personal record of my share in the war would be satisfactory to me did it not include special mention of this remarkable man and eminent soldier. Like his great friend Henry Wilson in England, he was at one time head of the Staff College in France. Shortly before the war he paid several visits to England. It was on the occasion of one of these that I first made his acquaintance. All the world knows the splendid work he did in the first weeks of the war, and it gave me the greatest pleasure and satisfaction to find myself so closely associated with him in the northern theatre. I hope it is not too much to say that, during this time, our acquaintance ripened into a fast and firm friendship, which has increased and expanded ever since.

I regard General Foch as one of the finest soldiers and most capable leaders I have ever known. In appearance he is slight and small of stature, albeit with a most wiry and active frame. It is in his eyes and the expression of his face that one sees his extraordinary power. He appreciates a military situation like lightning, with marvellous accuracy, and evinces wonderful skill and versatility in dealing with it. Animated by a consuming energy his constant exclamation *"Attaque! Attaque! Attaque!"* reflected his state of mind, and there can be no doubt that he imbued his troops with much of his spirit. Of all the generals in this great struggle he most resembled in audacious strategy his great master—Napoleon.

Personally I owe a great deal to his invaluable help and cordial co-operation. In the darkest hours of our work together—and there were many such—I never knew him anything but what I have described—bold, hopeful, and cheery; but ever vigilant, wary, and full of resource.

Several local attacks were delivered against the 1st Corps which were repulsed with loss, and I saw little reason to fear that the temporary weakening of our line would have any ill-effects.

The 1st Cavalry Division was now also *en route* for the northern theatre.

On the 5th reports had reached me from Bridges, in Antwerp. He was certainly pessimistic as to the possibility of the fortress holding out until we could relieve it. He told me that the Germans had 16-in. howitzers in position against the forts.

There were indications today that considerable German forces were collecting against Foch's left, near Lille, and the flanking movement was making very little progress. German cavalry were reported to be in Hazebrouck.

At Fère-en-Tardenois I received a visit from President Poincaré. He thanked me for all the work the British Army had done in France, and spoke a great deal about the situation at Antwerp. He told me he thought the action of the British War Office in sending troops into Antwerp was a mistake, and expressed great surprise that the control and direction of all the British troops in France was not left entirely in the hands of one Commander-in-Chief.

On the 8th, General Headquarters moved to Abbeville, at which place the 2nd Corps had nearly completed their detrainment. They were concentrating north-east of Abbeville, and their leading troops were on the line Oneux—Nouvion-en-Ponthieu.

The 3rd Corps had been relieved on the Aisne by French troops, and their entrainment at Compiègne was proceeding.

We left Fère-en-Tardenois at 8.30 on the morning of the 8th, and reached General de Castelnau's Headquarters at Breteuil about one. He told me that his 4th Corps was again being very hard pressed, and that the enemy was attacking violently all along his front. The General had just heard that two of his sons had been killed in action, and was naturally in a very sad and depressed frame of mind.

I then went on to General Foch's Headquarters at Doullens, which I reached about four in the afternoon. He gave me a great reception with a guard of honour.

He took a very optimistic view of the situation, said that the enemy was making no headway anywhere, and that he was gradually getting round the German flank on the north. It gave me a great hope for the future to find him so confident of success.

I explained my plans to him briefly as follows: the 2nd Corps, having completed its detrainment north of Abbeville, was to march to the line Aire—Béthune. The Corps should arrive there on the 11th; the 3rd Corps was to detrain at St. Omer about the 12th; the cavalry was to move in advance of the 2nd Corps to sweep round by the front and northern flank to clear the ground.

I returned to Abbeville that evening. I found that an officer had arrived from Ostend by motor with a letter from Rawlinson, in which he explained the situation in the north, the details of which we know.

I remained at Abbeville and its neighbourhood on the 9th.

The British move to the north was now in full swing. Abbeville is an important railway junction, and as I looked down from some high ground commanding a view of all the lines of railway, it was as though every set of metals had its procession of trains as far as the eye could reach. That a flank movement of some magnitude was proceeding must have been apparent to any observer. Some enemy aircraft flew over the ground on which I stood, and I felt sure that the Germans must have had warning of our approach to the north. But if the movement was ever properly reported, very little attention was paid to it, for the subsequent activities of the cavalry and the 3rd Corps were most certainly a surprise to the enemy.

Spiers, too, came in and told me that the left of Foch's Army (de Maud'huy's Corps) was holding its own well.

That day I had a long interview with Allenby, and arranged with him to form the cavalry into two divisions, the 1st under de Lisle, the 2nd under Gough. The two, forming the Cavalry Corps, to be, of course, under Allenby's command. I directed him to make Aire by the 10th with the 2nd Cavalry Division, the 1st to follow in support.

I told him that his role in the immediate future would be to clear the country to the north and north-east, reconnoitring woods, etc., and securing passages over waterways. I warned him that he must be prepared to turn round and support the 2nd Corps if it became necessary, but added that I hoped not to have to call upon him for this.

An air officer (not, however, Sykes) whom I had sent towards Antwerp returned and reported the fall of the fortress. He told me of the great difficulty which had been experienced in withdrawing the Naval Brigade.

On this afternoon (October 9th) I had a message from Rawlinson. He told me that 8,000 French were holding Ghent. He was sending two brigades under Capper to the place in order to cover the retreat of the Belgians to Bruges, and, with the same object, he was directing a brigade of Byng's cavalry on the Lys towards Courtrai.

A wire having arrived from Kitchener putting Rawlinson under my command, I sent the latter instructions.

He was told to hold the line of the Lys if he could, but not to risk a big fight. If he could hold on to these positions I promised to connect up with him by the 13th or 14th. If, however, he were forced to retire, he was directed to do so in the direction of St. Omer, where the 3rd Corps was now detraining.

On the afternoon of the 9th, the 2nd Corps were approaching the line Béthune—Aire, the infantry travelling in motor lorries lent by General Foch. These lorries and motor omnibuses were much used in the ensuing operations, and proved of great value in adding to the mobility of the troops.

On the 10th, orders were sent to Rawlinson to the effect that the troops under his command (namely, the 7th Division and the 3rd Cavalry Division) were to form the 4th Corps, and that, as soon as the 8th Division came out it would go to him, and Byng's cavalry would be withdrawn.

I was much perturbed at hearing that there was delay on the part of the French in relieving the 1st Corps on the Aisne; Joffre, however, assured me that all Haig's troops should reach St. Omer so as to enable me to get them into line by the 17th or the 19th, and with this I had to be content.

When I visited Smith-Dorrien at his Headquarters at Hesdin, I found that he would not be able to reach the line assigned to him on this night, as the motor lorries were late, and his mounted troops and horses were very tired. I directed him to rest for the night and march at 9 a.m. next morning.

After leaving the 2nd Corps I went to St. Pol and had a long talk with General de Maud'huy (commanding the 10th Army). I learnt from him that things were not going so well north of Loos. He had been obliged to fall back before the attack of the XIXth German Corps, which had come up from Valenciennes. He expected to be forced further west, but promised me to hold a line extending from Béthune to the south-east up to 12 noon on the 12th, if by then the 2nd Corps could have arrived at Béthune.

De Maud'huy was among the best Army Commanders that France had produced in the war. I look back with much pleasure and gratification to my long association with him. He was of a most cheerful and buoyant temperament and a *bon camarade* in every sense of the word. His skill and dash as a leader are well known.

On leaving him I returned again to Smith-Dorrien, and begged him to hasten his move. He promised to deploy into his new position as early as possible on the following morning.

On this day (October 10th) instructions were sent to Allenby to take the 1st Cavalry Division to join the 2nd near Aire early the next day, and to act on the left front and flank of the 2nd Corps. The Forêt de Nieppe was said to be occupied by German cavalry in some strength.

After a long interview with Foch, we concerted together plans of which the following is a brief outline.

It was agreed that, by the 13th, the British and French troops would be in a position to make a combined advance east. On that day we were to make the line Lille—Courtrai.

The French left was to secure the passage of the Scheldt at Lille; the British centre was to be directed on Courtrai, and was to make good the passage of the Lys at that place.

The road Béthune—Lille—Tournai was to be used by the French, and all roads north of it by the British.

The 4th Corps and Belgians were to be on the left of the advance.

On the evening of the 11th the cavalry had cleared the Forêt de Nieppe (south of Hazebrouck), and were in touch with the Divisional Cavalry of the 6th Division east of that place. They extended thence south-east to the left of the 2nd Corps.

The 2nd Corps had reached the line of the canal, and I directed Smith-Dorrien to wheel up his left the next morning in the direction of Merville and move east to the line Laventie—Lorgies, which would bring him on the immediate left of the French 10th Army.

One division of the 3rd Corps was moving on Hazebrouck.

Rawlinson reported that Capper with two brigades was still in Ghent. His aircraft had brought word that two divisions of the enemy were moving on Alost—Termonde—Lokeren, and that five pontoon bridges had been constructed by the Germans at Termonde. He said he had received my instructions and would carry them out as far as he was able to.

The 3rd Cavalry Division was at Thourout.

The French cavalry were very energetic on the 11th. Conneau's Cavalry Corps pushed back the German cavalry to the line Vermelles—Richebourg—Vieille Chapelle. De Mitry's Cavalry Corps assembled and drove the German cavalry back to the line of the Lawe at Vieille Chapelle and Estaires.

By the night of the 11th, the Cavalry Corps under Allenby had made good a great deal of ground to the north, and were halting between Wallon-Cappel (west of Hazebrouck) and Merville. Moving thence on the morning of the 12th, they carried out invaluable work during the subsequent two or three days. Allenby liberally interpreted his orders and made a magnificent sweep to the north and north-east, driving the enemy back all the way.

Of all the splendid work performed by the cavalry during the war, little can compare (in results achieved) with this advance. It was only surpassed by their immortal stand on the Wytschaete—Messines ridge on those ever-memorable days and nights of October 31st and November 1st.

By the evening of the 12th, Gough, with the 2nd Cavalry Division, had attacked and captured the Mont des Cats position, which was a strategic point of great importance lying six miles north-east of Hazebrouck. There was great opposition by the enemy cavalry, which was supported by *jäger* and strong infantry detachments; but Gough carried all before him in fine style.

The 1st Division under de Lisle halted before Merris, after severe fighting which drove the enemy back many miles.

On the 13th, the cavalry made a further great advance, driving the enemy before them, and on the evening reached the line Mont Noir—Boeschepe—Berthen. The position of Mont Noir was vigorously defended by the Germans, but they were finally driven out by the 2nd Cavalry Division under Gough, who handled his troops with great skill and determination.

On the 14th, the 1st Cavalry Division reached the area Dranoutre—Messines and pushed advanced detachments to Warneton. The 2nd Division moved to the Kemmel—Wytschaete area, sending advanced detachments to Werwick.

I sent instructions to Allenby to make a strong reconnaissance of the Lys from Estaires to Menin on the 15th, and report the result as quickly as possible to me at the Headquarters of the 3rd Corps.

Late at night on the 12th, the 3rd Corps (4th and 6th Divisions and 19th Brigade) moved to the area east and south of Hazebrouck. The infantry were moved in motor omnibuses.

On this day General Headquarters were moved from Abbeville to St. Omer. On my way there I went to Hazebrouck to see the Commander of the 3rd Corps. Pulteney is a very old friend and comrade of mine, to whom I should like to devote a few lines of this story.

The keenest of soldiers from his early youth, he was Adjutant of his battalion of the Scots Guards. Thence he sought service in Africa, where he did excellent work, although he suffered severely from the climate.

I had the good fortune to be closely associated with him in the South African War, and there had experience of his fine qualities as a soldier and leader of men. I was delighted to find him with me as one of the three Corps Commanders who fought with the First Expeditionary Force sent to France.

Throughout my period of Commander-in-Chief he wholly justified the estimate which I had formed of his capacity and capability in the field. He enjoyed the full confidence of the officers and men who served under him. Possessed of iron nerve and indomitable courage, he remained imperturbable and unmoved in face of the most difficult and precarious situations. No matter how arduous the task imposed upon him he never made difficulties, but always carried out the role assigned to him with energy and skill. It had been my hope to see him in command of an Army, for which I feel sure he was thoroughly qualified; but my withdrawal from France prevented my carrying out my intentions with regard to him.

His conduct of the operations which I am just about to describe was characterised by his customary skill, boldness and decision. The great results which accrued from the First Battle of Ypres may be fairly traced back to his initial leading of the 3rd Corps in the series of successful advances which were the most prominent and important amongst the opening phases of that great combat.

On reaching Hazebrouck, about 4 p.m. on the 13th, I was told that the 3rd Corps was engaged with the enemy some miles east of the town. Repairing with all speed in that direction I came up with the rear of the 6th Division, which had been heavily engaged almost up to that moment, but now was preparing to advance. My car got hopelessly blocked amidst ammunition wagons and all manner of traffic, and in trying to extricate it we found ourselves badly bogged in a ploughed field.

Leaving the motor to struggle back, I tried to see what was going on from some high ground close by. Rain was falling heavily, and the atmosphere was foggy and misty. I watched as best I could for some little time what was going forward, until I felt assured that the tide of battle was flowing very favourably for us. I then got back as quickly as possible to Headquarters at St. Omer, where reports were awaiting me. I learnt that the town had been heavily bombed by hostile aircraft during the day. Much damage was done to buildings, and several soldiers and civilians had been killed and wounded. It was a somewhat unpleasant welcome for us, but the effect of it was completely wiped out by the news I received from Pulteney of the victory he had attained.

The enemy opposed to him consisted of one or two Divisions of cavalry, at least a Division of infantry (19th Corps) and several *jäger* battalions. Pulteney found them posted in a strong position covering Bailleul, with their left resting on Bleu (close to Vieux Berquin) and their right on Berthen. The British attack opened at 1.30 p.m., and by nightfall the 6th Division had captured Bailleul and Meteren, whilst the 4th Division captured and occupied a strong position facing east one mile to the north of the 6th Division.

This was an excellent day's work performed by the 3rd Corps; and the captured ground was of great value in the subsequent operations.

About noon on the 14th, the 3rd Corps continued the advance, and after some considerable fighting secured, by 7 p.m., the line Bleu—east of Bailleul—Neuve Église.

On the 15th I directed Pulteney to make good the River Lys between Armentières and Sailly-sur-la-Lys, and endeavour to gain touch with the 2nd Corps.

By nightfall the 3rd Corps had made the line Sailly-Nieppe.

Between the 11th and the 15th, the 4th Corps under Rawlinson was constantly engaged in assisting and covering the retreat of the Belgian Army. During this time the German forces from Antwerp were concentrating westwards in ever-increasing strength. The 7th Division under Capper retired successively from Ghent to Aeltre, thence to Thielt, from Thielt to Roulers, and from Roulers to the south and east of Ypres.

The 3rd Cavalry Division under Byng was at Thourout on

the 11th, at Roulers on the 12th, at Ypres on the 13th, and on the 14th connected up with Gough's 2nd Cavalry Division in front of Kemmel, which position the two Cavalry Divisions captured and secured.

On the 15th the 7th Division was east of Ypres, with the 3rd Cavalry Division well out in advance of them in the direction of Menin and Courtrai.

The capture of the high ground about Kemmel proved to be of the utmost importance to us throughout the Battle of Ypres.

On the 12th the Belgian Army assembled in the area Ostend—Dixmude—Furnes—Nieuport, but on the 15th withdrew entirely behind the Yser to the north of Ypres.

The French Naval Division and other troops which had been covering the Belgian retreat were at Dixmude and Nieuport. A French Territorial Division from Cassel had been moved to Ypres.

On the 14th it was reported that about 10,000 German troops from Antwerp were moving on Bruges and Roulers, and that another German Division from Antwerp had reached Courtrai.

On the 15th, the enemy strengthened their line on the Lys, where part of the 19th and 12th German Corps were reported to be with their right on Menin, and, finally, the Germans were said to be advancing in four columns to the line Ghistelles—Roulers.

I now turn to the operations of the 2nd Corps, which, it will be remembered, was on the right of the British forces to the east of Béthune.

I visited Smith-Dorrien at his Headquarters almost every day between the 11th and the 15th. On each occasion I was more and more impressed by the exceptionally difficult nature of the country in this part of our field of operations.

If we draw a line on the map starting from Lens on the south and following north through Liévin, La Bassée, Fromelles, Armentières, almost to the valley of the River Douve on the north, the whole terrain for several miles to the east and west of that line strongly resembles the English Black Country. North of Liévin the ground is very flat, whilst mining works, slag heaps, factories and mining villages completely cover the surface in all directions.

There is a large mining population whose tenements (sometimes single houses, sometimes separate rows or cottages) cover the whole area. There are also towns of some size, such as Béthune, Noeux-les-Mines, Nieppe, and Armentières.

The ground, moreover, was of such a character as to render effective artillery support to an infantry attack most difficult. The roads were rough, narrow, badly paved, and very slippery in wet weather, which caused movements by motor to be a work of time and difficulty, particularly in the case of the heavy motor transport passing between the troops and their supply depots. This marked defect in the roads applied, however, to the whole area over which the British operations extended.

After some severe fighting, particularly by the 5th Division, the 2nd Corps reached the line Annequin—Pont Fixe—Festubert—Vieille Chapelle—Fosse on the night of the 12th.

On my way to Hazebrouck on the 13th, I saw Smith-Dorrien for a short time. He was holding his own, and during the day his left (3rd Division) made good progress, reaching Pont du Hem close to Laventie.

The French cavalry, which had been operating in advance of the 2nd Corps, had drawn back to the northern flank of the latter and were at Pont Rigneul. For some days subsequently they held the ground and kept up connection between our 2nd and 3rd Corps.

On the afternoon of the 14th, I again visited Smith-Dorrien at Béthune. He was in one of those fits of deep depression which unfortunately visited him frequently. He complained that the 2nd Corps had never got over what he described as the "shock" of Le Cateau, and that the officers sent out to him to replace his tremendous losses in officers were untrained and inexperienced; and, lastly, he expressed himself convinced that there was no great fighting spirit throughout the troops he commanded.

I told him that I thought he greatly exaggerated these disabilities. I pointed out that the cavalry, the 4th Division and the 19th Brigade were all just as heavily engaged at Le Cateau as the 2nd Corps, but that their spirit and condition, as I had seen for myself the day before, were excellent.

Even if, as I consider, his point of view was needlessly pessimistic, Smith-Dorrien was certainly confronted with a difficult task. He was on a very extended front, and the situation undoubtedly demanded skilful handling and great determination.

I arranged with Foch that the French should extend their line north, up to the line of the La Bassée canal. When this was done, the Commander of the 2nd Corps was able to shorten his line and keep one of his brigades back in reserve.

On this day General Hubert Hamilton, commanding the 3rd Division, was killed by a shell. His loss was deeply felt by his Division, who had the utmost confidence in him.

Hubert Hamilton was an old friend of mine, and it grieved me much to lose him. He was a fine soldier, possessing a most attractive nature, and I do not think he can have had an enemy in the world. I have always looked back with admiration to his leading of the 3rd Division in that critical period of the war.

I conclude this chapter with the arrival of the last detachment of the 1st Corps at St. Omer from the Aisne. There to the last they maintained the fine fighting record which they had earned, for on the 11th—shortly before their departure—they once again gallantly repulsed a heavy German attack with great loss to the enemy.

On the night of the 11th, the 2nd Division and 16th Brigade had been withdrawn from the trenches and had begun entraining *en route* for St. Omer, being followed shortly by the remainder of the 1st Corps.

The following Order of the Day was issued to the troops on October 16th:

Special Order of the Day
General Headquarters
October 16th, 1914
1. Having for 25 days successfully held the line of the River Aisne between Soissons and Villers against the most desperate endeavours of the enemy to break through, that memorable battle has now been brought to a conclusion, so far as the British Forces are concerned, by the operation which has once more placed us on the left flank of the Allied Armies.

2. At the close of this important phase of the campaign, I wish to express my heartfelt appreciation of the services performed throughout this trying period by the officers, non-commissioned officers and men of the British Field Forces in France.

3. Throughout nearly the whole of those 25 days a most powerful and continuous fire of artillery, from guns of a calibre never used before in field operations, covered and supported desperate infantry attacks made in the greatest strength and directed at all hours of the day and night on your positions. Although you were thus denied adequate rest and suffered great losses, in no case did the enemy attain the slightest success, but was invariably thrown back with immense loss.

4. The powerful endurance of the troops was further greatly taxed by the cold and wet weather which prevailed during the greater part of the time.

5. Paragraph 2 of the Special Order of the Day, August 22nd, ran as follows:

> All the regiments comprising the Expeditionary Force bear on their colours emblems and names which constantly remind them of glorious victories achieved by them in the past. I have the most complete confidence that those regiments, as they stand today in close proximity to the enemy, will not only uphold the magnificent traditions of former days, but will add fresh laurels to their standards.

I cannot convey what I feel with regard to the conduct of the troops under my command better than by expressing my conviction that they have justified that confidence well and nobly.

6. That confidence is everywhere endorsed by their fellow-countrymen; and, whatever may be before the British Army in France, I am sure they will continue to follow the same, glorious path till final and complete victory is attained.

J. D. P. French
Field Marshal
Commander-in-Chief, the British Army in the Field

CHAPTER 10

The Battle of Ypres

First Phase, October 15th to October 26th

Before continuing my narrative, which has now reached the opening stages of the First Battle of Ypres, let us consider what were the points at issue in this grave crisis in the history of the world. What were the stakes for which we were playing?

Let us suppose that from October 1914 up to the end of the war, the German right flank had been established at Dieppe, instead of at Nieuport. The enemy would have been in occupation of the whole of the Department of the Pas de Calais, including the seaports of Dieppe, Boulogne, Calais and Dunkirk.

How then would it have fared with the British Empire?

Discussing the question of the Channel tunnel, at a meeting of the Council of Imperial Defence, in May 1914, I suggested the possibility of submarines being despatched in sections by rail to certain ports and there assembled. The expert reply was that this would be quite impracticable. How has the experience of the war borne out this dictum?

It is as certain as anything can be, that, in the circumstances I have supposed, the Channel ports would soon have been full to overflowing with these craft, which, with such bases of operations, would have rendered the Channel a veritable *mare clausum*, so far as any attempt by our Navy to prevent invasion were concerned.

If, then, Napoleon entertained high hopes of success when he concentrated an army at Boulogne in 1805 for the invasion of this country, surely the Germans, in such circumstances as I have described, would have regarded such an enterprise with still greater confidence. And they would have been justified in so doing.

Then, as to aircraft. An examination of the map will show that London would be within about half the aircraft range of the German aerodromes as they existed if these latter were moved to Calais and its neighbourhood. Let those who have had experience of the full effect of air raids on London during the war judge what this might have meant. Had the western Channel ports been in German occupation, the horrors of these air raids would have been multiplied a hundredfold.

It is only necessary to add that, during the war, heavy artillery succeeded in making effective practice at ranges greater than the distance between Calais and Dover.

I think it is reasonable to deduce from this argument that the stakes for which we were playing at the great Battle of Ypres were nothing less than the safety, indeed, the very existence, of the British Empire.

Now, the Germans had two distinct opportunities of bringing about such a situation as I have contemplated—

(1) To reinforce their right much sooner than they did—even though, by so doing, they had to make slight and unimportant sacrifices elsewhere—and to take up a line of entrenchments resting on the sea at Dieppe, whence they could have run their trenches east and joined up with their main line before de Castelnau's flank movement could possibly have developed.

(2) By successfully attacking the British and French forces to the east of Ypres, and driving them back to the sea.

This latter alternative, as we know, is what they actually attempted; which mighty effort, together with our successful and prolonged resistance, constituted the First Battle of Ypres.

No one who has done me the honour of reading this book so far can suppose that I did not realise this danger.

I am free to confess, however, that, on October 15th, 1914, the day upon which I date the opening of the Battle of Ypres, I thought that the danger was past. I believed that the enemy had exhausted his strength in the great bid he had made to smash our armies on the Marne and to capture Paris. The fine successes gained by the cavalry and the 3rd Corps, narrated in the last chapter, did much to confirm these impressions on my mind.

I could not bring myself to suppose for one moment that, with such resources as the Germans afterwards showed that they had at this time in reserve, they could have let slip such an opportunity as we afforded them by our long delay on the Aisne and our perilous disregard of the danger in the north. One of their punishments will be the corroding contemplation of the "ifs" and "buts" of their stupendous gamble.

In my inmost heart, I did not expect I should have to fight a great defensive battle. All my dispositions were made with the idea of carrying out effectively the combined offensive which, as narrated in the last chapter, was concerted between Foch and myself.

There was only one reservation in my mind, and that concerned the danger of leaving a gap anywhere in our long line, or of failing to give a sufficiently close support to the weary but most gallant Army of the King of the Belgians. As will presently be shown, I had to run a terrible risk to safeguard against this danger, but I hold that the risk was justified.

Many of Napoleon's great campaigns developed in a totally unexpected manner, quite different to his original conception, but he always claimed that his constant success was due to the initial correct direction and impulse which he always imparted to his armies. Tolstoy states that the only directions he gave at Borodino, three in number, were never carried out, and could never, as the battle developed, have been carried out. I have not verified the great Russian novelist's statement, but it may well be true. History relates that in the Jena campaign of 1806, Napoleon, in three days, made three erroneous calculations of the Prussians' doings. Hamley says, in his *Operations of War*:

> On the 10th he thought Hohenlohe was about to attack him; on the 10th also he judged that the Prussians were concentrating on Gera; and on the 13th he mistook Hohenlohe's army for the entire Prussian force. Still, his plan, made on these suppositions, was in the main quite suitable

to the actual circumstances. And this, as is mostly the case, was owing *to the right direction* given to the movements *at the outset.* The preliminary conditions of a campaign seldom offer more than three or four alternatives; an attack by the centre or either flank, or some combination of these. If the enemy has made such false dispositions as to render one of these alternatives decidedly the best, the General who has the faculty of choosing it thereby provides in the best possible way for all subsequent contingencies. *A right impulse* once given to an army, it is in a position to turn events not calculated on, or miscalculated, to advantage.

As a humble but life-long disciple of this great master of war, I venture to make the same claim for the operations now about to be discussed.

The designation of the place where any great battle has taken place, and the limits of time within which it has lasted, were formerly much more easily defined than now.

In my first dispatch reporting the details of the Battle of Ypres, I think it was described as "The Battle of Ypres-Armentières," and, strictly speaking, that really would have been more correct.

I have mentioned this in order to draw attention to the fact that, although the most critical point throughout this living line of battle was east of the town of Ypres, yet the battle which was given that name was fought on a front of many miles, extending from the sea at Nieuport to the Béthune—Lille canal. Continuous and heavy fighting went on for days all along this line.

At the beginning of the operations which I am about to narrate, my plans were based generally on the agreement which I had come to with Foch on the 10th instant. Nothing had occurred, so far, to raise any great doubts in my mind as to the possibility of prosecuting the offensive which we had arranged to put in movement. At the time of the arrival of the 1st Corps, a few days later, increasing opposition had made itself felt all along the Allied front in the north, and reports reached us of a powerful offensive by the enemy towards Ypres and the Yser. In consequence of this, my appreciation of the situation was that I should have to make a very momentous decision between two most perilous alternatives.

But, for the moment, at any rate, I felt complete confidence. I met the Corps Commanders at Hazebrouck, and, in accordance with the plans which Foch and I had agreed upon, directed them as follows: the 2nd Corps on the right was ordered to continue in its present direction, making ground to the east. The 3rd Corps was to advance and make good the River Lys between Armentières and Sailly-sur-Lys, and to endeavour to gain touch with the 2nd Corps. The cavalry under Allenby were to make good the river towards Menin, and then, if possible, sweep round to the north and north-east. Rawlinson was to move with his right on Courtrai, keeping generally level with the 3rd Corps in the subsequent advance, should that prove possible; his cavalry under Byng were to move to the north of him.

I had told Rawlinson that, whilst conforming to the general move east, he must keep an eye on the enemy's detachments known to be at Bruges and Roulers. I told him I would deal with these later by means of the 1st Corps, but for the moment his left required careful watching.

In carrying out these orders some progress was made, and the troops reached the following lines by midnight: 2nd Corps.—Givenchy-les-La Bassée—Pont du Hem. 3rd Corps.—Neighbourhood of Sailly. The remaining parts of the line were much in the same position as before.

On the 16th I went out to see the cavalry. The day was wet and misty, and it was almost impossible to get artillery targets.

The 1st and 2nd Cavalry Divisions fought all day to gain the passage of the Lys from Warneton to Comines, but without success. The 2nd Cavalry Division gained a footing in Warneton, but was counter-attacked and driven out in the evening. Before I left Allenby, he told me he had great hopes of succeeding the next day. I remember watching some of this fighting from an artillery observation post established in a very roughly constructed hay-loft, through the rotten floor of which we were nearly precipitated some twenty feet to the ground.

On my way back I came to the Headquarters of the 3rd Corps. They were getting on fairly well and had made some progress, but they had not yet taken Armentières.

On this day the 2nd Corps was able to move forward with slight opposition to the line Givenchy—north-west of Aubers.

Of the 4th Corps, the 7th Division occupied the line Houthem-Gheluvelt-St. Julien, in touch with German outposts.

The 3rd Cavalry Division moved towards Roulers, and was slightly engaged with the enemy in the forest of Houthulst. In the evening they occupied the line Zonnebeke-Westroosebeke.

Reports pointed to an increasing hostile advance centred on Thourout.

My ideas as to an earnest offensive on our part were so far modified by what I had seen and heard, that I sent Wilson to Foch expressing my conviction that we could not hope to advance east on the lines which we had discussed on the 10th until our left was cleared. An offensive on that flank was the only move open to us. This, if successful, would drive the enemy back from Bruges, and possibly clear Ghent. I was anxious to know what support Foch could give me in the north. I told Wilson to assure Foch that the 2nd and 3rd Corps, as well as the cavalry, would continue their endeavour to make headway east, so far as circumstances permitted.

Foch replied that he had already two Territorial Divisions and two Cavalry Divisions, besides some six to seven thousand Marines, on the Yser. He could have another Regular Division there either by the 22nd or the 23rd, and he would then advance with all the forces at his disposal, in support of my left, and clear the country as far as Ostend and Bruges.

By the night of the 18th the 3rd Corps had captured Bois Grenier and Armentières, and were on the line Radinghem—Prémesques—Houplines, after an excellent advance for which Pulteney deserved great credit.

On the left of the 2nd Corps the 3rd Division had made some advance to the line Lorgies—Herlies. The 5th Division on the right was up against La Bassée, but could make no further headway. It was a most formidable stronghold.

The cavalry were watching the River Lys to Menin.

As to the 4th Corps, doubtless Rawlinson was restricted by the warning I had given him, and was naturally somewhat anxious about his left flank. His troops made but little progress towards the objective assigned to them.

I had good reasons to think that Menin was very weakly occupied on the 17th, and orders were sent to Rawlinson to move on and attack that place on the 18th. He did not, however, march. The embargo I had laid upon him as to his left flank was, perhaps, a sufficient justification; but I have always regretted that the cavalry did not get this very necessary support on the 18th, which might possibly have secured to us the line of the Lys from Menin upwards.

I do not impute blame for this to the commander of the 4th Corps. Such instances of disregard of orders occur in every campaign. Only when the full history of the war is known, and all the cards are laid on the table, can a right judgment be formed.

Nothing impressed me so much with the increasing power and weight of the enemy's opposition as my own personal experience on the afternoon of the 18th, when I went into Armentières to try and study the situation with a view to estimating future possibilities. A good outlook was afforded from some high buildings on the eastern edge of this place. The town was being heavily shelled, and the way in which large buildings were being smashed and turned into ruins proved that projectiles of large calibre were falling, and that a considerable force of *heavy artillery* was, therefore, in action against the town. It was evident that powerful reinforcements were coming up to the enemy.

I recall this afternoon in Armentières very vividly. Armentières has a manufacturing population, and the day being Sunday, everyone was wearing his best clothes. The scenes in the streets were extraordinary. Some of the men seemed to have gone mad with either rage or fear. Women rushed to and fro, screaming, with babies in their arms.

Close to the look-out post where I was standing, a priest in his altar vestments dashed out of a church with the sacred vessels in his arms, and tore in panic down the street in front of me, followed by large numbers of his flock. A great deal of damage was done to the town, and there were many casualties amongst the civilians.

By October 19th, the 1st Corps under Haig was fully concentrated in the northern theatre.

The 2nd Division was in the area Poperinghe—Boeschepe—Steenvoorde, the 1st Division between St. Omer and Cassel.

On this day I had to take a very grave decision, and I shall try and recall the working of my mind at the time, and the manner in which the problem I had to solve presented itself to me.

On October 10th and 11th, when I commenced operations in the northern theatre with the British Forces, I was, as I have said, decidedly optimistic as to the possibility of carrying out a strong offensive eastwards. Foch was equally confident, and we both thought that our concerted plans promised well.

My reason for forming this opinion was, in the first place, based upon my talks with Foch, who had already been on the spot for several days. He had been able to form some estimate of the enemy's strength between Arras and the sea. He considered that the Germans were in no condition to stem a determined advance by us. Reports had reached me of large transfers of German troops from this theatre to the Aisne and south of that river. Foch expressed himself as well satisfied with the progress already made by his own army, particularly the cavalry on his northern flank.

But I had other and more tangible reasons for hope and confidence. Between the 12th and the 15th, the cavalry and the 3rd Corps had gained important victories and made splendid advances. During these days it did not appear that Rawlinson in the north was ever heavily pressed. The 2nd Corps had made certain progress, though I have always thought, in regard to them, that more might have been done had they been directed with more determination and vigour.

The Germans themselves certainly thought so. We intercepted a wireless message sent by General von der Marwitz, Commanding the 4th German Cavalry Corps, who, in wiring to the Commander of the 6th German Army, commented upon the *weakness* of the 2nd Corps' attack, and the ease with which he had been able to withstand it.

After the 15th, however, the result of my own observations,

and the reports I continued to receive of the enemy's constantly increasing strength all along our line, caused me anxiety and induced me to send the message I have mentioned to Foch.

I was far from satisfied with the situation in the north. Although no reports had reached us of any great concentration of the enemy there, I had much reason to fear that troops were being moved east across Belgium to reinforce him. The French troops on the Yser were not numerous, and they included many Territorials, whilst the Belgians were completely tired out. On the right of the Belgians, as far as Menin, there were only the 3rd Cavalry and 7th Infantry Divisions, both of which stood in need of rest and refit.

Ours was a tremendously long line to guard with so few troops available. If the enemy broke through the left flank all the British would be turned, the Belgians and the French troops with them would be cut off and the sea-coast towns would be gone.

When I looked further south, the prospect was no better. The enemy was daily and almost hourly getting stronger in front of our line, which was held by the cavalry and by the 2nd and 3rd Corps. The endurance of these troops had been heavily taxed, and I had practically no reserves. Moreover, they were extended on a front much too wide for their numbers, especially north of the Lys.

Bad as a complete break through by the enemy in the north would have been, a wedge driven through our lines south of Menin would have entailed still more disastrous consequences.

In a message which I received from de Maud'huy on the 16th, he expressed great fear that the Germans were intent on attacking between us and finally separating us. Had they accomplished this, the eventual alternatives before the British Army would have been to surrender or be driven into the sea.

I pondered long and deeply on the situation, and finally arrived at the following conclusion:—

If the enemy's threats against Ypres and the Yser were not strongly met by a corresponding offensive move, then a break through at some point in that neighbourhood by the Germans was a practical certainty, and the seaboard would be theirs.

On the other hand, although from the south of Ypres to La Bassée the situation would remain very precarious, I conceived that it might be possible to hold on till support could arrive.

Since the solution of the problem, as presented to my mind, resolved itself into a balance of *certain disaster* against a disaster which, although much greater in degree, was still *not* a *certainty*, I determined to guard against the former; and on the evening of the 19th I sent for Sir Douglas Haig and gave him his instructions.

I explained the situation as clearly as possible, and showed him on the map where and how we thought the enemy's troops were distributed. I said that at the moment I did not think there was much more than the 3rd German Reserve Corps, with possibly one or two Divisions attached, between Ostend and Menin, but that all reports pointed to an early arrival of strong reinforcements from the centre and east of Belgium.

I pointed out to Haig how much importance I attached to the clearing of Ostend and Bruges before these reinforcements could arrive. I said I hoped that, with the assistance of the French and Belgian troops on the north, and Rawlinson on his right flank, he would be able to effect this object and perhaps, with luck, throw the enemy back on Ghent. I told him that this was what I particularly wanted to bring about, but that he would have to be guided by the course of events. I informed him of Wilson's visit to Foch on the 16th, and Foch's promise that he would strongly support us on the north. Orders were then issued to the 1st Corps, of which the following is a summary:

> The 1st Corps will advance *via* Thourout with the object of capturing Bruges. If this is proved to be feasible and successful, every endeavour must be made to turn the enemy's left flank and drive him back to Ghent. The situation, however, is very uncertain, and in the first instance it is only possible to direct the 1st Corps with its right on the line Ypres—Roulers. Should the forces of the enemy, reported to be moving west between Iseghem and Courtrai, seriously menace the 4th Corps, it is left to the discretion of the Commander of the 1st Corps to lend this Corps such assistance as may be necessary.

It had been arranged by the Admiralty that some battleships were to be held in readiness at Dover, to co-operate with our movements on the north coast should opportunity offer.

My advanced Headquarters were now established at Bailleul, and a long discussion I had there on the 19th with Pulteney and Smith-Dorrien showed that our front south of Menin was being still more severely pressed.

An attempt by the 4th Corps to advance on Menin ended in failure.

The Germans were also fairly active in the north. They pushed back de Mitry's French Cavalry Corps towards Staden and Zarren, and heavily attacked the Belgians at Nieuport, but our Allies held their ground well.

The events of the 20th showed still greater pressure by the enemy. The 3rd Cavalry Division was driven back to the line Zonnebeke—St. Julien—Pilkem by infantry and guns advancing from Roulers.

The centre of Allenby's Cavalry Corps fell back on Messines, which place was heavily shelled.

In order to cement the connection between the 2nd and 3rd Corps (now only maintained by Conneau's French cavalry) I sent the 19th Brigade to be placed at Pulteney's disposal.

Haig sent two battalions of the 4th Guards Brigade to support the centre of the 4th Corps between Byng and Capper.

On the 21st, all my worst forebodings as to the enemy's increasing strength were realised. Intercepted wireless messages established the certainty that the comparatively small German force which on the night of the 18th we judged to be between Ostend and Menin, was now reinforced by no less than four Corps, namely, the 21st, 22nd, 26th and 27th Reserve Corps. These Corps had been hastily formed, and were not composed of the best troops, They were also weak in numbers and artillery as compared with other Corps.

Although I looked for a great addition to the enemy's numbers within a few days from the 18th, the strength they actually reached astounded me. This, taken with the speed in which they appeared in the field, came like a veritable bolt from the blue.

My only comfort lay in the certainty that my direction of the 1st Corps to the north was sound and best calculated to meet these new and startling conditions.

All hope of any immediate offensive had now to be abandoned. It was simply "up to us" to hold on like grim death to our positions by hard, resolute fighting, until relief in some shape could come.

It may well be asked how I expected such relief to be afforded, and whence it could arrive. What hope could be justified in face of such overpowering odds?

As far as reinforcements went, all I had to look to was the Indian Corps, one Division of which (the Lahore) detrained on the 19th and the 20th at St. Omer, and was now concentrating at Wallon-Cappel, west of Hazebrouck. A wire from Lord Kitchener on the 22nd offered me another Territorial Battalion to replace the London Scottish on the lines of communication, if I wished to use the latter at the front. I had also available the Oxfordshire Yeomanry Cavalry, which had been landed at Dunkirk.

These were all the British reserves which could possibly be available for some time. Doubtless, if we could keep our positions for two or three weeks, much larger reinforcements would be forthcoming. But, even so, it did not appear that there was any prospect, in the near future, of attaining definite results by an effective offensive. Nevertheless, I remained hopeful and confident of the final result.

On the 23rd I issued the following special Order of the Day to the troops:

> The Field-Marshal Commanding-in-Chief wishes once more to make known to the troops under his command how deeply he appreciates the bravery and endurance which they have again displayed since their arrival in the northern theatre. In circulating the official information which records the splendid victories of our Russian Allies, he would remind the troops that the enemy must before long withdraw troops to the East and relieve the tension on our front. He feels it is quite unnecessary to urge offic-

ers, non-commissioned officers and men to make a determined effort and drive the enemy over the frontier.
H. Wilson
Major-General
7.30 p.m. Sub-Chief

This, then, was my great hope. It was to Russia and to the East that all eyes were turned at that time. Our Allies had scored a considerable success in that theatre.

With the failure of the second attack of the Central Powers upon Warsaw, we may take stock for a moment of Russia's achievement. Russia made no secret preparation for war, and the outbreak of hostilities had found her with her Army reorganisation incomplete and a serious shortage of equipment. She had to bring her men by slender communications many thousands of miles, but she was ready to strike a fortnight before Germany believed she could move. Her invasion of East Prussia had done much to relieve the strain in the West, and heavily she paid for her quixotry.

But, after Tannenburg, she made no mistakes. Von Hindenburg was enticed to the Niemen and then driven back to disaster at Augustovo; while in Galicia, Lemberg and all Eastern Galicia were won, and in two mighty battles three Austrian Armies were heavily beaten.

The Russian Generals showed that rarest of combinations— an omnipresent sense of a great strategic objective and a power of patiently biding their time and of temporarily relinquishing their objective when prudence demanded. A commander less wise than the Grand Duke Nicholas would have battled desperately for Cracow, lost a million men, and at the end of the year have been further from it than in September. But as it was, the first great advance was promptly recalled when von Hindenburg threatened Warsaw, and the second was also abandoned when it was at the very gates of the city.

The first Battle of Warsaw and the Battle of Kazimirjev were strategically admirable; and the subsequent fighting, from Kozienice westward, showed the stubborn valour of the Russian soldier. Not less brilliant was the long retirement from the Warta. There was some blunder of timing in the fighting between Lodz and Lowicz, for which Rennenkampf was held responsible; but there was no flaw in the retreat to the Bzura or the holding of the river line.

The Grand Duke Nicholas proved that he possessed that highest of military gifts—the power of renunciation, of cutting losses, of sacrificing the less essential for the more. We must remember that in all these first five months of war, the united strength of the Teutonic League outnumbered the Russians by at least half a million. Locally, as at the first Battle of Warsaw, the latter may have had the superiority; but in all the retreat from the Warta to the Bzura the Russian front was markedly inferior in weight of men to von Mackensen's forces. When we remember this, we can do justice not only to the excellence of the generalship, but also to the stamina and courage of the rank and file. Let it be added that reports are unanimous as to the behaviour of the Russian troops at that time, their chivalry towards the foe, their good humour, their kindliness towards each other and their devotion to their commanders.

In a decade the miracle of miracles had happened. Russia had found herself, and her Armies had become an expression of the national will. A correspondent wrote:

> There is as much difference in organisation, morale, and efficiency between the armies which some of us saw in Manchuria ten years ago and which crumpled up before the Imperial Guards of Japan at the Battle of the Yalu, and the military machine that these past few weeks has been steadily and surely driving back the armies of Germany and Austria, as there was between the raw American recruits who stampeded at the Battle of the Bull Run in 1861 and the veterans who received the surrender of Lee at Appomattox.

If then I am asked upon what I based my hopes during October, 1914, that is my answer.

The actual fronts and positions of the opposing forces from Nieuport and the sea to La Bassée, on the night of October 21st, were, according to our latest and best information, as follows:

Summary from Right to Left

	Front (approx.)	**Attacked by**
2nd Corps	6 miles	7th Corps
Conneau's Cavalry Corps	Filling gap, 1 mile	19th Corps and part of 7th Corps
3rd Corps and 19th Bgd	12 miles	
Cavalry Corps	4 miles	Part of 19th Corps and of 18th Corps
4th Corps	6 miles	1 Division of 13th Corps and 27th Corps
1st Corps	7 miles	26th Corps and part of 23rd Corps
Territorials, de Mitry's Cav. Corps, Belgians and French Marines	20 miles	23rd Corps, 22nd and 3rd Reserve Corps and Ersatz Division

On October 21st the 1st Corps came into line, and after hard fighting held at night the line Zonnebeke—Langemarck—Bixschoote, the left of the 1st Division being on the Yser Canal.

Some confusion and friction were caused by the withdrawal of de Mitry's Cavalry Corps to the west bank of the canal, thus uncovering the flank of the 1st Corps, who were also considerably delayed in their advance by French Territorial troops blocking the road. In spite of this, however, the 1st Corps delivered some powerful attacks with the bayonet, and in the afternoon the artillery of the Corps was in action for a long time against retreating hostile masses. They were splendid targets for one brigade in particular, which did tremendous execution.

The inevitable evils of divided command are clearly shown when Allied troops are mixed, and the limits of control cannot be properly defined. As will appear later, I made the most strenuous attempts to minimise this very serious drawback, either until rectified or considerably reduced by arrangements between the two Governments, but all in vain. I could get no hearing.

I was so strongly impressed with the danger of the confusion and congestion which the divided command was causing in the north, that I went myself on the evening of the 21st to Ypres, where I was met by Haig, Rawlinson, de Mitry, and Bidon (who commanded a French Territorial Division). Arrangements were there made by which the town was to be at once cleared of the French troops, and the left flank of the 1st Corps properly covered.

On the 21st I received a visit from General Joffre, who told me he was at once bringing up the 9th French Army Corps to Ypres.

Two battalions of the Lahore Division were sent at night in motor omnibuses to Wulverghem, to come under Allenby's orders in support of the cavalry.

The 3rd Cavalry Division was moved from the left to the right of the 7th Division to be in a position to assist Allenby's Cavalry Corps, which was being hard pressed on the left at Zonnebeke.

A fine piece of work was done by the 4th Division under Wilson on the morning of the 21st. The Germans had advanced and captured Le Gheer. The 4th Division retook it by a brilliant counter-attack and secured 200 prisoners.

I fix the close of the first phase of the Battle of Ypres as the night of October 26th. By the morning of the 27th the 9th French Corps had settled down in the trenches which they had taken over from the 1st Corps in the northern part of the Ypres salient.

Speaking generally, it may be said that, in the last days of this, the opening period of the battle, the northern portion of our line progressed slowly but surely, very heavy losses being inflicted on the enemy and many prisoners were captured.

To the south, however, between Zonnebeke and the La Bassée, a certain amount of ground was lost, but troops held staunchly to their positions, and there was never any break of a serious nature made in the line.

On the 22nd, the enemy, who had thrown a number of pontoon bridges across the Lys opposite the Cavalry Corps, appeared to be massing troops against that part of our line. The Lahore

Division having then reached Bailleul, I sent Egerton's Brigade to support the cavalry. I found there was no chance of getting the Meerut Division for some time to come, as they were being hopelessly delayed at Marseilles and Orleans.

At midnight on the 22nd both the 2nd and 3rd Corps Commanders were very anxious about their positions, and I therefore despatched the Lahore Division to Estaires, from which point it could support either Corps in case of urgent necessity.

On the 24th I paid a visit to General d'Urbal at Poperinghe. He had come to command the northern French Army. We discussed the situation together, and he seemed hopeful as to future possibilities.

D'Urbal impressed me as a man of striking personality. In figure and bearing he reminded me of the old Murat type of French *beau sabreur*. All his regimental service was passed in the cavalry. I was a great deal associated with him in the operations at Ypres and afterwards, when he commanded the French troops on the Arras front, and I can testify to his remarkable powers of command, his fine courage and his extraordinary tenacity. We were together in many critical situations, and I have passed some anxious hours in his company; but I never knew him other than helpful in the highest degree. Nothing ever ruffled the calmness of his demeanour, or prevented him from exercising that deliberate and well-weighed judgment which was a remarkable feature of his truly soldierlike character.

Dawnay came back from the 1st Corps on this night, and told me that late on the previous day the enemy had delivered a succession of counter-attacks against the front of the 2nd Division just as they were being relieved. The German infantry came on in dense columns singing "The Watch on the Rhine." They were simply mown down by our artillery and rifle fire. The ground was a veritable shambles, and the 1st Corps estimated that in the last three or four days they had put at least 8,000 Germans *hors-de-combat*.

Foch, with whom I had a long interview at Cassel on the morning of the 25th, appeared to be quite hopeful and sanguine about the situation on the canal north of Ypres. He told me that another French regular Division was to be brought up on either flank at Nieuport and Ypres, and he proposed later to move Conneau from the neighbourhood of Béthune. I told him I could hardly do without Conneau for the moment, and he agreed to leave him as long as I wanted him.

It is interesting to recall that General Conneau was once a cadet at the Royal Military Academy at Woolwich. He proved himself throughout the war to be a distinguished and able cavalry leader.

The first phase of the Battle of Ypres may be briefly summarised as the conclusion of the successive attempts, begun a month previously, to effect a great turning movement round the German right flank. The operations up to the night of the 26th certainly failed in their original intention of clearing the coast-line and driving the enemy from Bruges and Ghent, but they succeeded in establishing a line to the sea which, if it could be held, brought the Germans face to face with the challenge: "Thus far shalt thou go and no farther."

What this meant to them is proved by the desperate but abortive attempts they made to break through in the second phase of the battle.

Chapter 11

The Battle of Ypres

SECOND PHASE, OCTOBER 27TH TO OCTOBER 31ST

I regard the operations which were carried on by the British Forces in France during the days of which this chapter treats, as more momentous and fateful than any others which I directed during my period of service as Commander-in-Chief in the field. October 31st and November 1st will remain for ever memorable in the history of our country, for, during those two days, no more than one thin and straggling line of tired-out British soldiers stood between the Empire and its practical ruin as an independent first-class Power. I still look back in wonder on that thin line of defence, stretched, out of sheer necessity, far beyond its natural and normal power for defence. Right, centre, and left our men were tried and pressed as troops were never tried and pressed before.

A lofty tower of some antiquity still stood by itself on the top of a commanding hill just east of Kemmel. Its days even then were numbered, and after being heavily shelled, it was completely destroyed later in the battle. While this tower remained it made an excellent look-out post. I spent some time there on the 27th, when the crisis of the battle was approaching.

A glance at the map will show that from this point of view an observer with strong glasses can compass almost the whole battlefield of Ypres, where seven British infantry and three cavalry divisions were extended on a front of from 25 to 36 miles.

It was a bright October day with brilliant sunshine, and the line of fire could be seen all along the high ground encircling the Ypres salient to the north, the Wytschaete—Messines ridge to the east, and away to the south-east down to the Lys valley almost as far as Armentières, beyond which place the shell-bursts in the sky brought the right of the British battle line well into the picture.

For four or five days this line was being still further reduced in strength by the successful efforts of our troops to stem the tide of the enemy's advance, whilst on their side the Germans were being gradually reinforced to a strength which, by the 30th, reached about double our numbers.

In the great onslaught made by the enemy on October 31st and November 1st, sufficient recognition has never yet been given to the glorious stand made by the Cavalry Corps under Allenby, and when I speak of the gallantry of the cavalry, I hasten to add that the splendour of their work was equally shared by Shaw's 9th Brigade of the 3rd Division (1st Batt. Northumberland Fusiliers, 4th Batt. Royal Fusiliers, 1st Batt. Lines Regt., and 1st Batt. R. Scots Fusiliers), Egerton's Brigade of the Indian Corps (1st Connaught Rangers, 129th Duke of Connaught's Own Beluchis, 57th Wilde's Rifles, 9th Bhopal Infantry), the London Scottish, and the Oxfordshire Yeomanry.

For close upon 48 hours these troops held the Wytschaete—Messines ridge against the utmost efforts of no less than two and a half German Army Corps to dislodge them. Here was the centre of our line of battle, and, had it given way, disaster would have resulted to the entire left wing of the Allied line.

In almost the same degree I would allot the honours of those splendid days to the defenders of the Ypres salient, namely, the 9th (French) Army Corps, the 1st (British) Corps, and the 7th (British) Division.

It was only a slightly less arduous task which fell upon the 2nd Corps in this great battle, for they had a long line to hold, in a much more difficult country, and were subjected to powerful attacks by superior numbers.

There is, indeed, little distinction to be made between the troops who fought so bravely all along the line. All were doggedly tenacious; all were superhumanly brave. The fullest measure of mutual support was assured by the complete understanding and perfect loyalty which existed amongst leaders of all ranks, combined with the alertness shown by all commanders in filling up gaps in the line *without delay*, and in using the troops at their disposal with the utmost economy.

All said and done, however, the main element of success was to be found in the devoted bravery and the stern unyielding determination to "do or die," displayed by the rank and file of the "contemptible little army" and its reinforcements.

On the 27th I had received an urgent message from Haig about the exhausted condition of the 7th Division. During the day I went to Haig at Hooge and had a conference with him and Rawlinson. I decided to break up the 4th Corps for the present, and to send Rawlinson and his Headquarters home to supervise the preparation of the 8th Division pending its despatch to France.

The 7th Division, under Capper, was to be attached to the 1st Corps until the 8th Division arrived and the 4th Corps could be again reformed under Rawlinson. Byng with the 3rd Cavalry Division was placed under Allenby.

The 7th Division took over the ground south of the Ypres—Menin road, then occupied by some troops of the 1st Division which were withdrawn in reserve.

The further progress of the enemy between La Bassée and the sea was probably now in suspense, awaiting the arrival of reinforcements. We had reliable reports that the detraining of troops was rapidly proceeding at Lille and Courtrai.

During the next two days they began pouring in, and, by October 30th, from La Bassée to the north the following German Corps opposed us:

La Bassée to Armentières	7th, one Brigade of 18th, 19th
North of Armentières to east of Ypres	13th, 15th, 24th Reserve, 27th Reserve, and two Ersatz Divisions
East of Ypres to Dixmude	26th Reserve, 23rd Reserve, 22nd Reserve
Dixmude to Nieuport	3rd Reserve and 4th Ersatz Division

Roughly speaking there were some twelve German Corps opposed to seven of the Allies, whilst the enemy enjoyed enormous artillery superiority, both numerically and in calibre of guns.

The condition of the 2nd Corps was again causing me anxiety, and the Corps Commander was calling out for help and reinforcements. It had also given cause for apprehension to our Allies.

Willcocks arrived on the 27th, and took over command of the Indian Corps in the field.

On this day Prince Maurice of Battenberg died of his wounds. He was a young officer of great promise, and much beloved in his regiment, the 60th Rifles.

The 28th saw the loss of Neuve Chapelle by the 2nd Corps.

I met Smith-Dorrien and Willcocks together at Merville, and arranged for the Indian Corps to take over the line now held by the 2nd Corps. The 2nd Corps was to fall back to Bailleul in reserve.

On the morning of the 28th I had got a message from General de Maud'huy, commanding the 10th French Army on our right. It was sent through the French Mission, and was to the effect that he was very anxious about his left flank. He added some criticism of his own for my consideration.

The 6th Division under Keir scored a success on the 28th. On their front, just south of Armentières, they repulsed a severe counter-attack in which the enemy left several hundred dead in front of their trenches.

The supply of ammunition now began to cause me increasing anxiety, and my apprehension under this head continued more or less throughout the whole period of my Command in France.

October 29th witnessed the opening of that most critical stage in the first period of the war, to which I have already referred.

At nine in the morning of that day the centre of the Ypres salient, held by the 1st and 7th Divisions, was attacked in the neighbourhood of Gheluvelt by large masses of the enemy, who forced back our troops on the latter place. Well organised counter-attacks, which were splendidly led, repulsed the enemy during the day with heavy casualties. By nightfall the 1st and 7th Divisions had recovered all the ground they had lost, and the position that night (October 29) was somewhat as follows:

The Seventh and part of the First Division held a line which extended on the left from a point about five hundred yards north of the cross-roads on the Ypres-Menin road, and ran thence south through the cross-roads to the village of Kruiseij on the right, where the Seventh Division joined up with the cavalry. This line was well to the east of Gheluvelt, and consequently represented a considerable gain as compared with the ground held the day before.

The left or northern portion of Haig's line extended slightly to the west of Reutel and Poezelhoek (both these places being held by the enemy), and was continued by the Second Division to the east of Zonnebeke Station, where they joined the right of the Ninth French Corps. The attacking troops consisted of the Twenty-seventh German Reserve Corps and the Sixth Bavarian Division, which suffered a very severe check; their losses were known to be heavy. In the middle of the day I sent Haig the London Scottish, which was the only reserve I had left. They were moved in motor omnibuses to Ypres.

On the afternoon of the 29th I went to Cassel and had a long conference with Foch. The canal and the river Yser, from Ypres to the sea, were capable of wide inundation which would afford excellent cover and protection all along that battle front. From the first I had been most anxious that this inundation should be carried out; but there was great opposition to it. Whether this came from the French or the Belgians I did not know, but I am much inclined to think that the French generals, in their sanguine anticipation of an immediate advance east, feared that such an obstacle would hamper them. When I saw Foch on this afternoon, however, he was all in favour of the inundation. He told me he thought the enemy was very slack in the north, that fresh French troops were being landed at Dunkirk, and that he still expected to see his hopes of an early advance realized. It was impossible to be closely associated with Foch and not come under the spell of his sanguine temperament, which was always a great help to me, although on this occasion I knew perfectly well that the enemy was increasing in numbers on our front, and that it was utterly impossible for us at that time to do more than hold our own with the utmost difficulty.

At dawn on October 30 the Nineteenth Brigade (Second Battalion Royal Welsh Fusiliers, First Battalion Scottish Rifles, First Battalion Middlesex Regiment, and Second Battalion Argyll and Sutherland Highlanders) carried out a brilliant counter-attack with the bayonet, heavily repulsing the enemy on the right of the Third Corps.

An hour later Haig reported that he was being heavily shelled all along his front, and that the enemy was moving in great force to attack Byng's Third Cavalry Division on his right. Gough had sent two regiments and a battery of horse artillery to support Byng. One of these regiments (the Royal Dragoons) had, with great dash and gallantry, repulsed an attack on the château at Hollebeke.

I went early in the morning to Allenby's Headquarters at Kemmel, where Barrow (his Chief of Staff) reported the situation to me. I ascended the tower I have spoken of already, to get a view of the field, which by this time had been drawn nearer, but mist prevented good observation.

Hearing heavy firing towards Ypres, I went to Haig's Headquarters at Hooge. Whilst I was with Haig, Allenby came in.

It appeared that strong forces were attacking the 3rd and 2nd Cavalry Divisions under Byng and Gough respectively, in and around Hollebeke. Allenby had sent a brigade from the 1st Cavalry Division on his right to support Gough, who had also been obliged to recall the support which he had previously sent to Byng. Haig had sent the London Scottish to support Gough, and had brought down Bulfin with most of the 2nd Brigade to strengthen the 7th Division on his right. Furthermore, he had ordered Lord Cavan with the 4th (Guards) Brigade (2nd Batt. Grenadier Guards, 2nd Batt. Coldstream Guards, 3rd Batt. Coldstream Guards, 1st Batt. Irish Guards) to move south of the Menin road, ready to counter-attack towards Hollebeke.

By the evening the 2nd and 3rd Cavalry Divisions had fallen back to the canal, and the enemy was in possession of Hollebeke.

On Allenby's right the 1st Cavalry Division was heavily pressed at Messines; the enemy gained a footing in the village, but were driven out later in the evening.

On Haig's left the 6th Infantry Brigade (1st Batt. The King's

(Liverpool) Regt., 2nd Batt. S. Staffs Regt., 1st Batt. R. Berks Regt. and 1st Batt. K.R.R.) was attacked three times during the day, and on one occasion the enemy infantry reached the barbed wire, close to the trenches.

North of the 1st Corps and on the Yser, heavy fighting went on throughout the 30th, but the situation there remained practically unchanged.

Late on this night, orders were sent to Smith-Dorrien to move Shaw's (9th) Brigade of the 3rd Division to Neuve-Église (about 5 miles east-north-east of Bailleul), to come under Allenby's orders.

About 6 p.m. the line of the 11th Brigade (1st Batt. Somerset L.I., 1st Batt. E. Lancs. Regt., 1st Batt. Hampshire Regt. and 1st Batt. Rifle Brigade) in the 4th Division under Hunter Weston was broken at St. Yves, but the ground lost was brilliantly recaptured by the brigade later in the evening.

Such was the general situation at 2 a.m. on October 31st, at which hour I received a visit from Foch, who promised to let me have effective support for Haig on this day, namely, five battalions of French infantry and three batteries of artillery.

Shortly after dawn on this fateful 31st October, we had news that a serious infantry attack was developing on the left of the 4th Division in the valley of the River Douve. The 4th Division was able to extend its line some little way to the north of the river and thus release troops of the 1st Cavalry Division, which subsequently fought fiercely all day at Messines. Throughout the day the left of the 4th Division rendered valuable and efficient support, as did the artillery on Hill 63, about one mile north of Ploegsteert.

But the great events of the day took place between Gheluvelt on the north and Messines on the south.

Early in the morning Allenby reported that Messines was being heavily attacked, and that the 9th Lancers had been withdrawn after suffering severely; that the eastern exit of the town was held by the 4th and 5th Dragoon Guards, and that the situation was "decidedly critical."

A heavy attack had been delivered against the right of the 1st Cavalry Division shortly after 7 a.m., and an Indian Battalion of

Rifles (the 57th, attached to the 1st Cavalry Division) were driven from their trenches. The reserves, however, held on, and the Inniskilling Fusiliers retook the trenches which the 57th had lost.

At 9.30 a.m. large masses of infantry were reported to be advancing against the 2nd Cavalry Division between Oesttaverne and Roozebeek, and long columns of the enemy were seen on the road leading from the former place to St. Eloi.

Shortly afterwards I reached Allenby's Headquarters, which were now at Groote Vierstraat (between Mont Kemmel and Ypres). After we had discussed matters, Gough arrived. Explaining the situation to me, he said he was in occupation of the canal to the north-east of Hollebeke, whence he had been driven back the day before. Thence his line extended south till it joined the left of the 1st Cavalry Division. He was in complete possession of Wytschaete, but he asked Allenby for some further support on the canal. Kavanagh's Brigade (1st Life Guards, 2nd Life Guards and Royal Horse Guards), which had been returned by Haig, was sent to him.

Just then I got a report that the five battalions of French infantry, which had been promised by Foch, were now directed to make a counter-attack from Verbranden Molen towards the canal at the dangerous point.

The 2nd and 3rd Cavalry Divisions were heavily attacked during the day, but by dark they held the same ground as on the night before.

The most critical fighting of the day in this part of the line was at Messines, on Allenby's right.

By 9 a.m. the cavalry were driven out of Messines, holding only one or two houses on the eastern side. Owing to heavy pressure elsewhere, no support was available until Shaw's (9th) Infantry Brigade could arrive. It reached Kemmel at 10 a.m.

Gough sent the London Scottish to join the 3rd Hussars in support of Bingham's 4th Cavalry Brigade (Household Cavalry, composite regiment, 6th Dragoon Guards and 3rd Hussars) on the left of the 3rd Division. At the same time, three battalions of French infantry, supported by 12 guns, were just starting their attack from St. Eloi on Oesttaverne.

At about 11.45 a.m., two battalions King's Own Scottish Borderers and King's Own Yorkshire Light Infantry were sent forward to retake the Messines ridge.

General de Lisle, commanding the 1st Cavalry Division, was commanding at Messines. The Oxfordshire Yeomanry and an Indian battalion were the last reserves sent up to him.

About noon, when the 1st Cavalry Brigade were still clinging to the western edge of Messines, a counter-attack by the 3rd Hussars and London Scottish began on the north of the village. By 1 p.m., considerable progress had been made. The 3rd Corps had regained the trenches north of the River Douve to within half a mile of Messines.

The K.O.S.B. were on the right of the town, and the K.O.Y.L.I. on the left. The London Scottish and 3rd Hussars were engaged on the north of the latter, and an intense struggle for the convent and southern portion of the town, which was a point from which the lost ground could be recovered, was proceeding to our advantage.

At this hour the news appeared more hopeful, and I left Allenby in order to join Haig at Hooge, east of Ypres. A battalion of French arrived to support the troops fighting at Messines just as I was leaving. I learned later that the London Scottish attack reached the north edge of Messines shortly after 2 p.m.; that towards 4 p.m. the attack was checked on the Messines—Wytschaete road by heavy artillery; that fierce fighting went on in the streets, and that the town was severely shelled; but that, later, the Germans were driven completely out, and were holding the ridge to the east, including a ruined factory and some farms to the south.

At nightfall the line held about Messines was the same as in the morning.

As I passed through Ypres on my way to Haig, there were manifest signs of unusual excitement, and some shells were already falling in the place. It is wonderful with what rapidity the contagion of panic spreads through a civilian population. I saw loaded vehicles leaving the town, and people were gathered in groups about the streets chattering like monkeys or rushing hither and thither with frightened faces.

As we passed by the ancient Cloth Hall, the old Cathedral, and the other splendid examples of Flemish architecture for which this town was famed, I did not realise how soon the atmosphere of German "frightfulness" was to reduce all these noble buildings to a heap of ruins. Although today Ypres as a city has ceased to exist, I am thankful to know that no German soldier has ever set foot within its walls save as a prisoner. Here, as at Verdun, they did not pass; and the glory is that of every soldier in the ranks.

On reaching the eastern exit of the town, on my way to Hooge, I was stopped by a guard specially posted by First Corps Headquarters, with orders to prevent anyone leaving the city.

Satisfying them as to my identity, I proceeded on my way. I had not gone more than a mile when the traffic on the road began to assume a most anxious and threatening appearance. It looked as if the whole of the 1st Corps was about to fall back in confusion on Ypres. Heavy howitzers were moving west at a trot—always a most significant feature of a retreat—and ammunition and other wagons blocked the road almost as far as the eye could see. In the midst of the press of traffic, and along both sides of the road, crowds of wounded came limping along as fast as they could go, all heading for Ypres. Shells were screaming overhead and bursting with reverberating explosions in the adjacent fields.

This spectacle filled me with misgiving and alarm. It was impossible for my motor-car to proceed at any pace, so we alighted and covered the rest of the way to Haig's Headquarters on foot, nor did I receive any encouragement on the way to hope for better things.

The château of Hooge, where 1st Army Headquarters were situated, has long since been erased from the face of the earth in the severe fighting which had raged about it. But as I found it on that October afternoon, it was a typical modern red brick château, approached by a gate and a short avenue from the road. Shells were falling about the place, and the château was already beginning to show the effects of artillery fire.

I found Haig and John Gough, his Chief of Staff, in one of the rooms on the ground floor, poring over maps and evidently much disconcerted. But, though much perturbed in mind and very tired in body and brain, Haig was cool and alert as ever. Both he and Gough gave me a bad account of the state of affairs.

This is what happened on the front of the 1st Corps. In the morning the position along the line was normal. About 10 o'clock rather a disturbing situation developed south and south-east of Gheluvelt. A local counter-attack failed, and some trenches east of the village had to be abandoned. There was heavy shelling along the front of the 7th Division and of the 2nd Brigade (2nd Batt. R. Sussex Regt., 1st Batt. N. Lancs. Regt., 1st Batt. Northampton Regt., and 2nd Batt. K.R.R.), but no infantry attack.

At 10.30 a.m. the 1st Division line, north of the Ypres—Menin road, was forced to retire in face of a heavy infantry attack covered by artillery. Lomax, commanding the Division, ordered the 1st (Guards) Brigade (1st Batt. Coldstream Guards, 1st Batt. Scots Guards, 1st Batt. Black Watch and 1st Batt. Cameron Highlanders) north of the road to be ready to enfilade the enemy's advance.

By 11.30 a.m., thanks to strong support from our artillery, the situation about Gheluvelt became easier; but at 12.15 p.m. the enemy were again reported to be massing east of the village, and the situation once more became threatening.

The G.O.C. 1st Division made arrangements for calling on the 2nd Worcesters (5th Brigade, 2nd Division) for a counter-attack due south, if necessary. Shortly before this, owing to a report from the 2nd Cavalry Division that successive lines of German infantry were massing for attack against Oesttaverne, and in response to an urgent call by the Cavalry Corps, the 6th Cavalry Brigade (3rd Dragoon Guards, 1st Dragoons and 10th Hussars), one battery R.F.A. and one battery Howitzers, were sent at 11 a.m. to their support. The 7th Cavalry Brigade (1st and 2nd Life Guards and Royal Horse Guards) was moved at 10.30 a.m. to a point midway between Hooge and Zillebeke.

At 12.30 p.m. the Germans developed their attack against Gheluvelt in great force, and the line of the 1st Division was broken. A General Staff Officer from the 1st Corps, who was sent forward to discover the exact position of the 3rd Cavalry

Division, reached 1st Division Headquarters in time to find the situation critical, the line being broken and a part at least of the Division falling back rapidly along the main road. General Lomax ordered his reserves to hold the east edge of the woods just south-east of the bend of the road, while the 7th Cavalry Brigade was ordered to take up a line astride the road on the east side of the château grounds, behind which the 1st Division could rally.

At this time all was quiet on the front of the 2nd Division, while on the south the 7th Division, assisted by troops which General Bulfin had collected under his orders, were being heavily shelled. The retirement of the 1st Division exposed the left of the 7th Division and, owing to this, the Royal Scots Fusiliers (21st Brigade), who stuck to their trenches, were cut off and surrounded. A strong infantry attack was delivered against the right of the 7th Division at 1.30 p.m., a short time after the G.O.C. 7th Division had moved two battalions of his reserve in rear of his right.

On receiving a report of the situation on the front of the 1st Division, Haig issued the following order:

> The line Frezenberg—Westhoek—bend of Main Road—Klein Zillebeke—bend of canal to be held at all costs.

From Haig and Gough I learned that Lomax had been badly wounded, Monro, commanding the 2nd Division, temporarily disabled, and several Divisional Staff Officers killed at 1.15 p.m. that afternoon, when the Headquarters of the 1st and 2nd Divisions were shelled. On this General Bulfin was ordered to take command of the 1st Division, handing over the command of the 2nd and 3rd Brigades to General Lord Cavan, commanding the 4th (Guards) Brigade. Amongst the dead was poor Freddie Kerr, of the Highland Light Infantry, whom I had known very well at Aldershot. He was a rising man, and one of the most promising young Staff Officers in the Army. But the worst news was that the 1st Division had broken back and were in full retreat, only a mile or so to the east of where we were standing, with the Germans at their heels.

What grieved me almost more than anything else was that

the 1st Corps should at last be forced back after the glorious stand they had made. I felt that they had done far more than could be expected of any men, and that even if they were driven to the sea they had earned their country's lasting gratitude for the determined fight they had made. No shadow of blame could be laid upon them or their commander.

I sought to express what I felt to Douglas Haig in order to try and soften the cruel blow I knew this catastrophe would be to him and to his command. To me, indeed, it seemed as though our line at last was broken. If this were the case, the immense numerical superiority of the enemy would render retreat a very difficult operation, particularly in view of the fact that Ypres and the River Yser lay in our immediate rear. Our only hope now seemed to be to make a stand on the line Ypres—Messines; but it was a great question whether this would be possible in face of a close and determined pursuit. Personally I felt as if the last barrier between the Germans and the Channel seaboard was broken down, and I viewed the situation with the utmost gravity.

It was a dramatic half hour, the worst I ever spent in a life full of vicissitudes such as mine had been.

It had a truly dramatic climax.

At about 3 p.m. a Staff Officer galloped up to the front of the château with the news that the 1st Division had rallied and again moved forward. Gheluvelt was once more in our hands!

The 1st Division had rallied on the line of the woods east of the bend of the Menin road; the German advance by the road had been checked by enfilade fire from the north.

What had happened was that the attack against the right of the 7th Division had forced its 22nd Brigade to retire, thus exposing the left of the 2nd Brigade (1st Division). The G.O.C. 7th Division used his reserve, already posted in this flank, to restore the line, but, in the meantime, the 2nd Brigade, finding their flank laid bare, had been forced to withdraw. The right of the 7th Division thus advanced as the left of the 2nd Brigade went back, with the result that the right of the 7th Division was exposed, but managed to hang on in its old trenches till nightfall.

At 2.40 p.m. the situation appeared so serious that orders

were issued that although every effort should be made to hold on to the line originally given, if that should be impossible, the line Verbranden Molen—Zillebeke—Halte—Potijze was to be held to the last.

But, as the events turned out, the pendulum was swinging towards us once more. On the Menin road a counter-attack delivered by the left of the 1st (Guards) Brigade and the right of the 2nd Division against the left flank of the German line was completely successful. By 3.30 p.m. Gheluvelt had been retaken with the bayonet by the 2nd Worcesters, admirably supported by the 42nd Brigade R.F.A. The left of the 7th Division, profiting by the recapture of Gheluvelt, advanced almost to its original line, and connection between the 1st and 7th Divisions was re-established.

I could not then discover who was actually responsible for this dramatic success or to whom the chief credit was due. The rally had been centred on the 2nd Worcesters (5th Brigade, 2nd Division), who behaved with the utmost gallantry.

It was not until some time after the battle that I ascertained that the original moving spirit had been Brigadier-General FitzClarence, V.C., Commanding the 1st Guards Brigade (1st Division).

Captain Thorne, who was Staff Captain of the 1st Guards Brigade on October 31st, made the following statement:

> On October 31st, 1914, the 2nd Batt. Worcester Regt. were in reserve to the 2nd Division who were on our left. About 8 a.m., finding the 1st Brigade rather pressed and having no reserve of our own, General FitzClarence got the loan of one company of the Worcesters, and this was placed along the railway line to Bercelaere, just north of Gheluvelt, to cover our right flank and to catch any Germans emerging from the village. This they did most successfully. Then a little later, when General FitzClarence found out how badly things were going on the right of the Scots Guards, he at once decided that an immediate counter-attack was to be made, and sent me off with orders to get hold of the remaining three companies of the Worcesters, and instruct the C.O. to counter-attack on the Scots Guards' right; the latter were holding the château.

The three companies then went up through the company lining the railway, through the château garden, drove the Germans out of the village north of the main road, and re-established the line. It was undoubtedly entirely on General FitzClarence's initiative that this counter-attack was made, as he gave me the order personally.

Major Hankey, who was commanding the 2nd Batt. of the Worcester Regt. on that day, fully corroborated Captain Thorne's account. He wrote:

> I feel perfectly certain that by shoving us in at the time and place he did, the General saved the day. If he had waited any longer, I don't think I could have got the battalion up in time to save the South Wales Borderers, and fill up the gap.

This most distinguished Irish Guardsman, FitzClarence, was killed a week or two later in the same part of the field, and his loss was most deeply felt.

I determined that every possible effort must be made to prevent the recurrence of such a situation as I had just witnessed, and at once hurried off to find Foch. He was with d'Urbal, and we all went thoroughly into the situation.

Foch told me that on the morning of the next day (November 1st) a French mixed force, up to the strength of a Division, would concentrate on the line St. Eloi—Wytschaete at daybreak, and advance from that line to attack the left flank of the forces in front of Haig. Similarly the 9th French Corps on Haig's left would be ordered to attack south-east against the enemy's right.

I sent Barry (one of my A.D.C.s) and Brinsley FitzGerald (my Private Secretary), who were both with me throughout the day, back to Haig with a full account of my interview with Foch. They returned later with the information that the line of the 1st Corps had been completely re-established, and that just before dark Kavanagh's 7th Cavalry Brigade (1st and 2nd Life Guards and Royal Horse Guards) had done some good work in driving back the enemy. At the end of the day the brigade again became available to close a dangerous gap which had occurred on the right of the 7th Division. In the woods the Household Cavalry encountered large numbers of Germans, whom they cleared out, capturing many prisoners and inflicting heavy losses. Haig reported that they were of great assistance in restoring the line.

Throughout this great day (October 31st) the flank of the 1st Corps had held fast to their ground. But the wooded country which intervened enabled superior forces of the enemy to penetrate to a dangerous extent between them.

In fighting such as this it was inevitable that troops should become much intermingled and mixed up. It was not only so as between larger or smaller units of the same Army, but also by reason of the fervent loyalty and fine feeling which has happily always been so strongly marked a feature amongst the Allies.

Throughout the day no effort was spared by any of the units engaged to afford each other the utmost mutual support without any regard to nationality, nor was there a moment's hesitation and time lost in waiting to get orders from superior authority.

Not many hours of darkness had elapsed, however, before new anxieties arose in connection with the line held by the cavalry on the Wytschaete—Messines ridge.

Events hardly less momentous than those of October 31st were before us.

CHAPTER 12

The Battle of Ypres

THIRD PHASE, NOVEMBER 1ST TO NOVEMBER 10TH.

The importance attached by the Germans to the fighting of October 31st and November 1st was emphasised by the presence of the Emperor at Courtrai. An intercepted wireless message informed us that he was to go to Hollebeke, no doubt with the intention of heading a "triumphal entry" into Ypres.

Our airmen endeavoured to give him as warm a reception as possible, and we had information that his quarters were changed at least once in consequence of their activity.

I issued an Order of the Day to the troops, announcing the presence of the august visitor on our front, and urging them to give His Majesty a good demonstration of what the "contemptible little army" could do. Right splendidly did they respond.

Throughout the night of the 31st-1st, the 2nd Cavalry Division was heavily attacked all along the Wytschaete-Messines ridge. The enemy gained a footing in the village of Wytschaete, broke through the line north of Messines and turned the left flank of the trenches held by the London Scottish. With devoted gallantry the reserve company of this battalion made repeated charges with the bayonet, which checked the enemy's advance and enabled the battalion to hold the position. This it did until daylight. The Germans were then discovered to be well round both flanks, and a retirement became inevitable. This was carried out very steadily under heavy rifle and machine-gun fire in the direction of Wulverghem.

At 3 a.m. the 12th Lancers, the Northumberland Fusiliers, and the Lincolns made a counter-attack and re-established the original line. The cavalry fought on foot with the bayonet in the narrow streets of the village, and were reported to me as equal to the best infantry in such work.

By 6.30 a.m. the enemy had been reinforced, and were able to drive back the 2nd Cavalry Division with the troops attached and reoccupy Wytschaete. This loss, coupled with the enemy's seizure of the ridge north of Messines, rendered the latter place untenable by the 1st Cavalry Division. They retired slowly to an entrenched line north of Wulverghem.

Somewhat the same kind of situation arose here now as on the day before at Gheluvelt. Since the night of October 30th the Cavalry Corps and attached troops had been holding on to the Wytschaete—Messines ridge against overwhelming numbers of the enemy. They were utterly exhausted, and the French marching to their succour were still some way off.

At 5 a.m. two battalions of the 2nd Corps were despatched from Bailleul to Neuve-Église, and further reinforcements were ordered to follow them an hour later. These troops had only themselves just got back into reserve, after a most trying and exhausting experience on the right of our line lasting for nearly three weeks. They also stood in dire need of rest, but they were the only reserves of any kind at my disposal.

At 10 a.m. on the 1st, the exhausted 2nd Cavalry Division was retiring on Mont Kemmel, which they were in no condition to hold if the enemy pressed on vigorously after them. But once again, as on the 31st, the situation was saved by a desperate effort. Some battalions of French infantry attacked on the left of the 2nd Cavalry Division and checked the enemy's advance, which was finally held off until, some time later, the head of the 16th French Army Corps arrived and regained the western end of Wytschaete.

The 3rd Corps had reported early in the morning that the position of its left flank was rendered precarious by the loss of Messines. With the support furnished by the 2nd Corps, as narrated above, Pulteney was able to draw back his left towards

Neuve-Église and form a flank facing north, covering the important artillery position on Hill 63. This move had threatened in flank the German advance on the Wytschaete—Messines ridge, and assisted greatly in securing the retirement of the cavalry in good order.

At 12.15 p.m. the situation was as follows:

The 1st Cavalry Division occupied an entrenched position running to the east and north-east of Wulverghem, in touch on the right with the reconstructed line of the 3rd Corps and on the left with the 2nd Cavalry Division.

After the successful advance of the French, the 2nd Cavalry Division was drawn in to the south of Wytschaete, and its left was in touch with the 16th French Corps holding the western border of that village.

The 1st Corps was also heavily attacked on November 1st. On the front held by the 1st Division, part of the 1st Brigade was driven from its trenches; but the position was retaken by counter-attack, and in the evening the line held was the same as on October 31st. The 1st Division was much exhausted and weakened by heavy losses. The 7th Division remained only 2,000 strong. The 3rd Cavalry Division was given temporarily to the 1st Corps, and assisted to hold the position. The 9th French Corps on the left of our 1st Corps was unable to make any progress during the day.

Information came in towards evening that the enemy was again massing against Gheluvelt. I went to Vlamertinghe to consult with Foch and d'Urbal, who told me that nine French battalions and some batteries would reach Ypres early on the morning of the 2nd. Foch promised me that he would at once dispatch two battalions of Zouaves to support Haig's centre.

Reviewing the situation as it presented itself on October 31st and November 1st, 1914, I believe that the vital interests of the British Empire were in great danger on both these days. That is to say, the whole coast-line from Havre to Ostend was within an ace of falling into the hands of the enemy.

In recalling the fateful hours of those two wonderful days and nights, I think we were perhaps in the greatest danger between

2 a.m. and 11 a.m. on Sunday, November 1st. Had the French 16th Corps arrived only an hour later than it did, the German advance from the line Wytschaete—Messines would have gained such volume, strength, and impetus, that nothing could have saved Mont Kemmel from falling into their hands. A vital wedge would have been driven into the very centre of our line.

The enormous numerical and artillery superiority of the Germans must be remembered. If they had turned the situation to full account, we should have seen all the French, British, and Belgian troops lying to the north of an east and west line through Mont Kemmel, cut off and hemmed against the coast.

The greatest threat of disaster with which we were faced in 1914 was staved off by the devoted bravery and endurance displayed by the Cavalry Corps under a commander, General Allenby, who handled them throughout with consummate skill. The same high praise must be given to those two redoubtable divisional leaders, Hubert Gough and de Lisle.

The cavalry was admirably supported and helped by Shaw and Egerton with the splendid battalions of infantry which composed the brigades they commanded, and none of us will ever forget how those French battalions on the left of the 2nd Cavalry Division checked the enemy by their gallant and determined advance at the most critical moment.

It is no disparagement, however, to the other troops engaged if I lay stress on the fact that it was the cavalry alone who, for more than a fortnight previously, had been disputing foot by foot every yard of the ground to the River Lys. They had fought day and night with the utmost tenacity, and the battles of October 31st and November 1st were but the climax to a long and bitter spell of heroic effort.

For the information of non-military readers, it is necessary for me to explain that a cavalry division fighting on foot is at a great disadvantage as compared with an infantry division. When horses cannot be used in the fighting, they have still to be looked after, and this takes many men away from the fighting line. A cavalry division consists ordinarily of three brigades, but when employed in the trenches they get little more than half that number into the firing line. They have nothing like the same gun power as an infantry division. But the mobility of the cavalry arm will always be found to compensate in large degree for these manifest disadvantages. Taking into account the losses they had suffered, they can hardly have opposed 2,000 rifles to the onslaught of what has been computed at more than two German Army Corps.

Of late years our custom has been to train our cavalry to fight on foot, and in the present war we have reaped the fruit of this wise policy. But the instinct which must be inculcated in the horse soldier to regard his horse as his chief reliance, must always disqualify him to some extent for the role which our cavalry were called upon to fulfil throughout the momentous issues in the history of the war of which this chapter treats. I may mention in passing that it was this same cavalry spirit, or instinct, with which the British cavalry is so strongly imbued, which enabled them to show to such splendid advantage in the mounted combats of the earlier phases of the war.

I must add a few words as to the fine part played in the fighting of November 1st by the Oxfordshire Hussars and the London Scottish. They were the first Territorial troops who fought in the war.

After disembarking at Dunkirk the Oxfordshire Hussars took part in the important operations connected with the Belgian retreat from Antwerp, and rendered most valuable aid in the defence of the Wytschaete—Messines ridge when that piece of ground was held with such marvellous tenacity by the Cavalry Division against overwhelming odds.

As for the London Scottish, their services on these two days are well summarised in a memorandum sent in to me by Allenby. He wrote:

> The London Scottish came under my orders on the evening of October 30th, 1914, and were detailed to the support of the 2nd Cavalry Division on the following morning. They went into action at 10 a.m., October 31st, with a strength of 26 officers and 786 men, and occupied trenches in conjunction with the 4th Cavalry

Brigade. They held these trenches throughout the day, being subjected from time to time to heavy artillery and machine-gun fire. From 9 p.m. onwards during the night October 31st—November 1st, the Germans attacked the trenches of the London Scottish continuously, and at 2 a.m. they succeeded in turning the left in large numbers. The situation was restored at the point of the bayonet by the Reserve Company. By daylight on November 1st the Germans had, however, turned both flanks, and it became necessary to retire. The retirement was directed on Wulverghem, and was carried out steadily under heavy rifle and machine-gun fire. At 8 a.m. the same morning, the London Scottish went forward again to take their places in the trenches alongside the 1st Cavalry Division, and there they remained until relieved at dusk that evening.

Throughout these operations, which lasted for two days, viz., October 31st and November 1st, the losses of the London Scottish amounted to 278, or about 34 per cent, of their strength. Rarely, if ever, have second line troops sustained unshaken so high a percentage of casualties.

E. H. H. *Allenby*

Lieut.-Gen., Commanding Cavalry Corps

I sent the following message to the Officer Commanding the London Scottish:

I wish you and your splendid regiment to accept my warmest congratulations and thanks for the fine work you did on Saturday. You have given a glorious lead and example to all Territorial Corps fighting in France.

I saw the battalion personally a few days later, and said a few words to the men on parade. How they had suffered was only too pathetically apparent. Whilst there was work to be done and an enemy to be held at bay no other thought filled any of their minds than to die fighting, if necessary, to the last man. But when these Territorials returned for a term of well-earned rest to their cantonments, with the excitement and danger behind them, a severe reaction came upon them. The heavy losses amongst their friends and comrades bowed them down with grief; for they necessarily lacked as yet the professional training and stoicism of men whose real business is war.

This exhibition of natural feeling only excited in me a deeper admiration for the splendid courage and endurance they had displayed when unsustained and unassisted by the influence of that iron discipline which only a long course of military training can inculcate. They were urged only by the spirit of *noblesse oblige*, and the higher ideals which inspire all who have taken up arms against the Germans in this war.

* * * * * * * *

On November 2nd, the 16th French Corps and Conneau's French Cavalry Division were holding the Wytschaete—Messines ridge, with a detachment of our 1st Cavalry Division supporting Conneau.

The troops who had fought so well on the 1st were absolutely tired out. They had suffered tremendous casualties and could not be counted on for the moment even as a reserve. They were withdrawn to rest and refit.

It was with great difficulty that the French troops were able to maintain themselves on the ridge. The Germans were very active, and the fight constantly swayed backwards and forwards. The western edge of the plateau and the outskirts of the villages marked the extreme limit of the Allied advance line.

For some days I had felt considerable anxiety as to the condition of the 1st Corps (1st and 2nd Divisions and the 7th Division).

I had constant messages from Haig asking that his tired troops might be given some rest after all their hard work; but I was driven almost to my wits' end to find means of giving him the relief he sought. His Chief of Staff (John Gough) came to my advanced Headquarters at Bailleul and discussed the subject fully with me.

I thought perhaps Foch might be able to help me; but when I went to interview him he said that, whilst the present crisis lasted, he could not spare a single man for this purpose. All I could do was to send two very tired brigades of the 2nd Corps up to Ypres on the morning of the 5th to relieve the 7th Division, who then came back into billets round Locre in a shattered condition.

The next day the remainder of the 2nd Corps (which was resting) followed to Ypres to afford what further relief was possible to the 1st Corps. The 2nd Corps was now scattered in detachments along the whole line, and the only reserves available were two or three lately arrived Territorial Battalions and the worn-out 7th Division, reduced to less than a brigade in strength.

Willcocks about this time felt anxiety as to the line his Indian troops were holding, and sent his Chief of Staff to me at Bailleul to ask if he could be reinforced. Under the conditions then existing, I was most anxious that the Indian Corps should hold its own without assistance and, after calling into consultation other officers of great Indian experience, I refused to do so, pointing out that he had four battalions of the 2nd Corps in close reserve behind him.

My faith in the Indian troops was justified, and a day or two later he reported that the Indians were doing well and that he was full of confidence in them.

On the night of the 3rd, I issued two Special Orders of the Day to the troops. They ran as follows:

Special Order of the Day
By Field-Marshal Sir John French, G.C.B., G.C.V.O., K.C.M.G. Commander-in-Chief, British Army in the Field.
1. The sphere of operations over which the British Army in France has been operating is now much contracted and rendered more compact. Since October 21st it has been possible to keep a considerable force in general reserve.
2. For several days past the enemy's activities against our front have been sensibly slackened, and it is quite possible that we may have entered upon the last stage of the great battle in which we have been engaged since October 11th. At this moment I am anxious to address a few words to the splendid troops I have the great honour to command. In view of the magnificent way in which the troops of the British Army have fought, the hardships they have had to endure, and the heavy losses they have suffered, it is right that all ranks, collectively and individually, should form a just and reasonable conception of the general situation and the object which we are endeavouring to attain.

3. It is necessary for this purpose to realise in the first place the true limits of the theatre of war as a whole, and then to take a comprehensive view of the entire course of operations as they have proceeded up to the present moment, in order to estimate the value of the results attained.

4. It must clearly be understood that the operations in which we have been engaged embrace nearly all the Continent of Central Europe from East to West. The combined French, Belgian and British Armies in the West and the Russian Army in the East are opposed to the united forces of Germany and Austria acting as a combined Army between us. Our enemies elected at the outset of the war to throw the weight of their forces against the Armies in the West, and to detach only a comparatively weak force, composed of very few first-line troops and several Corps of the second and third line, to stem the Russian advance until the Western forces would be completely defeated and overwhelmed.

5. The strength of our enemies enabled them from the outset to throw greatly superior forces against us in the West. This precluded the possibility of our taking a vigorous offensive, except when the miscalculations and mistakes made by their Commanders opened up special opportunities for a successful attack and pursuit.

The Battle of the Marne was an example of this, as was also our advance from St. Omer and Hazebrouck to the line of the Lys at the commencement of this battle. The role which our Armies in the West have consequently been called upon to fulfil has been to occupy strong defensive positions, holding the ground gained and inviting the enemy's attack; to throw these attacks back, causing the enemy heavy losses in his retreat, and following him up with powerful and successful counter-attacks to complete his discomfiture.

6. While we have been thus engaged, the Russian Armies in the East, numbering some three to four millions of men, have had time to mobilise and concentrate their immense forces scattered over all parts of their vast Empire. Our Eastern Allies have already inflicted a series of crushing

defeats on the Austro-German forces, and are now rapidly advancing on East Prussia and Silesia in great strength.

7. The value and significance of the splendid role fulfilled since the commencement of hostilities by the Allied Forces in the West lies in the fact that at the moment when the Eastern Provinces of Germany are about to be overrun by the numerous and powerful Armies of Russia, nearly the whole of the active army of Germany is tied down to a line of trenches extending from the Fortress of Verdun on the Alsatian frontier round to the sea at Nieuport, east of Dunkirk (a distance of 260 miles), where they are held, much reduced in numbers and morale, by the successful action of our troops in the West.

8. What the enemy will now do we cannot tell. Should they attempt to withdraw their troops to strengthen their weakened forces in the East, we must follow them up and harass their retreat to the utmost of our power. If they make further futile attempts to break through our lines, they must be again thrown back with greater and greater loss. The Armies of Russia are at their Eastern gates and will very soon be devastating their country and overthrowing their Armies. The great fight which you have so splendidly maintained against superior numbers in the Western theatre will be decided and completed by our brave Allies in the East, and I think that we on this side have reason to hope that we have completed the most severe and arduous part of our task. We must, however, be prepared for all eventualities, and I feel sure no effort will be relaxed to meet with the same undaunted front any situation, however unexpected, which may arise.

9. I have made many calls upon you, and the answers you have made to them have covered you, your regiments, and the Army to which you belong, with honour and glory. Your fighting qualities, courage and endurance have been subjected to the most trying and severe tests, and you have proved yourselves worthy descendants of the British soldiers of the past who have built up the magnificent traditions of the regiments to which you belong.

You have not only maintained those traditions, but you have materially added to their lustre.

It is impossible for me to find words to express my appreciation of the splendid services you have performed.

J. D. P. French
Field-Marshal
Commander-in-Chief, the British Army in the Field
November 2nd, 1914

Special Order of the Day
By Field-Marshal Sir John French, G.C.B., G.C.V.O., K.C.M.G. Commander-in-Chief, British Army in the Field
General Headquarters
November 2nd, 1914

The Field-Marshal Commanding-in-Chief has watched with the deepest admiration and solicitude the splendid stand made by the soldiers of His Majesty the King in their successful effort to maintain the forward position which they have won by their gallantry and steadfastness. He believes that no other Army in the world would show such tenacity, especially under the tremendous artillery fire directed against it.

Its courage and endurance are beyond all praise. It is an honour to belong to such an Army.

The Field-Marshal has to make one more call upon the troops. It is certainly only a question of a few days, and it may be of only a few hours, before, if they only stand firm, strong support will come, the enemy will be driven back, and in his retirement will suffer at their hands losses even greater than those which have befallen him under the terrific blows by which, especially during the last few days, he has been repulsed.

The Commander-in-Chief feels sure that he does not make his call in vain.

J. D. P. French
Field-Marshal
Commander-in-Chief, the British Army in the Field

During the early days of November, strong French reinforcements began to reach Ypres. The 20th French Corps detrained in that area on the 4th and 5th.

It was about this time that both our Intelligence Departments and that of the French became very optimistic on the subject of a great withdrawal of the Germans from the Western Front. The Russians were going on from one success to another, and large entrainments of German troops were reported at Roulers, Thourout, Tourcoing, and other places.

Whatever may have been really going on, our hopes were, as usual, doomed to disappointment, for the pressure on our front became greater and greater. But our eyes were always turned towards the East, and, as I have explained in a former chapter, the Russian "Will-o'-the Wisp" continued to uphold us and keep our eyes centred upon it.

Several Territorial units now began to be landed in France, amongst others the Artists' Rifles, the Honourable Artillery Company, the Queen's Westminsters and Hertfordshire Territorials, and the Warwickshire Battery of Horse Artillery. I spent a morning riding about amongst them, and was deeply impressed by the wonderful spirit which pervaded them. The only thought they had was to prepare themselves in the shortest possible time to take their part in the fighting at the front.

The Hertfordshire Battalion was commanded by an old friend of mine, whom I can never think of as other than "Tom Brand," under which patronymic I had served with him for a long time both in peace and war, and learnt his great soldierlike qualities. By this time, however, he had succeeded his father, the famous Speaker of the House of Commons, and had become Viscount Hampden. I watched him at the time of which I am writing exercising to the full the power, which he possessed in an extraordinary degree, of instilling the real fighting spirit in the men he commanded and afterwards led with such great skill and gallantry.

It was a power which he possessed in common with his intimate friend, Lord Cavan, who fought for a long time side by side with him in France. These two men bore a strong resemblance to one another in the marvellous influence they seemed to exercise over those under them. Both men struck me very much. Lord Cavan, like Hampden, was "a dug-out" and commanded first a brigade and then a division of the Guards, until he was selected for the command of an Army Corps, with the utmost gallantry and success.

Closely associated with my early recollections of the Territorials in France is the Artists' Rifles. They were, before the war, classified, with some few others, as an Officers' Training Corps. Our losses in officers in the campaign up to then had been prodigious, and I was trying to devise some means to fill up their ranks. What I saw of the Artists' Rifles and the men of which the Corps was composed, induced me to think of turning them to this purpose.

They were commanded by a most valuable and efficient officer, Colonel May. Him I consulted about it, and with his help an Officers' Training School was established, which was the first of many which have since sprung into existence. The Artists' Rifles were instrumental in quickly meeting some of our pressing needs in this important respect, and may be said to have laid the foundation of that Officers' School of War whose ramifications were soon to extend not only behind all the fighting lines, but throughout the United Kingdom. It is interesting to recall the fact that the conversion of certain picked Territorial battalions into Officers' Training Corps before the war was another of Lord Haldane's brilliant conceptions.

* * * * * * * *

Some fine work was done on the evening of the 6th by Kavanagh's 7th Cavalry Brigade, Cavan's 4th Guards Brigade and Lawford's 22nd Brigade of the 7th Division. Moncey's detachment of French troops, posted on the right of the 1st Corps, had been driven back over the canal, and a serious position was created.

Our troops counter-attacked with great effect, Lawford's Brigade (2nd Batt. The Queen's, 2nd Batt. R. Warwickshire Regt., 1st Batt. R. Welsh Fusiliers, and 1st Batt. S. Staffs Regt.) capturing a good many prisoners and machine guns. The counter-attack was successful, and the situation was restored.

We paid dearly for this success, however, in the loss of some very valuable lives. Amongst others Gordon Wilson, commanding the Blues, and Hugh Dawnay, commanding the 2nd Life Guards, were killed. Wilson was an excellent cavalry leader. He had done splendid work with the 3rd Cavalry Division ever since they landed, and his death left a big gap.

Up to three or four days before his death, Hugh Dawnay had been my liaison officer with the 1st Corps. The occasion of his going back to his regiment arose in this way. The 2nd Life Guards were getting very weak in officers, and he had an idea that he ought to be with them. He felt this very deeply, and told me so in a conversation we had together on the subject. The first time he spoke to me about it I told him that, whilst I sympathised with all he said, yet I considered it was his duty to remain where he was. I reminded him of the highly important work he was doing so well, and told him that it would be most difficult to replace him in that work, whereas it would be comparatively easy to put his regiment right as regards officers.

The next day he came back to me and repeated his request with great earnestness. He told me he could never be happy or contented in his mind if at this juncture he did not take his place beside his brother officers in his old regiment. It would indeed have been difficult for any soldier to refuse such a request, or fail to understand and enter into Dawnay's feelings.

I felt that it was weak of me to give way to him, but I did so on the understanding that his absence was only to be temporary. Of course, he might easily have been killed in the performance of his Staff duties, nevertheless when I heard he had fallen I felt that, in the interests of the service, I had done wrong in allowing him to go.

It is necessary to steel one's heart against any kind of sentiment when conducting a great war, and in the loss of one of the finest and most valuable young Staff Officers I have ever come across, I learnt a lesson never to be forgotten.

On several subsequent occasions similar requests were made to me without avail, notably in the case of my friend Clive of the Grenadiers, whose services and help I can never recall without admiration and gratitude.

On the night of the 6th came the information that the Austrians had been badly routed and driven across the San river by the Russians. Up went our hopes again like quick-silver; another week gone and we expected to see the Germans on our front weakened and reduced by the necessity of sending troops to save Silesia.

Our hopes and plans were fully discussed at a meeting held on Sunday, November 8th, at Foch's Headquarters at Cassel. Foch was in one of his most sanguine moods, and I must confess to having strongly felt the infection of his hopeful disposition. Our military barometer, however, went up and down as swiftly and suddenly as that of a ship in a typhoon.

What filled my immediate thoughts was the dire necessity of relieving the tired-out troops in the Ypres salient, and this was the point I impressed most strongly upon Foch who, it seemed to me, found it difficult to talk of anything but *"Attaque! Attaque! Attaque!"*

He gave me some help in this matter; indeed, as much as he could, I feel sure, but not before most of those gallant troops were called upon to withstand the new and terrible onslaught which I shall describe in the next chapter.

On the 9th we received the following gracious message from His Majesty the King:

To Sir John French
Expeditionary Force
November 9th, 1914
The splendid pluck, spirit and endurance shown by my troops in the desperate fighting which has continued for so many days against vastly superior forces fills me with admiration. I am confident in the final results of their noble efforts under your able command.
George, R.I.

The following reply was sent:

To His Majesty the King
Buckingham Palace
London
November 9th, 1914
Your Majesty's most gracious message has been received

by the officers and men of Your Majesty's Army in France with feelings of the deepest gratitude and pride. We beg to be allowed to express to Your Majesty our most faithful devotion and unalterable determination to uphold the highest traditions of Your Majesty's Army and carry the campaign through to a victorious end.
French

Throughout the phase of the battle narrated in this chapter, fighting went on with varying success all along the line from La Bassée to the sea. Ploegsteert Wood was the scene of many violent engagements. The 6th Division and 19th Brigade to the south were constantly at grips with the enemy. All along the valley of the Douve and the Wytschaete—Messines ridge the enemy was continuously active. But the point in the line which caused me the greatest anxiety was the dent between the 1st (British) and the 16th (French) Corps at the canal to the north of Hollebeke. It is not too much to say that only by the display of the greatest gallantry and endurance on the part of the 3rd Cavalry Division and the other troops engaged at that point was the enemy prevented from getting dangerously near our communications.

CHAPTER 13

The Battle of Ypres

FOURTH AND FINAL PHASE, NOVEMBER 11TH
TO THE END OF THE BATTLE

Each of the four phases into which I have divided this very brief and incomplete narrative of the Battle of Ypres is marked by one important and far-reaching crisis.

In the beginning of the battle came the arrest of the German advance on the Channel ports, and the brilliant repulse of the enemy back to the Lys by the cavalry under Allenby and the 3rd Corps under Pulteney. The second phase is distinguished by the crisis of October 31st, while in the third phase occurs the memorable stand of the cavalry and other troops under Allenby on the Wytschaete—Messines ridge.

The great feature of the fourth and last phase was the desperate assaults made against the Ypres salient on the 11th and 12th November, in which the flower of the Prussian Guard participated, having received the Emperor's personal command to make certain of finally breaking our line.

It was in the same conference room at Cassel in which I had been with Foch on the 8th, and where, as I have said, we mutually indulged in day-dreams of imminent victory, that, on the evening of November 10th, I received the reports which warned me that another great crisis was at hand.

Foch informed me that an attack on a great scale had just begun against his line between Ypres and the sea. He had received reliable reports that the enemy had brought up five fresh corps from the south. He said that the Germans had already gained possession of the village of Dixmude, but had not yet crossed the Yser, which French Marines and Belgians were holding against them. He added that he was being heavily pressed and was losing ground near Langemarck, and declared that he must move Conneau's Cavalry Division (holding the line opposite Messines) north to support him, and he asked me to put Allenby in to relieve Conneau. I agreed to this, and gave orders accordingly.

Early on the morning of the 11th, Haig reported that his position was being heavily shelled, and that he was threatened with a powerful attack. Two fresh German Army Corps had come up in his front, namely, the Guard and the XVth.

In short, the Germans were about to deliver their final desperate blow, which they hoped and believed would at last open up to them the road to the sea.

The situation was met by Haig with the same grim determination, steadfast courage and skilful forethought which had characterised his handling of the operations throughout. A volume might easily be written of this day's fighting of November 11th, but it is only possible in these pages to glance at the particular points in the line of battle where the fighting was fiercest, and where the issues were most vital at different hours of the day.

Up the Menin road came the first tremendous onslaught at 9.30 a.m. on the front held by the 1st (Guards), 7th, and 15th Brigades. At the first clash of arms the Germans pierced our line with a rush. This was splendidly disputed by the Royal Fusiliers under McMahon, their devoted and gallant leader, who was killed; while the battalion was almost annihilated. Reserves, however, quickly came up, counter-attacks were organised and delivered, and the line was re-established.

About noon the critical point changed to the right at the canal, where the French were driven out of their trenches and fell back on Verbranden Molen. General Vidal called on our 1st Corps for support and help. The heavy fighting in the neighbourhood of the Menin road had used up most of his reserves, and the enemy were still clinging to the woods in that part of the line and threatening renewed attacks; but, in spite of this,

Haig was able to render the French sufficient help to enable them to make a little headway, though the situation in this part of the line was in doubt and caused anxiety all day.

About 1.30 p.m. a fresh attack of great violence was delivered further north against the 5th Brigade. This was thrown back mainly by our artillery fire.

About 3 p.m. the enemy began to mass in the woods about the Menin road, near the centre of our line. On attempting to advance, however, they were caught between two fires, from the north-east and south-west, the Oxfordshire L.I. and the Northamptons turning them out of the woods at the point of the bayonet.

Severe fighting went on till nightfall, units becoming much intermixed. The losses were very heavy indeed, the 1st (Guards) Brigade mustering at night only four officers and 300 men.

The final result of this magnificent defence was that the attack was repulsed with terrible loss to the enemy, and the original line practically held throughout, save for the loss of some few and unimportant trenches.

Brigadier-General FitzClarence, V.C., to whom reference has already been made, was killed. His name has justly become famous for many gallant deeds, but more particularly in connection with the crisis of October 31st.

The success of this great defence, like those which preceded it, was due in the first place to the quick grasp of the situation by Sir Douglas Haig, who so skilfully handled the scanty forces at his disposal, and economised his few reserves with such soldier-like foresight. Mutual support at critical moments was ensured by the wholehearted co-operation of commanders of all units, great and small. No words can express my sense of the gratitude which the country owes to the young officers, to the non-commissioned officers, and to the rank and file of this invincible army. When all has been said, it was their courage and endurance which spoke the last word.

Whilst we were thus fully occupied about the Menin road, the French were also being attacked all along their line to the north of Ypres, but the enemy was held off.

In accordance with the arrangements made with Foch, the

Cavalry Corps took over the line opposite Messines on the morning of the 11th, when Conneau's cavalry marched north. Allenby was reinforced by two battalions of the 8th Division, these battalions being replaced by two Territorial battalions.

In the evening de Lisle's (1st) Cavalry Division was sent to reinforce Haig, to whom were also dispatched the Hertfordshire Territorial battalion and two yeomanry regiments from St. Omer.

The situation north of Hollebeke at the canal (which the Germans had now crossed) was a source of much anxiety to me, and I made strong representations to Foch as to the necessity of strengthening his troops at that important point. He promised to reinforce Vidal at once with three battalions of chasseurs.

On the evening of the 11th, Field-Marshal Lord Roberts arrived at my Headquarters on a visit, accompanied by his daughter, Lady Aileen (now Countess) Roberts. It is needless to say with what enthusiasm the Field-Marshal was welcomed everywhere.

The martial fire, which was the life-long characteristic of this great soldier, burnt as brightly within him during these last few days of his life as when he earned his Victoria Cross on the eastern battlefields over 60 years before. His presence, particularly at this critical time, in the midst of the army he loved so well—love which they returned to the full—acted as a timely inspiration and incentive to our weary and hard-pressed troops.

That the tremendous energy of the great soldier remained unimpaired to the last was proved to me on the night of his arrival. He dined at my Headquarters' mess, and after dinner I had a long conversation with him on the situation. It was getting late, and I suggested that, as he had a hard day before him on the morrow, he should go to his quarters and get some rest.

He asked me when I generally got to bed. I told him that I took rest when I could, but never knew exactly when it would be possible. I added as an example of this that a conference was fixed for that night between 12 and 1 o'clock, when we hoped all the reports would be in. Nothing that I urged could dissuade him from remaining up and attending that conference, which he followed with his usual clearness of mind and acute perception, although it lasted into the small hours of the morning.

The early dawn of the next day saw him perfectly fresh, going out to visit his beloved Indians.

On the evening of Friday the 13th the Field-Marshal was suddenly taken very ill on his return home from visiting troops in the front, and he died on Saturday, the 14th, at about 8 p.m.

On the morning of Tuesday, November 17th, a military funeral service was held at St. Omer, which was attended by everyone who could get there. Generals Foch and de Maud'huy represented the French Army. The Indian Princes attached to the Indian Corps were also present, and the Maharajah Sir Pertab Singh took his place on the motor hearse and acted as a personal guard over the remains of the great chief on his last sad journey to England.

General de Maud'huy paid an impressive tribute to the dead Field-Marshal in the following General Order which he issued to the 10th Army, dated November 16th, 1914.

General Order No 44
Lord Roberts, Field-Marshal in the British Army, died yesterday at General Headquarters of the British Army.
The illustrious conqueror of Afghanistan and South Africa had come, in spite of his great age, to visit the battlefields where at the present time his valiant soldiers are fighting. Up to the moment when death struck him down, he pursued the object to which he devoted his whole life, the greatness of England.
The General Commanding the 10th Army is voicing the feeling of all ranks under his command, both officers and men alike, when he says to Marshal French and to the General Officer Commanding the Indian Corps, that the 10th Army fully shares in the mourning of our Allies today.
May the example afforded by the famous British Marshal up to the end be understood and felt by us all. Lord Roberts has died in an hour of mighty battles, in the midst of the troops which he loved so well. No end can be more enviable, none more glorious for a soldier.
De Maud'huy

During the 12th the enemy attempted renewed attacks on

either flank of the 1st Corps, but was repulsed with great loss. Although the troops holding the Ypres salient were hard pressed and got little rest until they were relieved by the French, still it may be said that these attacks were practically the last of the really determined and nearly successful efforts made by the Germans during the First Battle of Ypres.

The French were able to retake some of the ground they had lost, although the enemy still held on to Dixmude.

From November 12th onwards, the chief anxiety I had was to get relief and rest for the troops which had been fighting so desperately in the Ypres salient, particularly the 1st Corps. I had long interviews with Foch, and represented to him the necessity for French troops to take over the whole of the ground there, at any rate for a time. At first he said there would be a great difficulty in doing this; but finally he promised to meet my wishes and agreed to start carrying out the relief on Sunday, the 15th, at latest.

On this I told Haig that no more troops would be sent to him, but that he would be gradually withdrawn into reserve as he was relieved by French troops. The 1st Corps troops were to be withdrawn before any others, and brought into reserve as quickly as possible. Foch was as good as his word. On the night of the 15th, the French 9th Corps took over some of Haig's trenches and released two brigades of the 1st Division, as well as some artillery. These all came into reserve on the 16th at Locre and Westoutre.

On the 13th our front on the Ypres salient was heavily shelled from 10 a.m., and infantry attacks commenced at 1 p.m. up the Menin road and against the 6th and 7th Brigades (1st Batt. The King's (Liverpool) Regt., 2nd Batt. S. Staffs Regt., 1st Batt. R. Berks Regt., 1st Batt. K.R.R. and 3rd Batt. Worcester Regt.; 2nd Batt. S. Lancs., 1st Batt. Wilts Regt., and 2nd Batt. R. Irish Rifles). The latter had their line broken, but it was restored by a counter-attack. The enemy lost heavily.

Heavy attacks were made early on the 14th against the 9th Brigade (1st Batt. Northumberland Fusiliers, 4th Batt. Royal Fusiliers, 1st Batt. Lincs. Regt. and 1st Batt. R. Scots Fusiliers) in the same area, and later these developed along the whole front, but the Germans were everywhere driven back.

On the 15th the Indian Corps became heavily engaged between Armentières and La Bassée. Some trenches were lost and regained during the day, and the enemy made no progress. On the early morning of this day a very gallant piece of work was carried out on our Ypres front by a storming party which was led by Co.-Sergt.-Major Gibbon of the 5th Battn. Northumberland Fusiliers. On the previous evening the enemy had gained possession of some buildings within our line. A gun was brought up by a cleverly-concealed route to the closest range, the buildings were battered down and our position restored at the point of the bayonet.

On the 17th the Ypres salient was again the scene of heavy encounters. There was severe fighting, but we had a very successful day, inflicting great loss on the enemy south of the Menin road.

The 21st marked the end of the Battle of Ypres, and I had the satisfaction of seeing our troops completely evacuate the Ypres salient. The whole of the 1st Corps and the cavalry were in reserve. The fourteen battalions of the 2nd Corps, which had been moved up to support the 1st Corps in the north, marched to rejoin their Corps north of Bailleul.

* * * * * * * *

I cannot close the narrative of this great battle without particularly emphasising the part which was played by the 1st Corps. They were thrown in suddenly to fill up the gap through which the Germans were preparing to pour in troops in order to seize the Channel seaboard. They were called upon to advance and make good their ground in the teeth of numbers three or four times their own strength and against a much more powerful artillery. For five weeks they fought day and night continuously against vastly superior forces, and against artillery always far above their own in strength and numbers.

In the great campaigns of the past we find special units singled out and handed down to fame, such as "The Light Division" under Crawford in the Peninsular War or "The Brandenburg Corps" under Prince Frederick Charles of Prussia in the Franco-German War of 1870. I think we may rest assured that history will label the 1st British Corps in this war with some such distinguished sobriquet. Well and truly did they earn it.

I append the record of the losses of the 1st Corps in the battle up to November 21st, when they were relieved. It speaks more eloquently than any words of mine of the great role it played in this tremendous struggle.

FRANCE.

CASUALTIES OF THE FIRST BATTLE OF YPRES.

	Killed (including Died of Wounds and Died other causes).		Wounded.		Missing (including Prisoners).		Total.	
	Off.	O.R.	Off.	O.R.	Off.	O.R.	Off.	O.R.
1st Corps (1st and 2nd Divisions), Oct. 15th to Dec. 21st, 1914, inclusive.	127	1,666	316	7,669	74	3,663	517	12,998
7th Division (Oct. 27th to Nov. 7th, 1914), inclusive	49	425	114	1,328	83	1,644	246	3,397 + (a) 734 + (b) 765
7th Brigade (less 3rd Worcesters, but including 1st Gordons), Nov. 5th to 20th inclusive.	8	91	12	315	—	94	20	500 + (c) 327
9th Brigade (less 1st Scots. Fusiliers, but including 2nd K.O.S.B.), Nov. 5th to 20th; 1st Royal Scots Fusiliers, Nov. 10th to 20th.	3	110	16	358	4	393	23	861 + (d) 310
15th Brigade (viz., 1st Bedfords, 1st Cheshires, with 2nd Duke of Wellington's added Nov. 5th to 20th; 1st R.W. Kent and 2nd K.O.Y.L.I., Nov. 12th to 20th.	10	128	18	420	5	275	33	823 + (e) 131
56th Field Coy. Divisional Mounted Troops of 3rd and 5th Divisions, Nov. 12th to 20th.	—	4	—	27	—	—	—	31
Total	197	2,424	476	10,117	166	6,069	839	18,610 + 2,264

(a) 2nd Scots Fusiliers, unclassified, 27/10 to 4/11/14.
(b) 1st S. Staffs, unclassified, 20/10 to 7/11.
(c) 2nd S. Lancs, unclassified, 20/10 to 24/10.
(d) 4th Royal Fusiliers, unclassified, 11/11/14.
(e) 1st Scots Fusiliers, unclassified, 10 to 12/11.

C2 Cas—6/11/17.

CHAPTER 14

Entry of the Territorial Army

On November 16th the Prince of Wales joined the Army in the Field. It was the first time since the days of the Black Prince that the Heir Apparent to the Throne had taken the field in war. His Royal Highness was received by the troops with delight and acclamation. The courage, devotion and endurance which he has since displayed on active service have secured him the love and admiration of every officer, non-commissioned officer and man of His Majesty's Army, and his name will descend in history, bright with the honour which he won in the field.

Early in the month a certain amount of heavy artillery began to arrive in France. Special positions were selected and prepared all along the front, and the few guns we had were interchanged between them as occasion required.

It was from such crude beginnings that we reached the wonderful developments in the use of heavy artillery which have been witnessed during the progress of the war. It is of some interest to compare the number of 6-in. guns and over which we had at that time, with the number which were deployed on the same front later in the war.

During the latter part of the First Battle of Ypres the weather was very wet and stormy. The rain gave place to cold northerly winds, and on the afternoon of November 19th there was a heavy fall of snow. That evening a hard frost set in which lasted for several days. The men in the trenches began to suffer severely.

It was at this time, the third week of November, 1914, that the serious evil known as "Trench Feet" first made its appearance in the Army in France. The cases were at first labelled "Frost Bite," but as they were subsequently found to occur without any fall of the temperature to freezing point, this term was evidently a misnomer. Indeed, cases have occurred during the month of August.

The condition is caused by prolonged immersion in water, and certainly can occur when the temperature of the water is as high as 50°F. It is seldom caused unless the immersion is as long as 24 hours, but the cooler the water the less is the time required to produce it. In most cases the temperature of the water has been below 40°.

In addition to cold water, the onset is favoured by—
(a) Prolonged standing in one position, as is often the case with men deep in mud.
(b) Tight puttees and tight boots.
(c) Exhaustion and want of food.
(d) A natural tendency to feeble circulation, *e.g.*, men who suffer from chilblains.
(e) Lying out, after being wounded, in wet and cold weather.

The condition observed varies very much according to the severity of the case:
(a) The feet may be merely very painful and tender.
(b) Much more often they are very swollen and cold, with but little feeling in them.
(c) Frequently the whole foot is like a big "chilblain" and is very hot, red and swollen. *Blisters* are common in all such feet.
(d) The toes may be black and the foot blue.
(e) The toes especially, and the foot much more rarely, may die and become gangrenous.

Except in slight cases, the men affected are quite unfit for duty for two or three months at least, especially for duty in trenches in cold weather. If men are sent back to duty too soon, a short exposure at once brings back all the trouble in an aggravated form. Of course, if gangrene occurs, the man is permanently invalided.

The only *real* preventative is to arrange that the men do not remain deep in mud or cold water for prolonged periods. If this is not possible, cases of *trench feet* are inevitable. Apart from avoiding this, the primary cause, various subsidiary causes can be guarded against; and, from the experience gained in dealing with the condition, the following instructions were formulated and communicated to the officers in charge of the men:

(1) Boots and puttees should not fit tightly and must be taken off once *at least* every 24 hours and the feet well rubbed and cleaned, dry socks put on.

(2) The feet should be kept as clean as possible so as to avoid septic complications in case of blistering.

(3) *Rubber thigh-boots* should be supplied to all men in waterlogged trenches, and these should be large enough to take two pairs of socks.

(4) Trench-boards should be provided, or brushwood or straw laid down.

(5) Men should be kept dry by the use of mackintosh over the shoulders.

(6) Hot food should be supplied whenever this is possible.

It is, of course, evident that all these precautions are often quite unobtainable. In the Ypres region in the winter of 1914-1915 many men stood for days and nights up to the middle in water, and some of the communication trenches were impassable because of the depth of the water. Indeed, a good many men were drowned.

The treatment varies with the severity of the case. Rest with the feet up and careful washing of the feet is all that is at first needed in slight cases. If there are blisters or sores these must be treated. Later on various forms of electrical treatment and massage are of use. In all but slight cases treatment does not prevent the man being unable to walk for many weeks without pain.

The number of men invalided for trench feet during the winter of 1914-1915 was over 20,000. The 27th Division lost 3,000 men the first week they were in the trenches in February. With good trenches and proper care trench feet should be of rare occurrence. If under these conditions they are numerous, someone is to blame. As a result of the experience gained during the winter of 1914-1915 and the adoption of the recommendations issued, in the winters 1915-1917, in the Ypres salient, the trench feet cases did not average more than two a day in an army of over 200,000 men.

* * * * * * * *

It was in the closing days of the First Battle of Ypres that the bulk of the Territorial troops sent to France at that time entered the fighting line.

In the course of a telegram which I received from Lord Kitchener on November 2nd, the Secretary of State for War said:

> The total number of Territorial Battalions in France and ordered there is 19. I am selecting two more to make up one per Brigade.

These arrangements had been made in response to my urgent requests that whatever Territorial regiments of yeomanry or battalions of infantry were ready and available should be sent to France at once and incorporated with the regular forces there, and that we should not wait for the divisional formations to be prepared and completed.

The history of the Territorials is well known. The Volunteers, from which the Territorial Army sprang, came into being in the years just following the Crimean War.

For some 10 to 20 years afterwards the Volunteers may be said to have met with little better than derision. It was said that they only wanted to wear a uniform and play at soldiers, and hardly anyone believed in the wonderful spirit which really animated them from the start. The military and other authorities gave them but little help and hardly any encouragement, in fact they refused to take the Volunteers seriously.

In spite of all these drawbacks this wonderful force, under the leadership of such men as the late Lord Wemyss, Lord MacDonald, and others, went steadily on, struggling against adversity, but increasing in strength all the time. The great patriotic spirit which has always been the soul of the Volunteers, was kept alive by their great leaders in face of slights and neglect, but it was reserved for Lord Haldane to devise the scheme which was to make the fullest use of the Volunteers and bring them to the zenith of their reputation. He realised that their patriotic ardour might be put to good purpose, and drafted the scheme whereby, whilst remaining volunteers, they were formed into a great Territorial Army, administered by the so-called Territorial County Associations, to whose energy and devotion the country owes so much.

The result of Lord Haldane's statesmanlike foresight has been clear to anyone who, during the past four years, has cast his eyes across the Channel and seen the splendid behaviour of our citizen soldiers in the field.

I have spoken already elsewhere of what I have always regarded as our great initial administrative mistake in the war, namely, the raising of an entirely new Army, when the machinery for expanding the Territorial Force—especially established by Lord Haldane for the purpose—I mean the Territorial County Associations—was already at hand and would have proved by far the most efficient and economical method of raising the troops required.

Lord MacDonald and those who are left of the early Volunteer soldiers must, in their old age, rejoice in the knowledge that they have lived to see the force, which they tended and nurtured against such appalling difficulties, actually for several months standing between the Empire and disaster.

Such a spirit as that which the Volunteers cultivated and maintained is bound sooner or later to make itself felt, and, as the years rolled on, the country came at last dimly and slowly to realise the Volunteers' true value. They figured in the field as early as 1882 in the Egyptian Campaign, and played their part afterwards in much greater numbers throughout the South African War.

After Lord Kitchener had made his call upon the country for the New Armies, the Territorials found themselves neglected and put in the shade.

It is true that by the terms of their engagement, Territorial soldiers were only available for home defence; but even in peace time a certain proportion of the force had volunteered to serve anywhere in case of war, and it was always anticipated that, when the necessity arose, a renewed call would be made upon the whole force to do likewise. The response to the call which was subsequently made upon them shows quite clearly that, had they been asked at first, they would have come forward almost to a man.

However, as it turned out, they were ignored and the call was never made upon them. Officers and men alike, naturally and inevitably made up their minds that they were not wanted and would never be used for any other purpose than that for which they had originally taken service, namely, the defence of the United Kingdom.

But the time for the employment of troops other than the Regulars of the old Army arrived with drastic and unexpected speed. The wastage of war proved to be so enormous that the fighting line had to be reinforced almost before the new Armies were in existence.

It was then that the country in her need turned to the despised Territorials.

The call came upon them like a bolt from the blue. No warning had been given. Fathers and sons, husbands and brothers, left families, homes, the work and business of their lives, almost at an hour's notice to go on active service abroad.

It seems to me that we have never realised what it was these men were asked to do. They were quite different to professional soldiers, who are kept and paid through years of peace for this particular purpose of war; who spend their lives practising their profession and gaining promotion and distinction; and who, on being confronted with the enemy, fulfil the great ambition of their lives.

Equally distinct were the Territorials also from what has been called the New Army, whose officers and men had ample time to prepare themselves for what they were required to do.

I wonder, sometimes, if the eyes of the country will ever be opened to what these Territorial soldiers of ours have done.

I say without the slightest hesitation that without the assistance which the Territorials afforded between October, 1914, and June, 1915, it would have been impossible to have held the line in France and Belgium, or to have prevented the enemy from reaching his goal, the Channel seaboard.

Between the beginning of November and the end of the Battle of Ypres, Territorial battalions were constantly arriving. A special training camp was formed for them at St. Omer under a selected commander. This post was admirably filled first by Brigadier-General Chichester, and later by Brigadier-General Oxley.

I have already told of the fine work done by the Oxfordshire Hussars and the London Scottish—the first Territorials to enter the line of battle.[1] Their splendid example was well followed, and the record they established nobly maintained by each unit of the Territorial Army as it successively took its place in the trenches.

Of these units, the Warwickshire Horse Artillery Battery detrained at St. Omer in the beginning of November. Of the cavalry, the Oxfordshire Hussars disembarked at Dunkirk about the middle of September; the Northumberland Hussars came to France in October; the Leicestershire, North Somerset, Essex and Northampton Regiments of Yeomanry during November; and the Surrey towards the end of December.

All these units received a course of training in the St. Omer camp of instruction. I often rode amongst them, and was much impressed by the fine material in men, horses and equipment of which they were composed, and with the rapid progress which they made.

I knew from my experience as Inspector of Yeomanry a good many years ago what efforts these Yeomanry Regiments had for a long time made to live up to the times and render themselves efficient. Although I now found that the old type of hunting farmer was not so fully represented in their ranks as formerly, yet a valuable leavening of this class still remained, and they were for the most part commanded and officered by county men of position and influence, accustomed to hunting, polo and field sports.

In a very short time we were able to use the Yeomanry in the front line. The Oxfordshire, Leicestershire, North Somerset and Essex were incorporated in brigades of the Cavalry Divisions, and the Northumberland, Northampton and Surreys were employed as Divisional Cavalry. The same practical value attached to the Warwickshire Battery of Horse Artillery, upon which Lord Brooke had expended so much time and energy for years preceding the war.

1: The North and South Irish Horse went to France much earlier than these troops but were employed as special escort to G.H.Q.

Twenty-three battalions of Territorial infantry were sent to France in 1914. Of these the London Scottish and the infantry battalion of the Honourable Artillery Company arrived in September. The 5th Border Regt., Artists' Rifles, 6th Welsh, 5th Black Watch, Queen's Westminsters, 10th Liverpools (Scottish), 13th London (County of London), 8th Royal Scots, 9th Highland Light Infantry, 5th Scottish Rifles, 9th London Regt., 4th Royal Welsh Fusiliers, 2nd Monmouths, Hertfordshire, 4th Seaforth Highlanders, 4th Suffolks, 6th Cheshires, and 6th Gordon Highlanders arrived in November, whilst the 7th Argyll and Sutherland Highlanders and the 12th London came in December.

These units were all put through a course of training at St. Omer. There was a great difference between individual battalions as regards their actual condition when they came out, and the time required to prepare them to take their places in the trenches.

Some were much better commanded and officered than others. There was a marked distinction to be noted in their physique and quality. But, on the whole, it may be fairly said that they promised to furnish most valuable reinforcements to our severely tried army. The energy they displayed and the progress they made were really wonderful.

As Inspector-General of the Forces between 1908 and 1912, I had constant opportunities of watching the training of the Territorial Army in the first years of its existence as such. I was familiar with the earnest and successful endeavours they had made to profit by the vastly improved conditions and status secured to them by Lord Haldane's wise and skilful administration. The same zeal which characterised them so remarkably as Volunteers was applied in greater force and with intensified confidence when, as Territorials, they were organised, commanded, staffed, equipped and trained on sound methods and up-to-date lines.

All this seven or eight years' experience operated to the greatest advantage when these Territorial battalions arrived in the theatre of war and commenced their final preparation to fill the gaps in our line, through which, as I have shown, the Germans must have penetrated had the Territorial Army not existed to step into the breach.

The H.A.C. was the first unit to follow the London Scottish. I inspected them at the front on November 9th—the day upon which they joined the Indian Corps—and they presented a splendid appearance. I never saw a finer lot of men. They afterwards established a record in the war which is well worthy of the fine old corps from which they spring.

The Queen's Westminsters and the 8th Royal Scots only embarked on the 1st and 4th of November respectively, yet their condition was so good that they were able to be sent to the front immediately after the H.A.C.

The Queen's Westminsters were sent to the 7th Division to relieve the Artists' Corps, which then became an Officers' Training Corps.

I saw a great deal of the Hertfordshires during the very few days they were training at Headquarters, and found them a particularly fine regiment. Although they only embarked on November 5th, they were at Ypres in the 1st Corps Reserve ten or eleven days later and before the end of the battle. The 10th Liverpools have a fine record. They embarked on November 1st and joined the 9th Brigade on the 25th of the month south of Wytschaete, where they were in the first line trenches on the 27th, between the Royal Fusiliers on the left and the 5th (Northumberland) Fusiliers on the right.

The 9th Highland Light Infantry were incorporated in the 5th Brigade (2nd Division) on November 24th, about ten days after their arrival in the country. The 2nd Monmouths, the London Rifle Brigade, and the 5th Scottish Rifles were incorporated in the 3rd Corps on November 19th, after some eleven or twelve days in the country.

Many other examples can be quoted to show how quickly these Territorial troops, following the lead given to them by the Oxfordshire Hussars and the London Scottish, accustomed themselves to the severe and trying conditions of war, and of what real value they were at this critical time.

The inexperience of regimental officers was, of course, the greatest difficulty we had to contend with when these troops first took the field. This was a most serious drawback in view of the vastly increased responsibility which falls upon leaders of all ranks in war as it is conducted today, but they improved beyond all expectation, and every week found them more efficient.

I have so far spoken of the Territorial Army in regard to its employment in units of regiments and battalions at a most critical time in the war, when reinforcements were badly needed. I come now to the time when, a few months later, they entered into the campaign as complete divisions.

The great mass of military opinion held that the highest practical unit in which Territorial soldiers could be organised was the brigade of four battalions. The regular gunner had no use for Territorial horse and field artillery. Engineer Volunteers had for some time existed, but only in small numbers and in particular localities. Although the Army Service Corps and the Army Medical Corps had for years been represented in the Volunteer Forces by small units and detachments, it was never considered that those services could be efficiently and practically performed by any but "whole-timers."

Backed up by the opinion and advice of a very few soldiers of experience, the Secretary of State for War cast all this prejudice to the winds, and determined upon a regular and complete divisional organisation for the Territorials. It was indeed a great and courageous decision.

"What!" exclaimed the gold-bedizened smart young horse artillery commander, "do you mean to say you are going to allot Territorial horse artillery batteries to your mounted brigade? You must be mad! It takes years even to approach the necessary degree of efficiency."

The field gunner, immersed in his latest developments to ensure the utmost accuracy of fire, the howitzer and heavy field artillery expert, the scientific and highly-trained sapper, all joined in the hue and cry, until Lord Haldane's conceptions almost collapsed and expired in a ferment of ridicule. But he remained steadfast. The mounted brigades received their Territorial batteries of horse artillery. Fourteen complete Territorial divisions were formed of three brigades of infantry, three brigades of field artillery, one brigade of howitzers, one brigade of heavies, field and signal companies of Engineers, companies of Army Service Corps and Army Medical Corps.

Lord Haldane had only some eight or nine years to wait for his reward. Within that time he saw his Territorials doing splendid and invaluable work as complete divisions in the field, and fighting with success against the most powerful and efficient army in the world. When I say he "got his reward," I may well be misunderstood. He got nothing but calumny and grossly unjust abuse; but the "reward" to such a man does not come in the ordinary way. He had proved the value of his great work, and that is all the reward he ever wanted.

It is to this organisation that I largely attribute the success of the Territorials in the field throughout the war. Each unit learned by degrees its own relative place and position in the great divisional machine. Enthusiasm was raised in the idea engendered in all ranks that they formed part of a great engine of war, furnished by their own counties and immediate neighbourhoods. At first, certainly, they were crude and untrained, but every day they improved through instruction, and developed great intelligence under a thorough and practical exposition of the objects to be aimed at.

The strength of the new arrangement lay chiefly in the fact that each division was commanded by an experienced general officer of the regular forces, assisted by a well-selected and competent staff of regular officers.

Six divisions in all arrived in France between November 3rd, 1914, and April 30th, 1915, namely, the 46th (North Midland), the 47th (London), the 48th (South Midland), the 49th (West Riding), the 50th (Northumbrian), and the 51st (Highland).

A prominent part was taken in the fighting of 1915 by all these divisions, as will be more fully recounted in subsequent pages.

CHAPTER 15

After the First Battle of Ypres

At this time all our ideas in regard to the framing of plans in the West were evolved and guided almost entirely by the progress of the campaign in Poland and Galicia.

After the battle of the Marne, when we were at the Aisne, we were still hopeful of effecting a great flanking movement which should lead to more or less decisive results, or at least clear Northern France and Belgium of the enemy's troops. It has been shown how the development of events obliged us to modify our hopes and anticipations until, at the close of the first battle of Ypres, we certainly felt at our own G.H.Q. that the Allied Forces in Great Britain, France and Belgium, could effect nothing of importance unless and until one of two things happened.

Either there must be a considerable augmentation of our forces, including a vastly increased supply of heavy artillery, machine guns, trench artillery and ammunition—*or*, the enemy's forces on the Western front must be so weakened by the necessity of sending troops to stem the Russian advance in the East, as to enable the Allies with their available forces to assume the offensive with success.

Now the only resources in regard to *personnel* upon which the Allies at that time had to depend for any considerable accession of strength was the British "New Army," whose entry into the line of battle must perforce be gradual. It could not be expected to make its weight felt for a long time to come.

After the fall of Antwerp I realised that, by taking up our position on the extreme left flank we should find ourselves very near to the coast, and a good opportunity would be afforded of gaining the co-operation of the Fleet. In other words, the paramount thought in my mind was that the British and Belgian forces, co-operating with the British Fleet, should constitute in themselves the left flank of the Allied line in the West.

Whilst on the Aisne I had a visit from Mr. Winston Churchill, who was then First Lord of the Admiralty. He arrived on the night of September 26th and left on the 28th. Winston Churchill had been for several years one of my most intimate friends. I saw much of him during the South African War, but it was not until about 1905 or 1906 that I really got to know him well. His complex character is as difficult to describe as it is to analyse. To those who do not understand him, the impetuous disposition, which is one of his strongest characteristics, is apt to throw into shadow the indomitable courage, tireless energy, marvellous perspicuity and quick virile brain-power which are the main features of Winston Churchill's extraordinary personality.

His experience and knowledge of public affairs must be unrivalled; for, at an age when most men are undergoing the grinding drudgery which falls to the lot of nearly all successful statesmen, lawyers, soldiers or ecclesiastics, he was holding the highest offices in the Government; and not even his most inveterate enemies can say that he has failed to leave his mark for good on every department he has supervised.

Possessing a combative nature, he engages constantly in political strife which is marked by the sharpest controversy, and it is, therefore, perhaps only his intimate friends who know the real manly, generous kindliness of his disposition and his perfect loyalty.

The perspective of history will show the part he has played throughout the Great War to have been consistently constructive and of direct value to the nation.

His visit to my Headquarters at this time was productive of great good. The Government were getting nervous of the military situation and of the arrest of our forward advance. With his characteristic energy and activity, Churchill visited and examined every part of the battlefield, and what he saw and heard put him in a position to send reassuring information to his colleagues.

I discussed with him fully my views as to the desirability of establishing the British Forces in a theatre where they could co-operate with the Navy and link up with the troops in Belgium. We examined the possibility of a failure to effect a decisive turning movement, and agreed in thinking that, in the last resort, we might still be able, with the flank support of the Fleet, to snatch from the enemy's possession the Belgian coast-line as far, at any rate, as Zeebrugge.

When he left me on September 28th it was with a complete understanding that he would prepare the Navy to fulfil this role, and a few extracts from letters which I subsequently received from him will show how well he redeemed his promise. On October 26th he writes:

> .... But, my dear friend, I do trust you will realise how damnable it will be if the enemy settles down for the winter along lines which comprise Calais, Dunkirk, or Ostend. There will be continual alarms and greatly added difficulties. We must have him off the Belgian coast even if we cannot recover Antwerp.
> I am getting old ships with heavy guns ready, protected by barges with nets against submarines, so as to dispute the whole seaboard with him. On the 31st inst. the *Revenge*, with four 13½-in. guns, can come into action if required, and I have a regular fleet of monitors now organised, which, they all say, have hit the Germans hard this week, a fleet which is getting stronger every day.
> If you could gain a passage off to the left, I could give you overwhelming support from the sea, and there you will have a flank which certainly they cannot turn. . . .

In a letter dated November 22nd, again:—

> .... If you push your left flank along the sand-dunes of the shore to Ostend and Zeebrugge, we would give you 100 or 200 heavy guns from the sea in absolutely devastating support. For four or five miles inshore we could make you perfectly safe and superior. Here, at least, you have their flank, if you care to use it; and surely, the coast strip, held

and fed well with troops, would clear the whole line out about Dixmude and bend it right back, if it did not clear it altogether.

.... We could bring men in at Ostend or Zeebrugge to reinforce you in a hard south-eastward push. There is no limit to what could be done by the extreme left-handed push and swoop along the Dutch frontier.... In a few hours I could have fifty 12-in. guns and seventy 6-in. firing on the enemy's right and rear. It is difficult for submarines to attack because of the sandbanks....

On December 7th the First Lord was again my guest at G.H.Q. We discussed the situation, and were completely in agreement as to the advisability of my projected coastal advance and close co-operation with the Fleet. I told him there was fear of disagreement with the French, and that political difficulties would certainly arise. He said he did not think that they were insuperable, and shortly after our conversation he left for England, promising to arrange everything with the Prime Minister and Kitchener.

Then came his letter, despatched on December 8th, after he had seen his colleagues in the Cabinet:

> .... Kitchener agrees entirely with your view. We held an immediate conference with the Prime Minister and Sir Edward Grey, and, as the result, the strongest possible telegram is being drafted. The Admiralty attach the greatest importance to the operation and will aid in every way. We are already making the necessary preparations on an extensive scale. Later I will let you have very full and clear details. The combination must be perfect.
> Kitchener proposes to let you have the 27th Division in time .... I hope you will continue to press the new plan hard, both here at home and on the French Generals.

I quote in full Sir Edward Grey's telegram, dated December 9th, to Sir Francis Bertie at Bordeaux:

> The military situation points to the advisability of shortly

taking steps to prevent the Germans withdrawing their best first-line troops from the Western theatre for employment against Russia and replacing them by second-rate troops.

As some forward movement to achieve this object may be decided on, I desire to bring to the serious attention of the French Government the very strong opinion held by His Majesty's Government that British troops should be so placed in the line as to advance along the coast in immediate co-operation with our Fleet, and thus enable us, if necessary, to land further forces at any critical juncture during the operation.

To obtain this result a slight change in the present position of Sir John French's forces in the line would be necessary. The British troops would have to be moved to the left of the Allied line, being replaced in their present position by the French troops now on the left. They would thus be again taking up the position in the line they held after moving from Soissons.

I would point out to the French Government that the people of this country realise that the Belgian coastal positions are now held by Germany as a menace to Great Britain. They would, therefore, regard any losses entailed by an active offensive taken by our troops against these coastal positions as fully justified. British public opinion will even demand that the menace should be removed, for the forts on the coast of Belgium are being prepared as a base of operations by sea and air against Great Britain especially, and this may in time hamper the safe transport of fresh troops from England to France.

Moreover, we feel sure that our co-operation with any contemplated French effort to drive the Germans back from their present positions would be rendered much more effective, and lead to more decisive and far-reaching results, if this preliminary step in the redistribution of the troops were now taken and our troops subsequently used in the manner indicated.

His Majesty's Government consider it most urgent and

important that this step should be taken, and you should ask the French Government to agree to it and to arrange with Gen. Joffre for carrying it out.

The French Government received these proposals very coldly. It was quite evident that they had no intention of leaving the British Forces in sole charge of the Allied left, but for the moment they agreed to regard the question as a military one and to refer it to General Joffre.

I had several conversations with him on the subject, but there appeared to be no disposition on his part to acquiesce in my plans.

This attitude on the part of the French was evidently well known in London, for, on December 13th, I received a letter from Winston Churchill in which he said: "Of course, we are disappointed here with the turn events have taken, but we shall do our best to help the French."

This meant that Joffre had rejected my scheme, but had substituted the idea of another kind of attack, to be made chiefly by the French, with fewer troops, in a different direction and with quite another objective. I will return to this presently, for such an operation actually took place and proved to be a very feeble substitute for what I had intended. Yielding thus to French representations, our Government began to weaken. Churchill adhered to his views throughout, but was not supported.

The terms of Sir Edward Grey's communication of December 9th were unanswerable. Everything which subsequently happened in the course of the war has proved it. The possession by the Germans of that strip of Belgian coast-line has been the sharpest of all thorns with which they have succeeded in pricking us. It has been one of the main causes of the prolongation of the war. Their vigorous and successful defence against all our attacks in the autumn of 1917 showed the value which they attached to the retention of this coast-line.

Lord Kitchener addressed a Memorandum to me in January, 1915, from which I quote *in extenso*:

The questions raised in your recent Memorandum of January 3rd, 1915 and in your appreciation of the situation in the various theatres of war, were considered by a War Council presided over by the Prime Minister, on Thursday, January 7th, and Friday, January 8th.

The principal questions discussed were—
1. The proposed advance to Zeebrugge. 2. The organisation of the New Armies. 3. The possibility of employing British Forces in a different theatre to that in which they are now used.

With regard to the proposed advance to Zeebrugge, the First Lord's telegram, No. 2623, sent to you on January 2nd, explained the difficulties imposed on the Admiralty by the development of Zeebrugge as a base for submarines, and the War Council realised that one of your principal motives in suggesting an offensive to effect the capture of Ostend and Zeebrugge was to ease the naval position.

On a general review, however, of the whole situation, naval and military, the Council came to the conclusion that the advantages to be obtained from such an advance at the present moment would not be commensurate with the heavy losses involved, as well as the extension that would be thus caused to the lines of the Allies in Northern Flanders. The Council was also influenced in this conclusion by the following considerations. The first of these was that the reinforcements of 50 battalions of Territorial troops, which you considered indispensable, could only be supplied at a considerable dislocation of the organisation of the future reinforcements to be sent to you. It must be borne in mind that the original organisation of the Territorial Force included no provision for drafts. Great difficulties have already been encountered in providing drafts for the 24 battalions already in your command; and, although arrangements for the necessary machinery to create a special reserve for the Territorials are in hand, it would not at present be possible to supply 50 more battalions with drafts without an entire reorganisation of the forces allotted to Home Defence, and this would modify the programme for reinforcements to join our Army in the future.

The second consideration was that it is impossible at the present time to maintain a sufficient supply of gun ammunition on the scale which you considered necessary for offensive operations. Every effort is being made in all parts of the world to obtain an unlimited supply of ammunition; but, as you are well aware, the result is still far from being sufficient to maintain the large number of guns which you now have under your command adequately supplied with ammunition for offensive purposes.

You have pointed out that offensive operations under the new conditions created by this war require a vast expenditure of artillery ammunition, which may, for even 10 or 20 days, necessitate the supply of 50 or 100 rounds per gun per day being available, and that, unless the reserve can be accumulated to meet expenditure of this sort, it is unwise to embark on extensive offensive operations against the enemy in trenches. It is, of course, almost impossible to calculate with any accuracy how long offensive operations, once undertaken, may last before the object is attained; but it is evident that the breaking off of such operations before accomplishment, owing to the want of artillery ammunition, and not on account of a successful termination or a convenient pause in the operations having been reached, might lead to a serious reverse being sustained by our forces.

The abandonment of the Zeebrugge project does not prevent you from co-operating to the utmost extent, compatible with your present resources, with any offensive movement contemplated by Gen. Joffre, and your previous instructions in this sense are in no way modified.

The Council further thought that there were certain indications, which should not be neglected, of German reinforcements reaching their Armies in the Western theatre in the near future, which may lead German Commanders to undertake a fresh attempt to force the lines you and the French Army hold. If this movement should develop, it could probably be better met and defeated by holding your present lines of prepared positions than by extending the line to the Dutch frontier and placing the Belgian Army in probably a more exposed position than they now occupy. You may rest assured that, as they become available, fresh troops will be sent to you with the least possible delay to strengthen your forces as far as is practicable. The 28th Division have already received orders to leave for France on the 14th inst.

The telegram from the First Lord of the Admiralty, dated January 2nd, referred to in the above memorandum, ran as follows:

The battleship *Formidable'* as sunk this morning by a submarine in the Channel. Information from all quarters shows that the Germans are steadily developing an important submarine base at Zeebrugge. Unless operations can be undertaken to clear the coast, and particularly to capture this place, it must be recognised that the whole transportation of troops across the Channel will be seriously and increasingly compromised. The Admiralty are of the opinion that it would be possible, under cover of warships, to land a large force at Zeebrugge in conjunction with any genuine forward movement along the shore to Ostend. They wish these views, which they have so frequently put forward, to be placed again before the French Commander, and hope they may receive the consideration which their urgency and importance require.

It will be seen from this that Mr. Churchill was not in accord with the views expressed in Lord Kitchener's memorandum.

The situation was well known to the Cabinet before the despatch of Sir Edward Grey's telegram of December 9th. It is clear that the points raised in the memorandum of January 9th were excuses used as a veil to screen the disinclination of the British Government to taking a firm stand against the attitude adopted by the French. But there was something more.

Lord Kitchener's objections can be easily answered. They may be generally stated thus:

(1) That the seizure from the Germans of this strip of sea coast would not be an adequate return for the heavy losses likely to be incurred in the operation.

(2) That the line then to be held would be unduly extended.

(3) That the reinforcement of the additional troops demanded "would only be supplied at a considerable dislocation of the organisation of the future reinforcements to be sent you."

(4) That the supply of gun ammunition on the scale demanded would be impossible.

(5) That embarking on such an enterprise would prejudice our power of resisting a possible German counter-offensive in the immediate future.

My answer to (1) is this: Had we been in possession of the Belgian coast-line between Nieuport and the Dutch frontier in the early part of 1915, and had we maintained it to the end of the war, the Germans would have been deprived in a great measure of the power they have exercised throughout with such success, to prosecute their submarine campaign. Any price we might have had to pay in the way of losses would have been well worth the object attained.

In a lesser degree this may be said of the enemy's aircraft enterprises. I claim that the naval history of this war clearly bears out my contention.

As to (2), the extent of the line to be held would depend upon the degree of success attained by the operations. If we had been able to make good our advance from the left flank (between Nieuport and Dixmude) by means of powerful naval support from the sea, the least we should have effected would have been to clear the Germans out of the triangle Nieuport—Dixmude—Zeebrugge.

If the operation had then to be suspended, we should have had to hold the line Dixmude—Zeebrugge instead of Dixmude—Nieuport. In actual distance the former space is about double the latter. But our position at Zeebrugge would have afforded a large measure of naval support, and the country to the south-west of that place lends itself to inundations. This would have enabled us to occupy the north-eastern portion of the line in much less strength. Further, it was just in anticipation of such a necessity that the extra troops were asked for.

Inasmuch, however, as such a situation would have forced upon the enemy the necessity of holding a dangerous and exposed salient which could be reached on the north side by our guns from the Fleet, it is more than possible that he would have effected such a retirement as would have considerably shortened our line.

(3) This contention is disputed; but even if it were true, it is no sound military argument against embarking on an operation which promised such valuable results.

(4) There is a complete answer to this objection. Some two or three months later, large trainloads of ammunition—heavy, medium, and light—passed by the rear of the Army in France *en route* to Marseilles for shipment to the Dardanelles.

(5) The best possible means of warding off an attack is to take a strong and powerful initiative.

I cannot characterise these reasons for rejecting my plans as other than illogical, and I feel sure they must really have appeared so to their authors.

Perhaps the true explanation which underlay all this is to be found in the following Memorandum of the War Council of January 9th, 1915. It runs as follows:

> The possibility of employing British forces in a different theatre than that in which they are now used
> The Council considered carefully your remarks on this subject in reply to Lord Kitchener's letter, and came to the conclusion that, certainly for the present, the main theatre of operations for British forces should be alongside the French Army, and that this should continue as long as France was liable to successful invasion and required armed support. It was also realised that, should the offensive operations subsequently drive the Germans out of France and back to Germany, British troops should assist in such operations. It was thought that, after another failure by Germany to force the lines of defence held by the French Army and yours, the military situation in France and Flanders might conceivably develop into one of stalemate, in

which it would be impossible for German forces to break through into France, while at the same time the German defences would be impassable for offensive movements of the Allies without great loss of life and the expenditure of more ammunition than could be provided. In these circumstances, it was considered desirable to find some other theatre where such obstructions to advance would be less pronounced, and from where operations against the enemy might lead to more decisive results.

For these reasons, the War Council decided that certain of the possible projects for pressing the war in other theatres should be carefully studied during the next few weeks, so that, as soon as the new forces are fit for action, plans may be ready to meet any eventuality that may be then deemed expedient, either from a political point of view, or to enable our forces to act with the best advantage in concert with the troops of other nations throwing in their lot with the Allies.

In fact, the idea became fixed in the minds of the War Council that a condition of stalemate was bound to occur on the Western front, and therefore other theatres which might afford greater opportunities of prosecuting a successful offensive must be sought.

I was asked for my views as to this, and I gave them in full. Space does not allow me to quote my memorandum on the subject *in extenso*, but my ideas will be gleaned from the concluding paragraphs, which run as follows:

> Assuming however, that all the foregoing arguments are brushed aside, it remains to be seen where any effective action could be taken. The countries to be considered are the following:
> (a) Russia.—Impossible, as there is no means of sending an Army there, the Baltic being closed. Archangel shut in winter and unsuitable at other seasons, and Vladivostok much too far away.
> (b) Denmark and (c) Holland.—One or other of these countries would have to declare war on Germany unless

her neutrality were violated, and in both cases the overseas communication would be so vulnerable to mine or torpedo attack as to be in the highest degree insecure.

(d) North German Coast.—Communications would be equally vulnerable.

(e) Italy.—Assumes that Italy is a friendly belligerent, in which case she would probably not require the assistance of British troops, as her own action should be sufficient to finish Austria. It is unlikely that Italy would be induced to join in simply by the offer of troops which her military intelligence must know would be better employed elsewhere.

(f) Istria and Dalmatia.—A very dangerous line of communication, and one which would be impossible in the face of a hostile Italy. The islands on the Dalmatian seaboard are specially favourable for the action of defending submarines and torpedo craft, while mines might render any approach to the coast out of the question. With an actively friendly Italy an advance through her territory would be more practicable, but, as stated in preceding paragraph, unnecessary.

(g) Through Greece to Servia, presumably *via*, Salonika, presumes Greece to be a friendly belligerent. Probably the least objectionable of any possible proposal, but necessitating the strict neutrality of Bulgaria, as otherwise the land communications would be very open to attack. A hostile Italy would also jeopardise the whole force.

(h) Gallipoli, Asia Minor, Syria.—Any attack on Turkey would be devoid of decisive result. In the most favourable circumstances it could only cause the relaxation of the pressure against Russia in the Caucasus and enable her to transfer two or three Corps to the West—a result quite incommensurate with the effort involved. To attack Turkey would be to play the German game and to bring about the end which Germany had in mind when she induced Turkey to join in the war, namely, to draw off troops from the decisive spot, which is Germany itself.

To sum up, my opinions are—

(1) That the impossibility of breaking through the German line in Flanders has not been proved, and that that operation is feasible provided a sufficiency of high-explosive shells and of guns is provided.

(2) That, even if it were proved impossible to break the German line, so large a margin of safety is needed that troops could not be withdrawn from this theatre. It is to be remembered that the Allies are in a much better position to await the outcome of events. Time is against Germany; she will not sit for ever behind her entrenchments, and the Allies must be prepared with an adequate force to strike her whenever she may attempt to break out or withdraw.

(3) That there are no theatres, other than those in which operations are now in progress, in which decisive results could be attained.

I have not gone into details in considering the question of the employment of forces in other theatres, as such operations were considered by the M.O. Directorate of the War Office when I was C.I.G.S., and I have no doubt that a full record of the conclusions which were reached are filed there.

General Joffre's final opinion is expressed in a memorandum, dated January 19th, 1915, of which the following is a summary:

1. I wish to call your particular attention to the following:
2. The French General Staff consider a German offensive possible—even probable—in the near future. The Germans are certainly making new formations; the 38th Corps has been identified in Bavaria.
3. Our front must therefore be made absolutely secure. If broken, for example, about Roye and Montdidier, the consequences for the Allies would be of the most serious description.
4. In addition to (3) we must place ourselves in the position of being able to assume the offensive.
5. Because of (3) and (4), reserves are absolutely necessary.
6. For these reasons, I am anxious for a rapid release of the Corps north of the British line.

7. We must never lose sight of the decisive result, and all secondary operations must give way.

8. Operations towards Ostend—Zeebrugge, though important, are, for the moment, secondary, and in my opinion should follow rather than precede the principal action, viz., the Collection of Reserves.

To resume:

(a) To beat the enemy it is necessary to have Reserves.

(b) These Reserves can only come from the north, as British reinforcements set them free.

(c) The German menace, not a vain thing, makes it necessary to collect these Reserves in the shortest possible time.

(d) The main object, viz., the defeat of the enemy, makes it necessary to delay the offensive towards Ostend—Zeebrugge.

I always disagreed with these views, and remain convinced that my plans should have been accepted and tried. I will only add, as a further argument against embarking upon operations in other theatres of war, that our military forces at that time, and for at least fifteen months afterwards, were not sufficient to enable us to carry on great operations in more than one theatre with the necessary power and energy required for success. They could only have resulted in what actually happened in 1915, viz., the series of feeble and on the whole unsuccessful attempts to break through the German line in France, and an absolute failure, compelling ultimate withdrawal of our troops, in the Dardanelles.

I have dealt at perhaps wearisome length with the strategic alternatives and the problems which presented themselves for solution after the close of the First Battle of Ypres. It has been necessary to do so in order that my countrymen may understand the situation as it actually existed at the time, and that they may appreciate what seemed to me conclusive reasons why greater progress was not made in 1915.

Divided counsels lead to half measures and indecisive action. Such counsels have always had, and always will have, the most deterrent and disadvantageous effect on any vigorous prosecution of a war, great or small.

CHAPTER 16

The Operations of December 14th-19th, 1914

For the plan sketched out in the last chapter, a certain amount of naval co-operation was secured. The Admiralty were always strongly in favour of my original proposal, and did not at all like the half-hearted operation which Joffre was substituting for it. They urged, with great force and reason, that the risks run by the ships in co-operation on the Belgian coast were increasingly great owing to the powerful fortifications erected by the Germans, and the presence of enemy submarines at Zeebrugge. Whilst, therefore, those risks might well be run in support of a real, strenuous, and powerful endeavour to wrench the coast-line from the enemy's grasp, the Admiralty felt that the Navy could not afford to sacrifice strength in hanging about day after day exposed to such risks, in the sole hope of rendering some slight help to an attack which had no great or decisive object in view. In proof of this, I quote the following telegrams which were received from the Admiralty. On December 20th, 1914, they wired as follows:

> We are receiving almost daily requests from the French for naval support on the Belgian coast. We regret we are unable to comply. The small vessels by themselves cannot face the new shore batteries, and it is not justifiable to expose battleships to submarine perils unless to support a land attack of primary importance.
> If such an attack is delivered, all the support in my Memorandum forwarded to you through Secretary of State for

War will, of course, be afforded. I would be glad if you would explain this to Gen. Foch, as it is painful to the officers concerned to make repeated refusals.

A previous wire had arrived on the 18th, the last few lines of which ran as follows:—

It is not justifiable to expose 'Majestic' to submarine risks unless to support a real movement, in which case every risk will be run and ample support provided.

And before this, on the 12th, the following was received:

Will you please put us in communication with the French General who will conduct the operation. . . . Meanwhile, all our preparations as outlined are proceeding. . . . but the serious risks to our ships, both from batteries and submarines, ought not to be incurred except in an operation of the first importance.

Admiral Hood, who afterwards fell so gloriously in the hour of victory at the Battle of Jutland, was then in command at Dover. He was responsible for the naval co-operation arranged for, and came to my Headquarters on the 13th to discuss plans. It was arranged that at daybreak on the 15th the advance from Nieuport was to be supported by two battleships, three monitors and six destroyers.

I urged the Quartermaster-General to do his utmost to provide more machine guns. At that time we had considerably less than one per company, and it was an arm in which the Germans were particularly well found. They must at that time have had at least six or seven to our one.

In the operations now under discussion, this disability was felt very severely. In discussing the progress of the fight with General d'Urbal on the 15th at Poperinghe, he told me that the slight and disappointing advance made by the French was due to their being everywhere held up by machine-gun fire. He said the enemy had received large machine-gun reinforcements, and he was then sending down special guns in armoured motors to endeavour to crush them.

From all parts of the line the same complaint came of the preponderance of the enemy's machine-gun fire.

The operations opened on the morning of the 14th by a combined attack on the line Hollebeke—Wytschaete ridge. It began when it was hardly daylight, at 7 a.m., by heavy artillery bombardment. At 7.45, the French right (five regiments of the 16th Corps) moved forward and captured the enemy's advance trenches on our left flank.

The 2nd Batt. Royal Scots and 1st Batt. Gordons (of Bowes' 8th Brigade, 3rd Division) then advanced on Petit Bois and Mendleston Farm. The Royal Scots seized and held the wood, which in the evening they entrenched on the eastern side. They captured about sixty prisoners, including some officers.

The Gordons at dusk had captured the enemy's trenches surrounding Mendleston Farm, but were again driven out of them by a powerful machine-gun counter-attack. They had to fall back on their own trenches.

The French 32nd Corps attacked to the north of the 16th on the line Klein Zillebeke—Zillebeke, and advanced some 200 to 300 yards. They repulsed a German counter-attack from Zandvoorde and captured the trenches in front of the château of Hollebeke.

As the French had not established themselves in the position agreed upon, the 3rd Division was unable to advance further, whilst the 5th Division (right of 2nd Corps) and all the 3rd Corps were confined the whole day to demonstration and holding the enemy.

I visited the *Poste de Commandement* of the 3rd Division Commander (Haldane) on the Scherpenberg—a hill near Bailleul, surmounted by a windmill—in the afternoon, and witnessed the fighting for some time. It struck me that the enemy artillery fire was much weaker than ours.

The operations were continued on the 15th, and I again spent some time on the Scherpenberg watching the progress of the fight, so far as the weather permitted any view; we were again prevented from advancing owing to the delay of the French on our left. Our joint plan was that successive points had to be taken from north to south. It is obvious that the movement had to commence on the French left, but from the first our Allies failed to execute their task and we had to wait for them.

The weather was terrible and the ground simply quagmire, whilst the rain, cold, and the awful mud of the holding soil paralysed any energetic attempt to drive the enemy back. A desultory fire was kept up at all points along the line; but no great activity appeared to be possible. The role of the 2nd Corps was quite plain and clear: it had to wait for the 16th French Corps to reach its allotted points.

Later in the day I went round to the 3rd Corps Headquarters and there met the Corps Commander (Pulteney), Du Cane, his Chief of Staff, and Allenby, Commanding the Cavalry.

I discussed the general course of the operations with them. I had in my mind the possibility of giving some impetus to the general advance by making an attack with troops of the 3rd Corps across the River Douve, and thus directly supporting an advance by Smith-Dorrien's right, perhaps supported by the cavalry. The mud and water in the valley of that river, however, presented insuperable difficulties.

During the night of the 15th-16th, troops of the 5th Division captured some trenches to the south of Messines. I was much perturbed at the slow progress we were making, as no better reports came from anywhere along the whole of the Allied line.

On the 16th I again visited the Scherpenberg, where I was met by Smith-Dorrien and Haldane. Smith-Dorrien assured me that the understanding between himself and the Commander of the 16th French Corps on his left (General Grosetti) to provide for mutual support and co-operation had been complete.

As our great aim was now to reduce the enemy's machine-gun fire, I directed Smith-Dorrien to send his pack artillery, which had recently been given him, close down behind the trenches and dig them well in.

De Maud'huy's attack north of Arras was begun on the 16th by a heavy artillery bombardment. The infantry attack followed on the 17th, but the results were disappointing, although a little ground was gained near Notre Dame de Lorette. Some slight progress was made by the French 21st Corps.

I tried to see Foch, but he was away from his Headquarters with de Maud'huy. I sent Henry Wilson after him to explain my views, namely, that our present plan must be modified, owing largely to the fact that we had considerably under-estimated the enemy's strength, particularly in the matter of machine guns. Foch sent Wilson back to tell me that he agreed in thinking that the present operations had not proved a success. He proposed to break them off as soon as we could reconsider our arrangements. He begged me, however, to continue demonstrating all along my front as much as possible, with a view to supporting the attack upon which de Maud'huy was now embarked.

It was at this time that one of the many instances occurred of the evils which attend divided command. There was undoubtedly a great opportunity on and about December 18th for a powerful attack opposite Wytschaete. I proposed to mass the 16th French and 2nd British Corps at this point, when I discovered that the 16th Corps was practically melting away on my left flank. Two brigades had been despatched to the north, and other units had been sent away to support de Maud'huy's attack on Arras. I was in complete ignorance of these moves until they were accomplished facts. I therefore had to give up all idea of a joint attack on any large scale for the present, and issued orders to Corps Commanders enjoining them to demonstrate on their immediate front, to keep the enemy occupied and seize any opportunity which might offer to capture hostile trenches.

Colonel Thomson (liaison officer with General de Castelnau) told me that the 2nd French Army had made some progress, the first line of the enemy trenches near Albert had been taken and the ground made good. Progress was also made near Roye.

Captain Spiers (11th Hussars), who was now my liaison officer with General de Maud'huy, came to me. He told me that a German counter-attack on Notre Dame de Lorrette had regained all ground lost by the enemy on the day before, but that the attack on Givenchy-les-La Bassée had succeeded only to the extent of capturing a trench west of the village, and that progress was being slowly made to the north. The ground won at St. Laurent was retained in spite of repeated German counter-attacks.

Some trenches north of Notre Dame de Consolation (east of Vermelles) were also taken and held.

I have had occasion to mention Spiers' name before. He has since deservedly risen to much higher rank. In my mind I always used to class him with Captain Colquhoun Grant of Peninsular fame—one of Wellington's most trusted scouting officers.

I have a most vivid and grateful recollection of the invaluable services performed by this intrepid young officer. He is possessed of an extremely acute perception, and is able to express himself and deliver his reports in the clearest and most concise terms. He was always exact and accurate, and never failed to bring me back the information I most particularly wanted. I seldom knew him at fault. He was a perfect master of the French language and was popular with the staffs, and made welcome by the various generals to whom he was attached. His unfailing tact, judgment and resource were very marked. His reckless, daring courage often made me anxious for his safety, and, indeed, he was severely wounded on at least five separate occasions.

I remember well his coming back to report to me late one evening. He spoke with his usual confidence and decision, and the information which he gave me proved to be very important and accurate, but I noticed that his voice was weak and he looked very tired and worn in the face. I sent him away to his quarters as quickly as possible, thinking he wanted rest. All this time he had a bullet in his side, and in that condition he had travelled back several miles to make his report. He fainted after leaving my room, and lay in considerable danger for several days.

To resume my narrative. The 3rd, 4th, and Indian Corps were all energetic in carrying out my latest orders, and demonstrated with considerable activity. On the 19th the 8th Division captured some trenches at Neuve Chapelle, and the 7th Division at Rouges Bancs, but of the latter, the 2nd Batt. Scots Guards, in the 20th Brigade, were driven back by a counter-attack; as also were the Devons.

Attacks were made very early in the morning by the Garhwal, Sirhind, and Ferozepore Brigades. Each was successful, and parts of the enemy's trenches were captured.

The Garhwal Brigade captured two machine guns and some prisoners, but had to return to their own trenches in the evening.

The 11th Brigade of the 4th Division, under Hunter Weston (1st Batt. Somerset L.I., 1st Batt. E. Lancs. Regt., 1st Batt. Hampshire Regt., 1st Batt. Rifle Brigade), made a concerted attack on the morning of the 19th on the edge of Ploegsteert Wood. Some houses were captured, but the mud and the wet made progress difficult. However, they maintained their position well.

The success of the Indian Corps was destined to be of but short duration. During the night of the 20th the enemy regained all the trenches they had taken except some sap-heads near Givenchy. The Germans attacked at daybreak all along the line between Givenchy-les-La Bassée and la Quinque Rue. The Sirhind Brigade were driven back on Festubert, and Givenchy was lost, but retaken in the afternoon.

On the front of the Meerut Division only the Garhwal Brigade on the left held its ground, and in the evening the situation was serious, the Germans occupying nearly all our line between Givenchy and Richebourg, whilst the Corps reserves were all engaged. In the evening the three brigades of the Indian Cavalry Corps were thrown into the fight.

At night Sir James Willcocks reported his troops as much exhausted, and urged their immediate relief; the 1st Corps was therefore ordered to send two brigades (1st and 3rd) up to the line occupied by the Indian Corps.

At 2.35 p.m. these two brigades advanced and partially restored the situation on the front Givenchy—Festubert, driving the enemy out of Givenchy. The 2nd Brigade (2nd Batt. R. Sussex Regt., 1st Batt. N. Lancs., 1st Batt. Northants Regt., 2nd Batt. K.R.R.) had now also been ordered up, and advanced in support of the Lahore Division.

On the evening of the 21st the 1st Corps were ordered to take over the Indian Corps' line. In the early hours of the 22nd the 1st Brigade (1st Batt. Coldstream Guards, 1st Batt. Scots Guards, 1st Batt. Black Watch, 1st Batt. Cameron Highlanders) made Givenchy secure. The 3rd Brigade (2nd Batt. R. Munster Fusiliers, 1st Batt. S. Wales Borderers, 1st Batt. Gloucester Regt., 2nd Batt.

Welsh Regt.) was unable to re-establish the original line on the left of the 1st Brigade, but occupied a line thrown slightly back.

The 2nd Brigade endeavoured to gain the old line at la Quinque Rue, but was unable to do so, and secured a position with its right in touch with the Meerut Brigade and in front of Festubert.

At 1 p.m. on the 22nd Sir Douglas Haig (commanding the 1st Corps) assumed command in this area.

On the 23rd the 27th Division, which had been despatched from England, completed its detrainment and concentrated in the area about Arques (near St. Omer).

On the 17th I received a letter from Kitchener from which I gleaned that the Cabinet were much perturbed by rumours of a contemplated invasion by the enemy, which apparently emanated from the Admiralty. The authorities at home were far from happy about the whole situation on the Western front, and it was greatly feared that our line might still be broken through by a determined German offensive.

I received orders to go home and consult with the Cabinet, and arrived at Folkestone about 11 a.m. on Sunday the 20th. Lord Kitchener met me there with his motor and we drove together to Walmer Castle, where the Prime Minister (Mr. Asquith) was then staying. I had not seen Kitchener since our memorable meeting at Paris, early in September, but he met me in the most friendly manner, and said many kind things about our work in France, of which he clearly appreciated the difficulties. We discussed the situation fully *en route*, and I remember his putting many questions to me about all the principal members of the Headquarters Staff. Whilst assuring him of my entire satisfaction with each and all of them, I reminded him that, if any fault was to be found, I and no one else was responsible.

In this and many subsequent conversations of a similar kind, I always maintained that a Commander-in-Chief can only be held in contempt who allows any member of his staff, or, indeed, any officer under his orders, to bear blame which must always most properly belong to *him* and to *him alone*. A chief in supreme command has always the absolute power of replacing any officer who fails in his duty. To *him* comes the principal credit and reward when things go well, and to *him* and him alone must the blame be apportioned when they do not. Until any officer under him is found by *him* to be unfit for his position, it is contrary to all efficient discipline to allow such officer to be censured or removed by any outside authority.

This principle is one of the most sacred traditions of the British Army. It is the foundation upon which there has been slowly and carefully built up that mutual confidence which exists between officers and men, which is the real secret of their wonderful fighting power. I recalled to Kitchener's memory our service together in South Africa, and reminded him how truly and faithfully he had always kept up this tradition in his own exercise of command.

After four months of the most ruthless war the world has ever seen, it was a curious sensation to find myself once again on English soil and in the midst of peaceful surroundings. It was one of those mild, balmy days which we very seldom get in the month of December, and the usual English Sunday atmosphere of rest and repose was over every object, animate and inanimate.

I could not help feeling deeply the extraordinary contrast which the scene presented to that which I had left behind me a few hours before. Except that one noticed a few men in khaki, there was nothing to indicate the terrific war which was raging all the time just across the Channel.

The people of this country have never truly realised the wonderful immunity from the horrors of war which they alone of all the belligerent countries have enjoyed. I wonder if it has really struck any large number of them that, after more than four years of desperate strife, we are the only people in Europe who can proudly claim that no enemy has ever occupied one square inch of all our vast Empire throughout the world, except for a short time in East Africa. The soil of Germany, Austria, Hungary, Turkey, Bulgaria, France, Russia, Italy, Serbia, and Romania has been repeatedly violated. It is truly a great record when we come to think that the sun never sets on the British flag.

On arriving at Walmer Castle I was very kindly and cordially welcomed by the Prime Minister. Entering the historic old stronghold, where the great Iron Duke breathed his last, I remember being at first seized with a pang of regret; for I thought his spirit would have rested in greater peace, if, under that famous roof, I could have told the first Minister of the King that we had once again planted the British flag in the face of the enemy on the field of Waterloo. It was a dream I had indulged in from the first, but, alas! like many others, it was destined never to be realised.

CHAPTER 17

The Close of the Year 1914

I had a long discussion with the Prime Minister at Walmer. Mr. Asquith possesses the rare quality of being able to discuss the most difficult and threatening situation with the utmost calmness and deliberation. He is a very attentive listener, and as he quickly appreciates and understands all that is told him, it did not take him long to become fully acquainted with the entire situation.

As I have said before, all the Cabinet were at this moment very anxious as to the general outlook, but neither by word nor gesture did the Prime Minister display the least want of hope and confidence.

During my sojourn in France I had received several most kind and encouraging letters from Mr. Asquith, in which he expressed his warm appreciation of all that we had done, and said how truly he realised the very trying circumstances which surrounded us. He personally reiterated these kindly sentiments; but it was evident that the Government had just begun to entertain doubts and fears which had induced them to call me into council. It was the faith inspired by this constant kindly sympathy, and his power as Prime Minister, which helped me to believe that the shortage in guns and ammunition which threatened ultimate destruction would be overcome. The glorious troops under my command had gone valiantly to their death when a few more guns and a few more shells would have many times saved their sacrifice. And still no sufficient supplies came.

The question of munitions and the fear of invasion formed the basis of our long conversation at Walmer. After lunch, I left with

Kitchener and travelled by motor to London. With deep sorrow I recall the fact that this was the last of all the many days of happy personal intercourse which I spent with my old South African chief. As a soldier and a commander in the field I had always loved and venerated him; in his capacity as a politician and Minister my sentiments and feelings towards him were never the same.

I am willing to admit that our differences—which were great and far-reaching—may have been to some extent my own fault; but, be that as it may, our subsequent relations, down to the time of his tragic death, were always clouded by a certain mistrust of one another.

It rejoices my heart, and alleviates the pain and regret which I feel, to look back upon this one day spent almost entirely *tête-à-tête* with him. On our way to London we had to pass by his country place at Broome, and he insisted on stopping for an hour to show me round it. To describe what I saw would only be a repetition of what is already very well known. As he stood in the midst of its beautiful scenery and surroundings, the true spirit of the great soldier shone out as distinctly and clearly as it ever did in the many and varied experiences we went through together in the South African War.

The eloquent and touching tribute paid to this great soldier's memory by Lord Derby in the House of Lords in June, 1916, brought out with telling force and happy expression Kitchener's deep affection for his "beloved Broome."[1]

Indeed, beneath that seemingly hard and stern exterior there existed a mighty well of sensitive feeling and even of romance,

---

1: A short speech which I made on this occasion in the House of Lords expressed my great appreciation of Lord Kitchener's capacity as a leader in the field. I told the House that, after I received intimation of my appointment to command in France, my first act was to seek out my old South African Chief and suggest to him that we should repair together to the Prime Minister and ask that he might be appointed to command, with me as his Chief of Staff. He could not be persuaded to do this. He was then on the point of leaving to return to Egypt, and had no idea that he was to be Secretary of State for War. I do not think Lord Kitchener was always credited by the country with the talent for command in the field which I know he really possessed, whilst, on the other hand, a role for which he was not well fitted was thrust upon him. As Commander-in-chief in France it would have helped him very much to have had a Secretary of State *other than himself* to deal with.

which it appeared to be the one endeavour of his life to conceal from the observation even of his most intimate friends.

All the next day, and far into the following, my whole time was employed in discussing the situation with the War Cabinet.

The principal ground for all their fears proved subsequently, in the course of the year 1916, to be only too well founded as regards the Eastern front. But the reports of large movements of German troops to the West, which really induced Mr. Asquith to send for me, were not true. Constant reports, however, continued to reach the Government from secret and reliable sources, that the Russians were even then running very short of ammunition, and that their condition, as regards the supply of war material generally, would certainly oblige them to evacuate the enemy territory they had already won, and even necessitate a retirement behind the Vistula, if not the Bug, with the loss of Warsaw and other important fortresses. The home authorities were undoubtedly influenced in forming this opinion by reports which, however, did not emanate from any part of the Western theatre of war, and I believe their judgment was generally hampered and warped by paying too much regard to unauthorised statements. The divergence of views which existed on various dates during the month of December is curiously illustrated by the following quotations from letters and telegrams.

On the 2nd, Kitchener wired to me:

> It is reported new corps are arriving in Russia and that some of the old corps lately between La Bassée and the sea have disappeared from that front. Can you ascertain what truth there is in this? It is thought possible the Germans may be replacing active corps by immature formations along northern portion of Allied lines so as to use their best troops in the Eastern theatre, where they are apparently developing great strength.

On the 18th he writes:

> The Russian news is very serious. I fear we cannot rely on them for much more for some time.

On the 26th I received the following telegram from him:

I think before you see Joffre it may be useful for you to know I am inclined to think Russians have been bluffing to a certain extent. I cannot get answers to my questions from Petrograd which would clear up the situation. For instance, amount of reserve ammunition in hand, which, according to Military Attaché here, who is kept entirely in the dark by his Government, ought to be very considerable.

A reason for a certain amount of bluff on their part might be that they are now negotiating to obtain from us a loan of forty millions. Anyway, their action in the field does not look as if they were as badly off as they make out.

All kinds of reports continued to arrive, insisting that masses of German troops were passing through Luxemburg and Belgium *en route* to the Western front; but these turned out subsequently to be either greatly exaggerated or to have no foundation whatever in fact.

The upshot of it all was that I received directions from the Prime Minister to seek out Joffre as soon after my return as possible, put these views and fears of the War Cabinet before him, and to report to them what he was prepared to do in order to meet the supposed threat. Before leaving I was received in audience by His Majesty the King.

On my journey back to the front, I pondered long and anxiously over all that had passed in London. I had plainly told the War Cabinet that I did not share these alarmist views, which I considered were not founded on any definite or reliable information, and I had warned them that these views disagreed altogether with our appreciation of the situation at the front. I by no means liked my mission to Joffre; but the orders received were imperative.

On the morning of the 24th, I had a long conference with Murray and Macdonogh, and we once more thoroughly examined the situation in all its bearings.

The daily official reports tended to show that the Russians were still holding their own well, and that there was no immediate fear of a retirement behind the Vistula. Even if pessimistic views held in London were warranted by the actual facts, it did not appear that there was any reasonable probability of the Germans ever being able to mass a sufficient force in the Western theatre to enable them to break through our line.

In accordance with the Prime Minister's decision, I arranged a meeting with Joffre at Chantilly for the 27th.

I found things were going on better in the north on the Yser. The Belgians had been able to resume active hostilities, and the 5th Belgian Division had made good the ground on the right bank of the river about Dixmude.

I began the last of the six Christmas days I have during my life passed in the field by visiting Foch. I told him of my mission to Joffre, and discussed with him the situation in the East. He said he felt sure that the Russians were exaggerating their deficiencies in ammunition, rifles, etc., in their representations both to the British and French Governments. He thought that they were afraid that the troops in the West were not displaying sufficient energy, and their idea was to stimulate this. Moreover, he said he was confirmed in this view by what the Russians were then doing in Poland and Galicia, which was also confirmed from German sources. He could not believe that, if they were, as they said, so short of ammunition, they could continue these aggressive tactics. He went on to speak of the work of the French at Arras, and said they had been much hampered by weather conditions, but that they were making some slight progress everywhere. He thought we might shortly find some opportunity for action in the neighbourhood of La Bassée.

On my return to Headquarters I met Haig and Smith-Dorrien, who had come to lunch, and I discussed with them my wish to form "Armies" immediately. I wished Haig to command the 1st, 4th, and Indian Corps as the 1st Army, and Smith-Dorrien the 2nd, 3rd, and 5th Corps as the 2nd Army. The cavalry was to remain at my immediate disposal. Orders to this effect came out on Christmas night.

Although I have never heard it actually confirmed, I believe a suggestion was made by the Pope to all the belligerent Powers that an armistice should be arranged for Christmas Day. It was further reported that the Central Powers had signified their assent, but that the Allied Governments refused to entertain the proposal. The suggestion was certainly never referred either to Joffre or to me.

Whether this statement was true or not, it is certain that, soon after daylight on Christmas morning, the Germans took a very bold initiative at several points along our front, in trying to establish some form of fraternisation. It began by individual unarmed men running from the German trenches across to ours, holding Christmas trees above their heads. These overtures were in some places favourably received and fraternisation of a limited kind took place during the day. It appeared that a little feasting went on, and junior officers, non-commissioned officers and men on either side conversed together in "No Man's Land."

When this was reported to me I issued immediate orders to prevent any recurrence of such conduct, and called the local commanders to strict account, which resulted in a good deal of trouble.

I have since often thought deeply over the principle involved in the manifestation of such sentiments between hostile armies in the field. I am not sure that, had the question of the agreement upon an armistice for the day been submitted to me, I should have dissented from it. I have always attached the utmost importance to the maintenance of that chivalry in war which has almost invariably characterised every campaign of modern times in which this country has been engaged. The Germans glaringly and wantonly set all such sentiments at defiance by their ruthless conduct of the present war; even from its very commencement.

Judging from my own experience, we never had a more chivalrous or generous foe than the Boers of South Africa, and I can recall numerous proofs of it.

For instance, I was in charge of the operations against General Beyers in the Western Transvaal during the latter part of December 1900. On the afternoon of Christmas Eve a flag of truce—that symbol of civilisation and chivalry in war which has been practically unknown during this war with Germany—appeared at our outposts, and a young Dutch officer was brought to my Headquarters carrying a request from Beyers regarding the burial of his dead.

Some important movements were then in progress, and I told him we must of necessity detain him there till the next day, but I hoped we would be able to make him as comfortable as possible. When he started back to his General on Christmas morning, I gave him a small box of cigars and a bottle of whiskey, asking him to present them to Beyers as a Christmas offering from me.

I had forgotten the incident when, a few days later, two cavalry soldiers who had been taken prisoners by the enemy marched back into camp with horses, arms and equipment complete. They brought me a note from Beyers, thanking me for my gift on Christmas Day and telling me that, although he had no whiskey or cigars to offer in return, he hoped I would regard his liberation of these men in the light of a Christmas gift.

When I told this story at the end of the war to my old friend and redoubtable opponent, General Christian Smuts, he expressed himself as very displeased with Beyer's improper use of what was not his own but his country's property. I pointed out to Smuts that it was the spirit which Beyers displayed which mattered—that spirit which was never more conspicuously displayed throughout the war than in the conduct of this same great soldier and statesman, General Smuts himself.

In the swift and kaleidoscopic changes which occur in world politics, the friend of today may be the enemy of tomorrow. Soldiers should have no politics, but should cultivate a freemasonry of their own and, emulating the knights of old, should honour a brave enemy only second to a comrade, and like them rejoice to split a friendly lance today and ride boot to boot in the charge tomorrow.

It is satisfactory to know that some such kindly and chivalrous spirit has at least made itself felt at times between the opposing flying services in the present war, for I have heard authentic stories which go to show that this has been the case.

On the 26th I met Willcocks and discussed the recent fighting of the Indian Corps with him. I considered that a certain amount of blame attached to the commanders of the units engaged, for embarking in an attack on trenches so far away from their own line before ensuring adequate support, especially in view of the muddy condition of the ground, and knowing, as they did, the exhausted state of the Indian troops and the effect of cold upon them. At first the General tried to combat this view; but he soon acknowledged the justice of my criticism.

I decided, regretfully, to make a change in the command of the Lahore Division. A commander very often, after having directed operations of a critical nature, needs rest and change of occupation to restore him to his full capacity for command.

I met Joffre at Chantilly on the morning of the 27th, as arranged. I explained the mission I had from the British Government, and told him of their fears of impending severe Russian defeats and of the possibility, which they thought might be open to the enemy, of withdrawing large numbers of troops and massing a force on the Western front strong enough to break our line and attain, after all, their original objectives, namely, Paris and the Channel ports. I told Joffre that the English Government were anxious to hear his views and ideas on the points raised.

The French Commander-in-Chief was much astonished to hear that such a view of the situation could be really and seriously entertained. But he added that, of course, the French General Staff had plans ready to meet any eventuality. He expressed the opinion that the time was not now opportune for the discussion of such contingent possibilities as these.

We then talked over the reported Russian deficiencies in munitions of war, and he entered into some most interesting details as to the state of the French manufacture of ammunition and guns. He told me that they were producing almost entirely high-explosive shells and hardly any shrapnel, and that an enormous improvement was being made in the pattern of fuse, from which great results were expected. The latest manufactured ammunition for the "75" gun had shown wonderful results, particularly in the matter of destroying wire entanglements.

Joffre went on to say that the Russians were in close touch

with the French factories, and were benefiting greatly by the experiments which had been carried out. Moreover, the French were able to supply the Russians with a considerable quantity of munitions of war. It took a long time to transmit; but he entertained great hopes that Romania and Bulgaria would soon be in such sympathy with the Allies as to permit the transport of material to Russia *via* Salonika. The reports he had received indicated that the Russians had sufficient ammunition at hand, if they remained on the defensive, for six weeks.

He expressed himself as fairly satisfied with the Russian position and outlook, and thought the Germans were being so heavily punished that whole corps would have to be reorganised.

These views were subsequently embodied in a memorandum which I sent to Lord Kitchener for the information of the War Cabinet.

I then arrived at an understanding with Joffre as to future plans. I again urged strongly upon him my conviction that an advance on the extreme north, in co-operation with our Navy, was the proper role for British troops to fulfil, and went over all the old arguments. In effect he rejected my plans again, although holding out hopes that, at a later stage, the French Army might co-operate in such an advance.

In the absence of support from my own Government, it was hopeless to say anything more. Joffre's plan was as follows. He meant to break through the enemy's line from the south at Rheims and from the west at Arras. He desired to mass as many French Corps as possible behind these two points; therefore, at all other points of the line the roles must be twofold: (1) to economise troops as much as possible in the trenches, so as to spare more men for action at decisive points, and (2) to organise good local reserves to keep the enemy in the front employed and prevent his sending troops to threatened points in the line.

As the history of the operations during 1915 will show, this general strategic idea was the foundation of all our efforts throughout that year. It brought about for the British Army the Battles of Neuve Chapelle, Ypres (second), Festubert, and Loos; and for the French other important actions, which, although local successes, did not result in achieving any appreciable advance towards the objectives which the plans sought to attain.

Those objects were not clearly defined till September, when we began our last combined attack to attain them and practically failed.

The attitude of our War Office in failing to speed up the manufacture of munitions of war and the practical collapse of the Russian Armies were to some extent responsible for the lack of success of our endeavours. But the detailment of troops and war material to the Dardanelles was undoubtedly the chief cause.

There was no other course for me to take, under the circumstances, than to fall in with Joffre's view; and in accordance with his plan I agreed to take over, in conjunction with the Belgians, the whole line from La Bassée to the sea, but only by degrees as troops became available.

Although Joffre at the time agreed in my wish to work the northern section entirely with the Belgian Army, it would appear that the French Government still insisted on keeping some hold on that part of the line with French troops.

On returning to my Headquarters I sent for Bridges, who was now my representative with His Majesty the King of the Belgians. On the morning of the 28th, we had a long conference on the subject of co-operation with the Belgian Army.

I had evolved a scheme in my own mind of amalgamating the Belgian and British Armies. I wanted to see Belgian brigades of infantry embodied in our own Army Corps at convenient sections in the line, and to apply the same process to the cavalry and artillery. This apparent surrender of independence was no doubt a heavy trial to impose upon the Belgian General Staff; but I believed it to be the surest and best method to adopt if we wished to get the highest efforts out of the two Armies.

When all is said, it must be acknowledged that the standard of training and war efficiency was higher in our troops than in the Belgian. This applied particularly to the leaders and the Staff; and, in spite of the drastic experiences of the Belgian Army during August and September, our own higher ranks certainly possessed a wider and more extensive experience in the field.

It can indeed hardly be doubted that a Division composed of two British infantry brigades and one Belgian would probably have done more, either in attack or defence, than such a unit composed entirely of Belgian troops.

Whatever views may be held on this point, it must be allowed that the scheme I proposed would have ensured a much greater unity of effort.

I talked it all over at great length with Bridges, and on leaving me he went back to put the proposal before the King of the Belgians. I entertained little hope of getting a favourable hearing; for, although I knew the King's lofty spirit and generous impulses would prompt him to make any personal sacrifice to attain greater power and efficiency for our united forces, yet I was also well aware of his difficulties with his own Ministers.

Two days later Bridges brought me His Majesty's answer. He told me it was possible the King himself might fall in with my suggestion. Ten thousand rifles would have to be retained for the "inundated" line, leaving 40,000 rifles available for the proposed amalgamation. This, I thought, would at once render the united Armies strong enough in the north to justify me in allowing Joffre to remove the 9th and 20th French Corps to the points where he so much needed strength for his own line.

This amalgamation of the British and Belgian Armies would certainly, have effected a great economy of force and fighting power, and have perhaps led to important results; but the scheme never came to fruition, both because the King of the Belgians was unable to gain the consent of his Government and because the French would not agree to the plan. Finally, I could get no support or help from our own people at home.

On the 27th, the French had some success at Carency (north of Arras), capturing several German trenches and advancing the line some 500 yards.

****

In spite of the "growls" in which I have so freely indulged, the close of 1914 yet found me in a hopeful and sanguine frame of mind. When the state of affairs which might have been came to be compared with the situation as it was, there was really very little reason for pessimism. We had scored one great offensive and another great defensive victory, and we had suffered no severe defeat.

The Germans were bound down behind their entrenchments from the North Sea to the Swiss frontier, and under the highest trial, the Allies had proved their ability to hold their actual lines inviolate.

Our Fleet had gained command of the sea, from which they had finally and completely driven the German flag. The spirit of the Allied nations was high and confident. On the other hand, had the enemy shown more of the skill and intrepidity of those great leaders of the past—Frederick, Napoleon, and von Moltke (whose teachings German writers of today claim that their commanders have so closely assimilated)—and the Allies a little less watchfulness and keenness, we might have seen Paris and the Channel seaboard in the enemy's hands, the British Army, irretrievably separated from its Allies, driven to the coast, and the French holding the southern provinces of the Republic with their capital at Bordeaux.

Finally, Russia, our great hope and mainstay for the future, was inspiring the utmost hope and encouragement amongst the Allies by the splendid deeds with which she heralded the close of the year. The last entry in my diary—December 31st, 1914—is as follows:

> Our night conference showed more and increasingly important Russian successes.

It was good to end the year with courage born of hope and confidence in the future. Time works wonders in all directions. Just as we could not foresee the utter collapse and failure of our great Eastern ally, so we could not discern the hidden forging of that sword of justice and retribution whose destined wielders were even then stirring from their fifty years of slumber and dreams of everlasting peace, to rise like some giant from the shores of the Western Atlantic and, with overwhelming force, to stride eastward and help lay low the German dragon once and for all time in the dust.

CHAPTER 18

Ammunition

From the beginning of the Battle of the Aisne up to the close of the Battle of Loos, at the end of 1915, the scanty supply of munitions of war paralysed all our power of initiative and, at critical times, menaced our defence with irretrievable disaster. Great anxiety on this subject overshadowed all my direction of military operations, and deep concern at the failure of the Government to appreciate and remedy our difficulties from this cause dominated all my work. In this chapter it is my object to make known some of the efforts I made to awaken both the Government and the public from that apathy which meant certain defeat. I exhausted every effort, by urgent official demands to the War Office, and personal appeals to Lord Kitchener and such Cabinet Ministers as I came in contact with. When these efforts got no response, I gave interviews to the press and authorised public men who visited me to urge this vital necessity in their addresses. Nothing less than my deliberate conclusion, after all these measures had failed and nine months of war had elapsed, that the Empire itself was in jeopardy, forced me to act in May 1915 as I did. I was conscious before taking this step, which meant the overthrow of the Government, that it also meant the end of my career in France, with all the hopes and ambitions that only a soldier can understand. But the consciousness of the great results achieved in this upheaval has been my reward, and I trust that a recital of my difficulties may, if occasion arise in the future, protect the British Army in the field from the recurrence of any similar situation.

During my term of office as Chief of the Imperial General Staff, from March 1912 to April 1914, I had urged these vital necessities upon the Government, but my demands were steadily opposed by the Finance Department and the Treasury. All our experiences in the South African War, and the warnings which the Manchurian campaign plainly gave, passed altogether unheeded in the years preceding the present war. I was always a strong advocate for the supply of high-explosive shell to our horse and field artillery, but I got very little support, and even such as was given to me was lukewarm in the extreme. I believe the Ordnance Board was not in favour of it.

As early as the middle of September 1914 the British Army in France was subjected to heavy bombardment from German 8-in. howitzers, to which they were quite unable to reply. At the same time the daily expenditure of artillery ammunition became far in excess of the receipts from home, and we were unable to maintain the stocks on the lines of communication up to anything like the proper war establishment. For example, the 18-pdrs. fired an average of 14 rounds a day, whilst the receipts were barely seven. The 60-pdr. guns and the 4.5-in. howitzers fired over 40 rounds a day, against a supply of eight or nine rounds at most. In private letters and telegrams I had repeatedly brought this to the notice of the Secretary of State, and a strong official memorandum on the subject was sent to the War Office on September 28th. A further communication to the same effect was made on October 10th; and on the 29th of the same month the War Office were officially told that the state of the ammunition supply had necessitated the issue of an order restricting expenditure to 20 rounds per gun daily, and that a further restriction to 10 rounds would be necessary if the supply did not improve. This was during the most desperate period of the First Battle of Ypres, when the average daily expenditure of 18-pdr. ammunition had amounted to 81 rounds per gun.

In some cases the expenditure per gun had reached the enormous total of 300 rounds daily. A proportion of at least 25 per cent. of high-explosive shells for 13 and 18 pdrs. was included in the demands to which I have referred above.

In a communication to the War Office on December 31st, the view was expressed that considerably more high explosive was necessary, and the following table was laid down as our minimum requirements to carry on the war with any prospect of success:

Required output of ammunition

Rounds per gun a day

13-pdr.	50 (25 H.E.)
18-pdr.	50 (25 H.E.)
4.5-in. howitzer	40 (35 H.E.)
6-in. howitzer	25 (all H.E.)
60-pdr.	25 (15 H.E.)
4.7-in. gun	25 (15 H.E.)
6-in. gun	25 (all H.E.)
9.2-in. howitzer	12 (all H.E.)

It was explained that this output was necessary for a period of active operations, and should be continued even during a lull, till a reserve of three or four times the amount laid down in war establishments had been accumulated. To this request there was no reply until January 19th. The War Office then declined to work up to more than 20 rounds a day, and refused a request for 50 per cent, of high explosives.

This amazing attitude at a most critical time compelled me to consider means by which the several members of the Government, and the public also, might be advised of this deplorable apathy which, if long continued, meant the destruction of our Army.

In this letter from the War Office, of January 19th, which I have already mentioned, an estimate was attached of the receipts which we might rely upon up to and including the month of May. This estimate was far below our requirements, whilst the actual receipts fell far short of it. The actual supply in May proved to be less than one half of the War Office estimate, which was the only one ever furnished for our guidance. Such failure made it quite impossible to make any reliable forecast of the condition of the ammunition supply at any particular date. This state of uncertainty rendered the formulation of plans for co-operating with the French most difficult, if not impossible.

During the winter of 1914-15 it was hoped to accumulate some small reserve of ammunition, but, during this period, all our efforts in this direction were of no avail, because the number of rounds per 18-pdr. gun throughout this period fell to less than five!

I had serious misgivings that the morale of the Army was becoming affected by this first long and weary winter of inactivity in the trenches, and to render the defence effective it was necessary to undertake an offensive operation.

Early in March a small reserve of ammunition had been accumulated, and the Battle of Neuve Chapelle was fought and won. Had proper steps been taken to increase the supply when my first strong appeals were sent in during September 1914, the offensive operation commenced so successfully at Neuve Chapelle might have been much further developed, and, indeed, possibly have led to great and important results. But the battle had to be broken off after three days' fighting because we were brought to a standstill through want of ammunition.

Immediately afterwards I again addressed the strongest representations I could frame to the War Office. I begged that His Majesty's Government might be informed that, if their object was to drive the enemy off French and Belgian territory during 1915, no progress towards this objective could be obtained unless and until the supply of artillery ammunition should enable the Army to engage in sustained operations. The only official reply which I received to this letter was an injunction to use the utmost economy, but a private letter, dated March 16th, was addressed by Sir James Wolfe Murray to Sir William Robertson, who was then my Chief of Staff. This letter was said to have been dictated by the Secretary of State, and its contents hinted very strongly that an impression prevailed at the War Office that we were wasting ammunition.

The operations at Neuve Chapelle used up all our available resources, and it became necessary to restore them by reverting for a time to a strictly defensive attitude.

It was, moreover, very clear that the Germans had early realised that the war was to be one calling for colossal supplies of munitions; supplies, indeed, upon such a stupendous scale as the world had never before dreamed of, and they also realised the vital necessity for heavy artillery. They began with an inferior field gun, and they never stopped to remedy this defect, but directed all their energies, from the first, to developing their heavy artillery. Whilst their total proportion of guns to bayonets was fully maintained, the proportion of field guns to bayonets was reduced, and all heavy guns enormously increased. Each month the development of heavy artillery became more accentuated until, towards the late spring of 1915, the greater number of projectiles fired by the Germans, whenever operations of any importance were taking place, were of 5.9 and upwards. This was in defence as well as in attack, and by this means the enemy endeavoured to shatter the morale of the attackers, as well as to inflict very heavy casualties.

The necessity for a great preponderance of heavy artillery was also recognised by the French long before our War Office could be persuaded to move in that direction. From early in the war they aimed at obtaining one heavy gun of 6-in. calibre and upwards for every field gun they held, without reducing the proportion to bayonets of the latter which obtains in the French Army. To meet these requirements the French were taking guns from their old warships and coast defence ships, and straining every nerve to get guns of heavy calibre into the field.

In May, 1915, the proportion of field to heavy guns above 6-in. calibre in the French Army was 2.3 to one. At this time the British Army had but 71 guns altogether above 5-in. calibre against 1,416 below it, and no adequate steps whatever had yet been taken to bring the proportion more nearly to the requirements of modern warfare. The supply of trench guns and mortars, with their ammunition, hand-grenades, and other most necessary munitions of war, was almost negligible, nor was there any active attempt to understand and grapple vitally with the new problems calling for the application of modern science to the character of warfare that had developed.

I have referred before to the disinclination of the War Office, prior to the war, to take up seriously the question of high explosives; the natural consequence was that the true nature of high-explosive shells, and the correct particulars which govern their construction, were not properly understood, as they had too little experience of them.

The deadly nature of modern rifle and machine-gun fire had brought about trench warfare, which enabled the troops opposite to one another to approach to ranges which were customary in the days of the Peninsula and Waterloo. The time-honoured grenades, which were so marked a feature in those days, were thus resuscitated.

Although the War Office received detailed reports from the Front as to the employment by the enemy of these new and unfamiliar weapons, no proper attention was ever paid to these reports. It was their duty to bring these old-time weapons up to date, and to compete with the new mechanical inventions constantly being devised by the great organisation of a thoroughly prepared enemy. But reports from the Front as to these new and unfamiliar weapons were received with a carelessness which bordered on incredulity. The critical days in the early part of November, and during the First Battle of Ypres, compelled me to devise a plan to meet the exigencies of this grave emergency. As the fighting settled into trench warfare, the inadequacy of our weapons to enable us to reply to an enemy thoroughly equipped with every contrivance for this sort of warfare became painfully apparent; while even our hand-grenades, by reason of their faulty construction, frequently did not explode. I was therefore compelled to conduct experiments in the field, and improvise new weapons as well as possible. For such work the Army had no organisation. In this I received invaluable assistance from my friend, George Moore. Mr. Moore is an American who has had wide experience of large construction developments in the United States. Although a young man, he was deeply versed in the method of scientific research as applied to mechanical invention. Add to this that he was a great personal friend of my own and passionately interested in the success of the Allies, and it will be seen how naturally I turned to him for help and advice in this terrible crisis. Under Mr. Moore's advice and direction, experiments were carried out with the maximum of speed, energy and resource, covering the field of the proper construction and use of high explosives, hand-grenades, trench mortars and bombs; and a number of factories and small plants were set up for the production, for use in the field, of properly constructed hand-grenades, bombs and trench mortars.

As a result of this work in the daily trench struggle that had then developed, we were rapidly enabled to acquire the accurate knowledge of the proper use of high explosives, and the appliances necessary to meet the enemy on his own ground under these novel conditions of warfare. Mr. Moore from time to time brought men in whom he had trust and confidence to help in the work. Among them I will only specifically refer to Colonel Lewis, an American, whose machine gun, bearing his name, proved of such enormous help in this war, and to Lieutenant Lawrence Breese. This gallant young officer of the Blues, to which magnificent regiment he belonged, did wonderful work, and conducted experiments the result of which was of the highest value; and, after several months of tireless energy, gave his life in carrying out one of these experiments. This hastily improvised organisation worked night and day in these trying times, with the results which enabled us, with success, to meet the enemy in trench warfare.

During this time I received visits at my Headquarters from prominent members of both Houses of Parliament, to whom I told, in course of conversation, the great anxiety I felt on the subject of the shortage of heavy guns and ammunition.

On March 22nd I gave an interview to the Press, which appeared generally in the English papers, from which I quote:

> It is a rough war, but the problem it sets is a comparatively simple one—munitions, more munitions, always more munitions; this is the essential question, the governing condition of all progress, of every leap forward.

On March 27th I gave an interview to *The Times*, in which I said as follows:

> The protraction of the war depends entirely upon the supply of men and munitions. Should these be unsatisfactory,

the war will be accordingly prolonged. I dwell emphatically on the need for munitions.

To the public men who visited me, I appealed that they should make known this grave necessity to the public in their speeches. I quote a line from a speech of the Earl of Durham, who, at my request, said: "What we want and must have is more and more munitions."

At a conference at Chantilly with Lord Kitchener, I reminded him of my constant representations on the subject of munitions, both officially and privately, and warned him that the danger would be fatal if instant action were not taken to supply our needs.

It must be remembered that all this time, when the British Forces in France were in absolute jeopardy owing to these deficiencies, trainloads of all kinds of ammunition were passing along our rear *en route* to Marseilles and the Dardanelles.

This was the situation when on April 22nd the Germans made their first attack with poisoned gas in the Second Battle of Ypres and, in a gigantic effort, again attempted to break through; and the defence called for the most desperate kind of fighting, only surpassed in intensity by the struggle in the First Battle of Ypres. Just about this time, the then Prime Minister, Mr. Asquith, made his famous Newcastle speech, in which he stated that the Army had all the ammunition it required. When I read this speech, after all my public and private appeals, I lost any hope that I had entertained of receiving help from the Government as then constituted. So that, on May 9th, 1915, when we commenced the Battle of Festubert, an operation undertaken to relieve the intense pressure on the troops at Ypres, my mind was filled with keen anxiety. After all our demands, less than 8 per cent. of our shells were high explosive, and we had only sufficient supply for about 40 minutes of artillery preparation for this attack. On the tower of a ruined church I spent several hours in close observation of the operations. Nothing since the Battle of the Aisne had ever impressed me so deeply with the terrible shortage of artillery and ammunition as did the events of that day. As I watched the Aubers ridge, I clearly saw the great inequality of the artillery duels, and, as attack after attack failed, I could see that the absence of sufficient artillery support was doubling and trebling our losses in men. I therefore determined on taking the most drastic measures to destroy the apathy of a Government which had brought the Empire to the brink of disaster. A friend was standing by my side on the tower, and to him I poured out my doubts and fears and announced my determination. He warned me that the politicians would never forgive the action I proposed, and that it meant my certain recall from the command in France. But my decision was made, and I immediately started for my Headquarters, fully determined on my future course of action.

If any additional proof were required of the hopelessness of any relief coming from the War Office, I found it waiting for me when I reached Headquarters that afternoon, in the shape of a telegram from the Secretary of State for War, directing that 20 per cent. of our scanty reserve supply of ammunition was to be shipped to the Dardanelles. I immediately gave instructions that evidence should be furnished to Colonel Repington, military correspondent of *The Times*, who happened to be then at Headquarters, that the vital need of high-explosive shells had been a fatal bar to our Army success on that day. I directed that copies of all the correspondence which had taken place between myself and the Government on the question of the supply of ammunition be made at once, and I sent my Secretary, Brinsley FitzGerald, with Captain Frederick Guest, one of my A.D.C.s, to England with instructions that these proofs should be laid before Mr. Lloyd George, who had already shown me, by his special interest in this subject, that he grasped the deadly nature of our necessities. I instructed also that they should be laid before Mr. Arthur J. Balfour and Mr. Bonar Law, whose sympathetic understanding of my difficulties, when they visited me in France, had led me to expect that they would take the action that this grave exigency demanded. Together with the correspondence, I sent the following memorandum:

(Secret)
Information regarding ammunition
1. Large quantities of high-explosive shells for field guns have become essential owing to the form of warfare in which the Army is engaged. The enemy is entrenched

from the sea to the Swiss frontier. There is no flank in his position that can be turned. It is necessary, therefore, for all offensive operations to start by breaking the enemy's line, which presupposes the attack of formidable field entrenchments. Shrapnel, being the man-killing projectile which is used against troops in the open, is primarily used in defence. In offensive operations it is used for searching communication trenches, preventing the enemy's reinforcements intervening in the fight, repelling counter-attacks, and, as an alternative for high-explosive shell, for cutting wire entanglements. It is, however, ineffective against the occupants of the trenches, breastworks, or buildings. It is, therefore, necessary to have high-explosive shell to destroy parapets, obstacles, buildings, and many forms of fortified localities that the enemy constructs, more particularly his machine-gun emplacements. Without an adequate supply the attack is impotent against the defenders of field fortifications, as the first step cannot be taken. Guns require 50 per cent. of high-explosive shell. Howitzers use high-explosive shell almost exclusively.

2. We have found by experience that the field guns actually engaged in offensive operations, such as Neuve Chapelle, fire about 120 rounds per gun per day.

Heavy guns and howitzers, according to their calibre, fire less in proportion. The guns of the whole Army are of course never equally heavily engaged at the same time, but the number of guns available and the amount of ammunition are the limiting factors when a plan of attack is being considered. There is, therefore, scarcely any limit to the supply of ammunition that could be usefully employed. The more ammunition, the bigger the scale on which the attack can be delivered, and the more persistently it can be pressed.

Demands must, however, be reasonable, and our position would be very greatly improved if our supply reached the figures in the attached Table "A" within three months. Up to the present it has been below these figures.

WANTED THREE MONTHS HENCE, SAY, AUGUST 1ST.

Table "A."

Nature.	Guns now in Country.	Rounds per Gun per Day.		Total Rounds required Daily.*	
		Shrapnel.	H.E.	Shrapnel.	H.E.
18-pdr.	700	12	12	8,500	8,500
13-pdr.	125	12	12	1,500	1,500
15-pdr. BLC.	200	12	12	2,500	2,500
4·7-in. gun	80	8	8	650	650
60-pdr.	28	8	8	250	250
5-in. howitzer	50	—	15	—	750
4·5-in. howitzer.	130	4	16	500	2,000
6-in. howitzer	40	—	12	—	500
9·2-in. howitzer.	12	—	12	—	150
				13,900	16,800
		Grand Total	-	30,700 daily.	
		Grand Total	-	921,000 monthly.	

* Round numbers are given. Expansion must be provided for at a similar rate. We need more guns and a correspondingly larger amount of ammunition.

3. Table "B" shows the percentage of high explosive of certain natures received since application for increased quantities was made between September and December last.

PERCENTAGE OF HIGH EXPLOSIVE RECEIVED SINCE FIRST APPLICATION FOR IT IN INCREASED QUANTITIES.

Table "B."

Nature of Gun.	Dec.	Jan.	Feb.	March.	April.	May.
	Per Cent.	Per Cent.	Per Cent.	Per Cent.	Per Cent.	Per Cent.
13-pdr.	Nil	Nil	Nil	Nil	Nil	Nil
18-pdr.	3·8	6·8	8·3	8·2	6·1	8
4·5-in. howitzer	44·4	68·5	88	75	59	65
60-pdr.	—	66	60	56	53	50
7-in. howitzer	55	59	51	77	69	50

Colonel FitzGerald and Captain Guest reported that on May 12th and 14th they had carried out my instructions and laid the facts before Mr. Lloyd George, Mr. Balfour and Mr. Bonar Law. On May 15th, Colonel Repington's article appeared in *The Times*. The world knows what then happened. The Coalition Government was formed, with Mr. Lloyd George as Minister of Munitions; and, though delays afterwards occurred, the problem was at last faced with the intelligence and energy that its gravity demanded, and I feel that for his work on munitions we owe unmeasured gratitude to Mr. Lloyd George. The successful solution of the problem came when he applied to it that matchless energy which has enabled him to come through the great ordeal as England's most valued leader in her direst hour.

For my unprecedented action I claim that no other course lay open to me. To organise the nation's industrial resources upon a stupendous scale was the only way if we were to continue with success the great struggle which lay before us, and I feel that the result achieved fully warranted the steps I took.

Maps

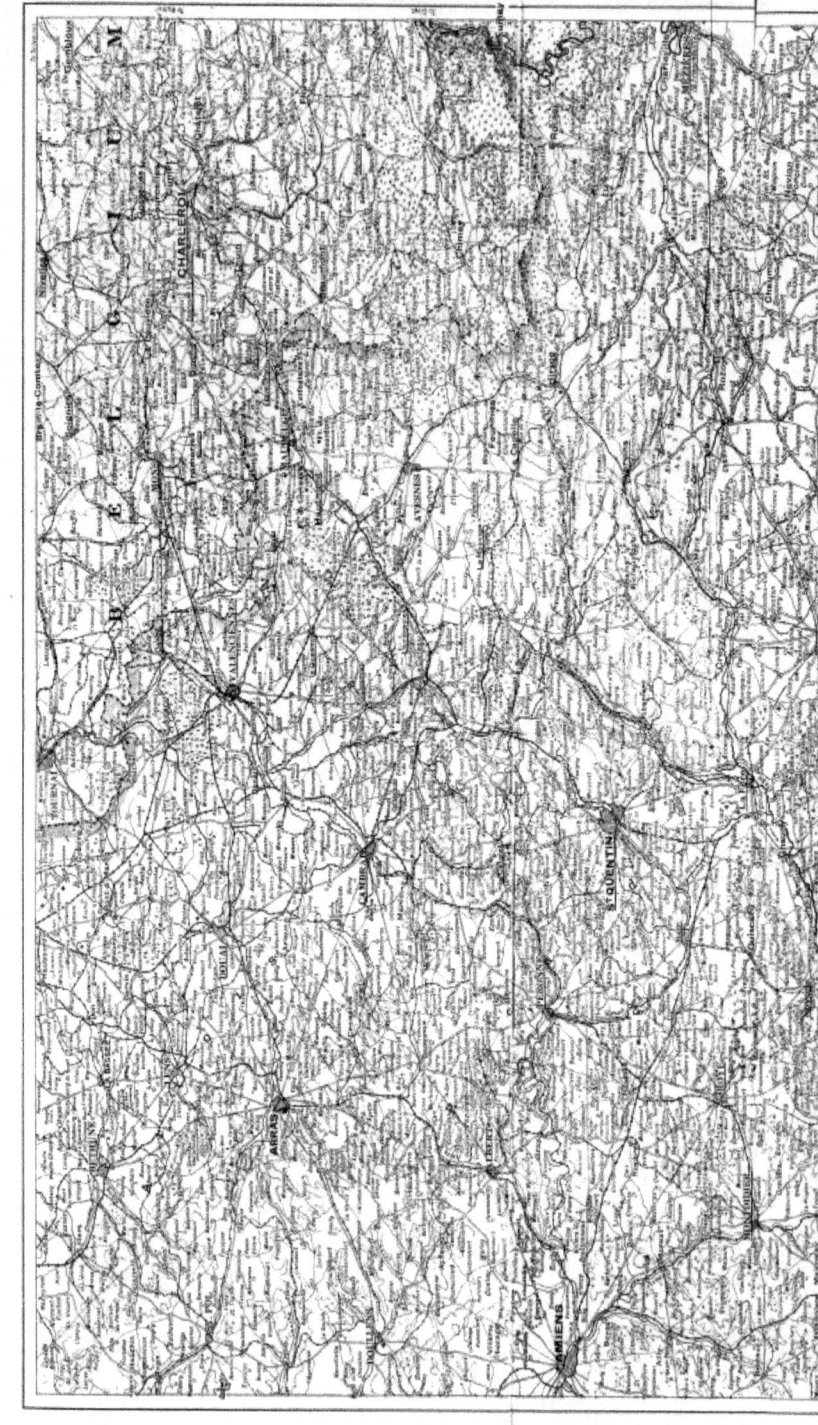

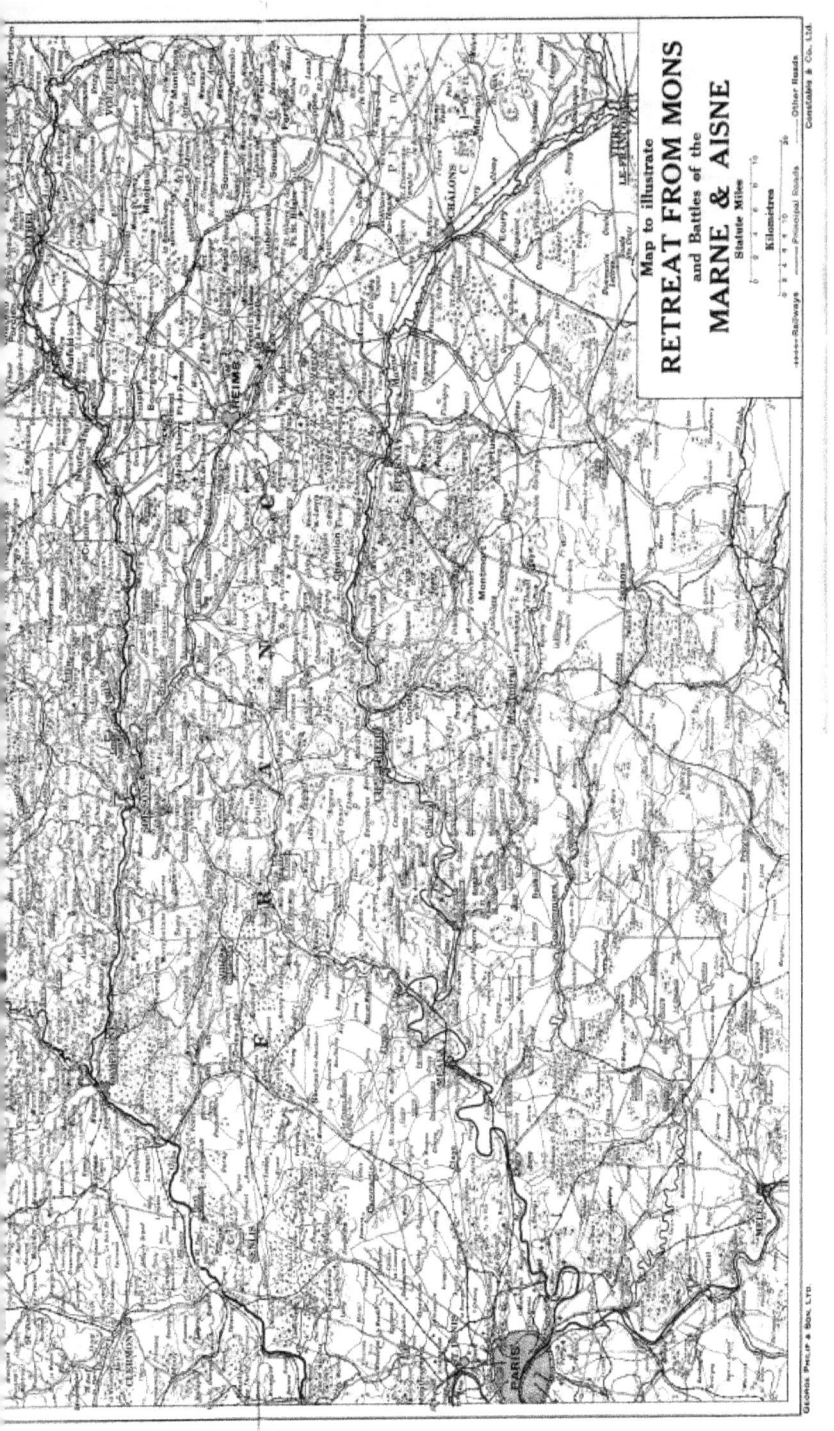

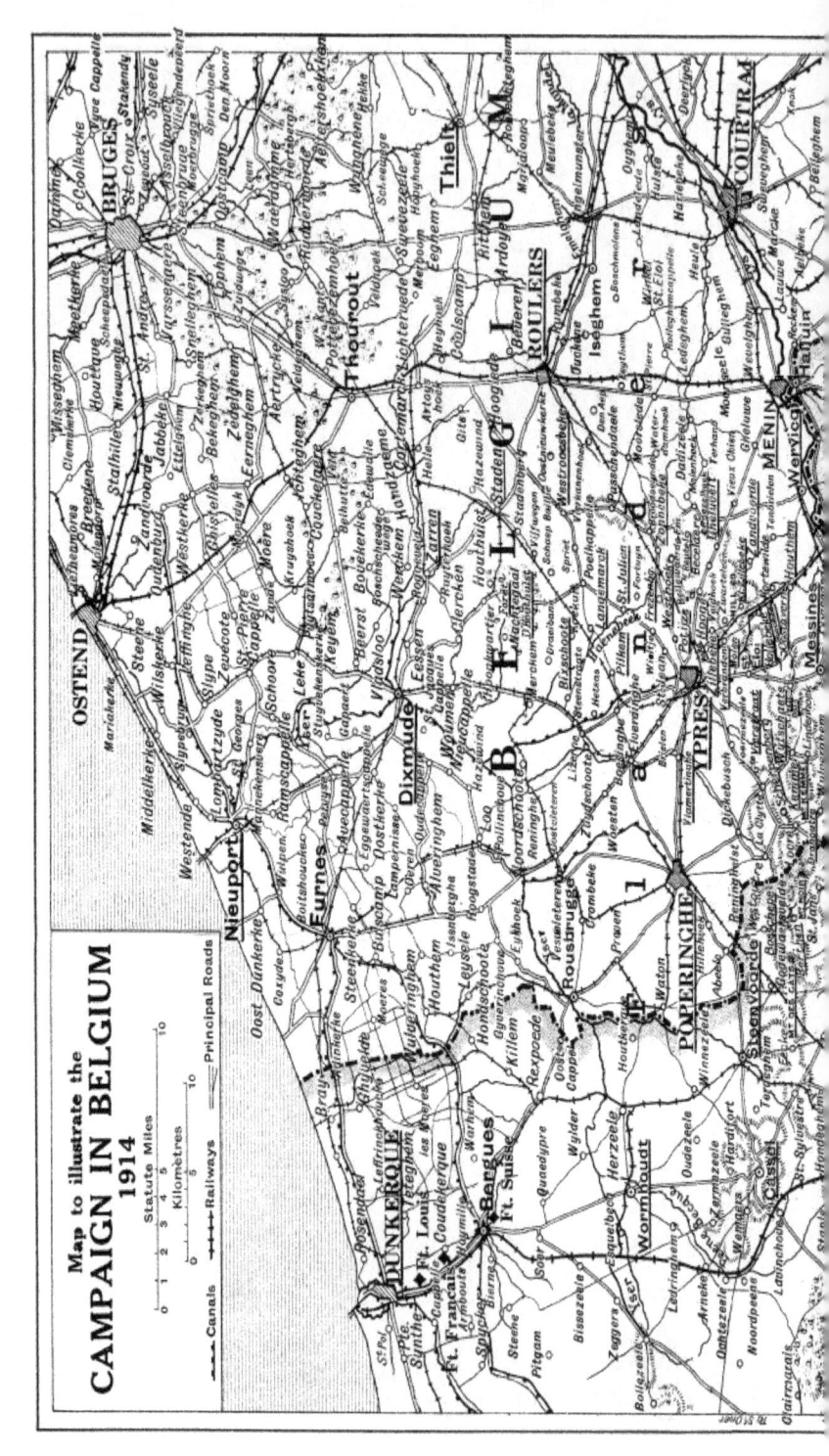

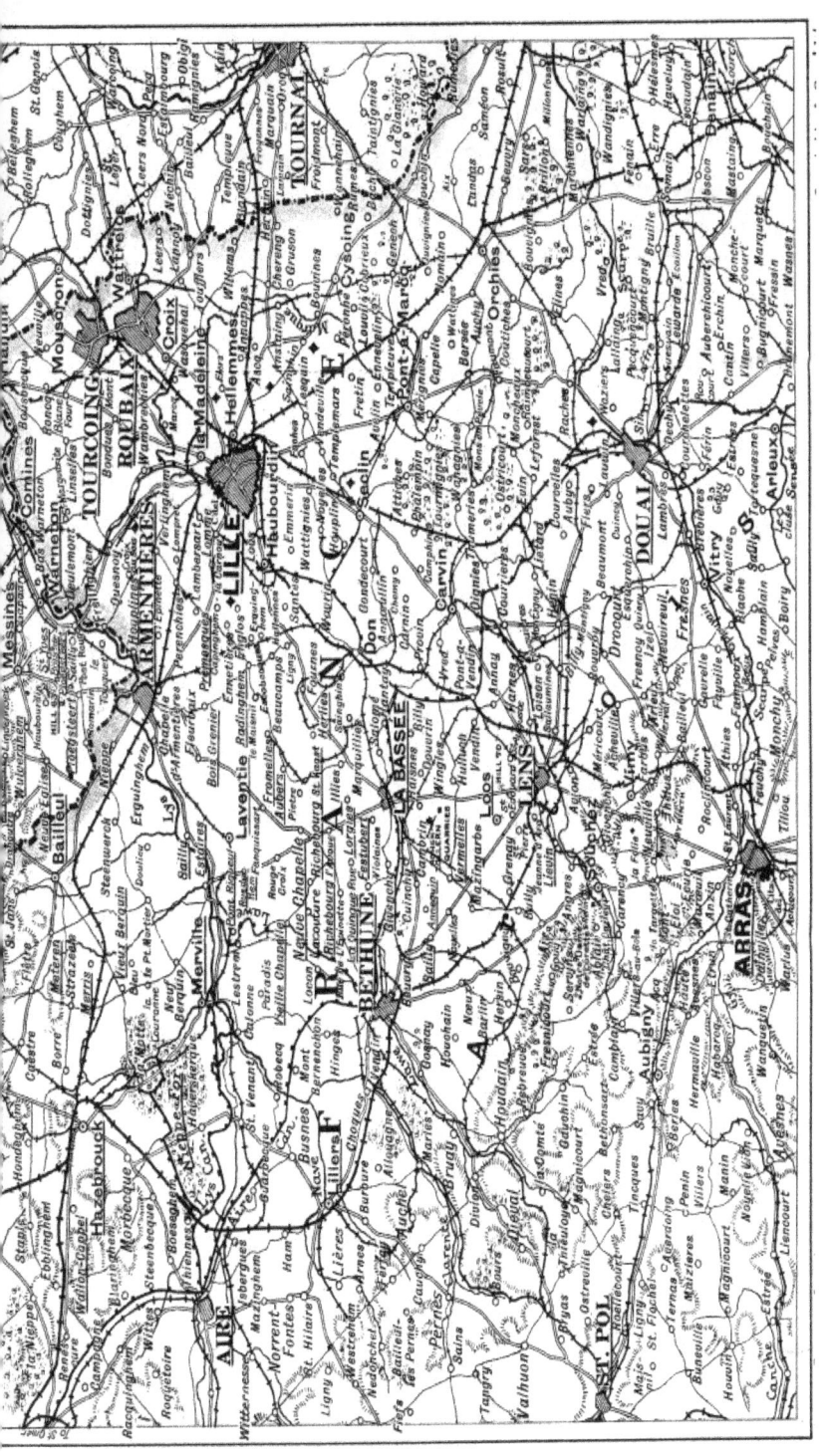

ALSO FROM LEONAUR
AVAILABLE IN SOFTCOVER OR HARDCOVER WITH DUST JACKET

DOING OUR 'BIT' by *Ian Hay*—Two Classic Accounts of the Men of Kitchener's 'New Army' During the Great War including *The First 100,000* & *All In It*.

AN EYE IN THE STORM by *Arthur Ruhl*—An American War Correspondent's Experiences of the First World War from the Western Front to Gallipoli and Beyond.

STAND & FALL by *Joe Cassells*—A Soldier's Recollections of the 'Contemptible Little Army' and the Retreat from Mons to the Marne, 1914.

RIFLEMAN MACGILL'S WAR by *Patrick MacGill*—A Soldier of the London Irish During the Great War in Europe including *The Amateur Army, The Red Horizon* & *The Great Push*.

WITH THE GUNS by *C. A. Rose & Hugh Dalton*—Two First Hand Accounts of British Gunners at War in Europe During World War 1- Three Years in France with the Guns and With the British Guns in Italy.

EAGLES OVER THE TRENCHES by *James R. McConnell & William B. Perry*—Two First Hand Accounts of the American Escadrille at War in the Air During World War 1-Flying For France: With the American Escadrille at Verdun and Our Pilots in the Air.

THE BUSH WAR DOCTOR by *Robert V. Dolbey*—The Experiences of a British Army Doctor During the East African Campaign of the First World War.

THE 9TH—THE KING'S (LIVERPOOL REGIMENT) IN THE GREAT WAR 1914 - 1918 by *Enos H. G. Roberts*—Like many large cities, Liverpool raised a number of battalions in the Great War. Notable among them were the Pals, the Liverpool Irish and Scottish, but this book concerns the wartime history of the 9th Battalion – The Kings.

THE GAMBARDIER by *Mark Severn*—The experiences of a battery of Heavy artillery on the Western Front during the First World War.

FROM MESSINES TO THIRD YPRES by *Thomas Floyd*—A personal account of the First World War on the Western front by a 2/5th Lancashire Fusilier.

THE IRISH GUARDS IN THE GREAT WAR - VOLUME 1 by *Rudyard Kipling*—Edited and Compiled from Their Diaries and Papers Volume 1 The First Battalion.

THE IRISH GUARDS IN THE GREAT WAR - VOLUME 2 by *Rudyard Kipling*—Edited and Compiled from Their Diaries and Papers Volume 2 The Second Battalion.

AVAILABLE ONLINE AT **www.leonaur.com**
AND OTHER GOOD BOOK STORES

ALSO FROM LEONAUR

AVAILABLE IN SOFTCOVER OR HARDCOVER WITH DUST JACKET

ARMOURED CARS IN EDEN by *K. Roosevelt*—An American President's son serving in Rolls Royce armoured cars with the British in Mesopatamia & with the American Artillery in France during the First World War.

CHASSEUR OF 1914 by *Marcel Dupont*—Experiences of the twilight of the French Light Cavalry by a young officer during the early battles of the great war in Europe.

TROOP HORSE & TRENCH by *R.A. Lloyd*—The experiences of a British Lifeguardsman of the household cavalry fighting on the western front during the First World War 1914-18.

THE LONG PATROL by *George Berrie*—A Novel of Light Horsemen from Gallipoli to the Palestine campaign of the First World War.

THE EAST AFRICAN MOUNTED RIFLES by *C.J. Wilson*—Experiences of the campaign in the East African bush during the First World War

THE FIGHTING CAMELIERS by *Frank Reid*—The exploits of the Imperial Camel Corps in the desert and Palestine campaigns of the First World War.

WITH THE IMPERIAL CAMEL CORPS IN THE GREAT WAR by *Geoffrey Inchbald*—The story of a serving officer with the British 2nd battalion against the Senussi and during the Palestine campaign.

STEEL CHARIOTS IN THE DESERT by *S.C.Rolls*—The first world war experiences of a Rolls Royce armoured car driver with the Duke of Westminster in Libya and in Arabia with T.E. Lawrence.

INFANTRY BRIGADE: 1914 by *Edward Gleichen*—The Diary of a Commander of the 15th Infantry Brigade, 5th Division, British Army, During the Retreat from Mons

HEARTS & DRAGONS by *Charles R. M. F. Crutwell*—The 4th Royal Berkshire Regiment in France and Italy During the Great War, 1914-1918.

TIGERS ALONG THE TIGRIS by *E. J. Thompson*—The Leicestershire Regiment in Mesopotamia During the First World War.

DESPATCH RIDER by *W. H. L. Watson*—The Experiences of a British Army Motorcycle Despatch Rider During the Opening Battles of the Great War in Europe.

AVAILABLE ONLINE AT
www.leonaur.com
AND OTHER GOOD BOOK STORES

ALSO FROM LEONAUR
AVAILABLE IN SOFTCOVER OR HARDCOVER WITH DUST JACKET

THE JENA CAMPAIGN: 1806 by *F. N. Maude*—The Twin Battles of Jena & Auerstadt Between Napoleon's French and the Prussian Army.

PRIVATE O'NEIL by *Charles O'Neil*—The recollections of an Irish Rogue of H. M. 28th Regt.—The Slashers— during the Peninsula & Waterloo campaigns of the Napoleonic wars.

ROYAL HIGHLANDER by *James Anton*—A soldier of H.M 42nd (Royal) Highlanders during the Peninsular, South of France & Waterloo Campaigns of the Napoleonic Wars.

CAPTAIN BLAZE by *Elzéar Blaze*—Elzéar Blaze recounts his life and experiences in Napoleon's army in a well written, articulate and companionable style.

LEJEUNE VOLUME 1 by *Louis-François Lejeune*—The Napoleonic Wars through the Experiences of an Officer on Berthier's Staff.

LEJEUNE VOLUME 2 by *Louis-François Lejeune*—The Napoleonic Wars through the Experiences of an Officer on Berthier's Staff.

FUSILIER COOPER by *John S. Cooper*—Experiences in the 7th (Royal) Fusiliers During the Peninsular Campaign of the Napoleonic Wars and the American Campaign to New Orleans.

CAPTAIN COIGNET by *Jean-Roch Coignet*—A Soldier of Napoleon's Imperial Guard from the Italian Campaign to Russia and Waterloo.

FIGHTING NAPOLEON'S EMPIRE by *Joseph Anderson*—The Campaigns of a British Infantryman in Italy, Egypt, the Peninsular & the West Indies During the Napoleonic Wars.

CHASSEUR BARRES by *Jean-Baptiste Barres*—The experiences of a French Infantryman of the Imperial Guard at Austerlitz, Jena, Eylau, Friedland, in the Peninsular, Lutzen, Bautzen, Zinnwald and Hanau during the Napoleonic Wars.

MARINES TO 95TH (RIFLES) by *Thomas Fernyhough*—The military experiences of Robert Fernyhough during the Napoleonic Wars.

HUSSAR ROCCA by *Albert Jean Michel de Rocca*—A French cavalry officer's experiences of the Napoleonic Wars and his views on the Peninsular Campaigns against the Spanish, British And Guerilla Armies.

SERGEANT BOURGOGNE by *Adrien Bourgogne*—With Napoleon's Imperial Guard in the Russian Campaign and on the Retreat from Moscow 1812 - 13.

AVAILABLE ONLINE AT **www.leonaur.com**
AND OTHER GOOD BOOK STORES

NAP-3

www.ingramcontent.com/pod-product-compliance
Lightning Source LLC
Chambersburg PA
CBHW031616160426
43196CB00006B/160